TEXAS
HIGH SCHOOL
FOOTBALL DYNASTIES

RICK SHERROD

Foreword by
G.A. MOORE

THE
History
PRESS

Published by The History Press
Charleston, SC 29403
www.historypress.net

Front cover, top: In 1927, Waco High School was the "first to four" state titles, defeating
Abilene High School 21–14 for the championship and securing the Tigers' fourth state
crown. This Waco team also achieved the first-ever Texas title three-peat and was selected
by the National Sports News Service as the 1927 national high school football champion.
Courtesy Texas High School Football Hall of Fame, Waco, Texas.

First published 2013
Second printing 2013

Manufactured in the United States

ISBN 978.1.60949.612.8

Library of Congress CIP data applied for.

To Mike Copeland and Joseph Gillespie—my friends and two of the Lone Star State's very finest.

CONTENTS

Foreword, by G.A. Moore   7
Acknowledgements   9
The Top 26   13
Introduction   17

1. It's Good to be King   31
2. The Petro-Dynasties   45
3. The Metro-Dynasties   87
4. The Micro-Dynasties   135
5. Mighty Mites   167
6. Six-Man Ball   203
7. Current Co-Regents   219

Conclusion   239
Appendix   241
Notes   243
Bibliography   245
Index   249
About the Author   255

FOREWORD

Dear Football Lovers,

I hope you will enjoy reading the contents of this book as much as I have. The great teams, coaches and dynasties are so well documented. I loved reading about some of the teams that I heard about growing up and many of the coaches I admired.

All of my life, I have enjoyed playing football, coaching football, watching football and talking football. Football, the joy of my life, has been my friend for more than fifty years. Because of this joy, my life has been like an exciting rollercoaster ride. I get up thinking about it, and I go to bed thinking about it. The awesome game of football brings challenges that can lift you to the clouds of heaven or drop you to the bottom of the ocean. But the thing that I like most about football is that it produces a "champion's heart."

Rick Sherrod has done a tremendous job in writing a book that will bring or restore great memories to the young and old about the greatest sport that exists.

—G.A. MOORE

ACKNOWLEDGEMENTS

I can be a difficult man to live with when I am in my "creative" mode, so perhaps I shouldn't have been surprised by the response from my lovely wife, Annette, when I first proposed the idea of writing *Texas High School Football Dynasties*. She reflexively replied, "Do you want to write another book, or do you want to be married?" At the time, I hoped that she was kidding. Apparently she was, because you are holding the book, and I remain happily hitched.

Many individuals provided support in the preparation of this volume: Dr. Darrell Floyd, Stephenville ISD superintendent; Joseph Gillespie and Michael Copeland, both Stephenville Yellow Jacket coaches and my valued friends; Mike Adkins, Ector County ISD director of communications; James Albritton of Salt Fork Images; Marco Alvarado, Lake Travis ISD director of communications; Robert Bedichek and Alan Pipkin, grandsons of Roy Bedichek (UIL director, 1922–48); Dale Caffey, Waco ISD director of communications; Kimberly Carmichael, UIL chief of staff; Debbie Wesson Cashell, Stephenville native; Will Collicott, project editor at the The History Press; Jym Daniel, territory manager for Lifetouch Austin; Debby Hayward, Plano ISD director of communications; Kris Hendon, Tarleton State University's interlibrary loan specialist; Shanon Hunt, creator of Lone Star Football Network (www.lonestarfootball.net); Bud Jones, Stephenville sportswriter and photographer; Marie Kirkham of Visual Services of Texas (Houston office); Brad Keith, sports editor of the *Stephenville Empire-Tribune*; Becky LeJeune, commissioning editor at The History Press; Randy Little and Tracy Little of Houston's H-M Oil Company; Gayle Lovvorn, New

Stamford American office manager; John Mace of Visual Sports of San Antonio; Michael Marugg of Stamford, Texas; Larry Mathis, longtime Brownwood High School faculty member and announcer at Lion home football games; Chris Moore, Garland ISD director of communications; Chad Morris, Clemson University offensive coordinator; Linda Briscoe Myers of the University of Texas at Austin's outstanding research facility, the Harry Ransom Center; Michael Odell, director, Stephenville ISD DAEP and Abilene native; Colin Shillinglaw, Baylor University director of football operations; Ellen Skipper of Stephenville's Skipper Real Estate (also an expert sports photographer); Louise Skipper of Skipper Real Estate; Steve Steed, Tarleton State University dean and Abilene native; T.J. Steed, software architect from Florence; Mike Truitt and Jake Truitt of Visual Services of Texas (Plano); Sara Vanden Berge, managing editor of the *Stephenville Empire-Tribune*; Linda Wiles of La Marque ISD; Alec Wills, computer applications specialist; and Diane Wrinkle of djWrinkle Photography.

I also received critical contributions from the following active or retired superintendents: Dr. Reece Blincoe (Brownwood), Ecomet Burley (La Marque), Don Fowler (Richland Springs), Don Gibson (Sonora), Ben Gilbert (Stephenville), Todd Gooden (Mart), Scott Kana (Sealy), Michael Miller (Converse Judson), Barbara Qualls (Ennis), Sandra Quarles (Daingerfield-Lone Star), Jennings Teel (Breckenridge) and Ronny Wright (Goldthwaite). Many former head coaches, current head coaches and/or athletic directors have generously supported this project: Tim Buchanan (Aledo), Hank Carter (Lake Travis), Sam Harrell (Ennis High School), Mike Jackson (La Marque), Wayne Hutchinson (Stamford), Gary Joseph (Katy), Danny Medina (Fort Hancock), Michael Miller (Converse Judson), G.A. Moore (Celina), Gary Proffitt (Goldthwaite) and Hal Wasson (Southlake). These coaches and administrators contributed invaluable information and stories and extended approval for publication of many of the Texas Sports Hall of Fame images included in this volume.

A debt of thanks also goes to the late Austin sports columnist and 2002 Texas Sports Hall of Fame (TSHF) inductee George Breazeale, whose wonderful work *Tops in Texas* did much to inspire the present book. Although my efforts are far narrower in scope and scale, Breazeale's earlier contribution influenced much of the way in which I organized and presented the material in my own book. The hospitality of Jay Black, curator of TSHF, made my picture research in Waco an efficient and enjoyable undertaking. Unless otherwise noted, this book's images come courtesy of Texas High School Football Hall of Fame, Waco, Texas. The remaining pictures have been provided by individuals or school districts that graciously approved their use. Unless otherwise noted, demographic data cited below is drawn from the 2000 U.S. Census. Although these figures are less recent than those available for 2010, the earlier census data seemed more relevant to most of the programs that have risen to dynasty status.

Three remaining individuals have played a very special role in nurturing both this volume and my writing career. My wife, Annette, has been a constant supporter and companion in my publications about social, local and family history. Her patience, kindness, encouragement and understanding—especially during the long hours when it seemed that I was married to my computer as much as I was to her—have made possible the modest contributions I have made to my fields of study. From earliest times, my father, Marshall Sherrod, has encouraged my interest and enthusiasm for sports in general and high school football in particular. His never-failing moral and financial support made my graduate studies of the 1970s a reality and still later enabled my literary dalliances across the decades when my otherwise paltry teacher's salary would have limited any personal achievements beyond the confines of the classroom. Finally, Ryan Schumacher, associate editor of *Southwestern Historical Quarterly*, directed me to The History Press as a likely publisher for this work. His friendship and counsel since we met in 2008 have helped me grow immeasurably as a researcher and a writer. To these three I owe an enduring debt.

Thanks to any and all of those individuals who took the time to examine either portions of this manuscript relevant to their individual knowledge and expertise or the manuscript in its entirety during its various stages of its preparation. Any errors that remain are my responsibility alone.

THE TOP 26

Conferences assigned according to relative placement by 2012 alignment standards

High School	Conference	Titles	Appearances (by year)	Title Runs	Win Percentage
Celina	1A, 2A and 3A	8	10 (1974, 1995, 1998–2001, 2005–08) *1 co-title	Four-peat (1998–2001)	80.0%
Southlake Carroll	3A and 5A	8	9 (1988, 1992–93, 2002–06, 2011)	Back-to-back (1992–93) and three-peat (2004–06)	88.9%
Abilene	5A	7	9 (1922–23, 1927–28, 1931, 1954–56, 2009)	Three-peat (1954–56)	77.8%
Brownwood	4A	7	8 (1960, 1965, 1967, 1969–70, 1977, 1978, 1981)	Back-to-back (1969–70)	87.5%
Plano	3A, 4A and 5A	7	9 (1965, 1967, 1971, 1977–78, 1986–87, 1993–94)	Back-to-back (1986–87)	77.8%
Katy	2A and 5A	7	11 (1959, 1994, 1997, 1999–2000, 2003, 2005, 2007–09, 2012)	Back-to-back (2007–08)	63.6%
Breckenridge	4A and 5A	6	6 (1929, 1951–52, 1954, 1958–59) *2 co-titles	Two back-to-back (1951–52, 1958–59)	100%
Converse Judson	5A	6	11 (1983, 1988, 1990, 1992–93, 1995–96, 1998, 2002, 2005, 2007)	Back-to-back (1992–93)	54.5%
Dangerfield	2A and 3A	6	9 (1968, 1983–85, 1998, 2008–10, 2012)	Three-peat (2008–10)	66.7%
Odessa Permian	5A	6	11 (1965, 1968, 1970, 1972, 1975, 1980, 1984–85, 1989, 1991, 1995) *1 co-title		54.5%

High School	Conference	Titles	Appearances (by year)	Title Runs	Win Percentage
Waco	5A	6	10 (1922–27, 1939, 1945, 1948, 2006) *1 co-title	Three-peat (1925–27)	60.0%
Wichita Falls	5A	6	10 (1937, 1941, 1949–50, 1958–61, 1969, 1971)	Back-to-back (1949–50)	60.0%
Richland Springs	Six-Man	6	7 (2001, 2004, 2006–07, 2010–12)	Back-to-back (2006–07) and three-peat (2010–12)	85.7%
Fort Hancock	Six-Man	5	6 (1986, 1988–92)	Four-peat (1988–91)	83.3%
La Marque	4A	5	10 (1986, 1993–98, 2003, 2006, 2010)	Three-peat (1995–97)	50.0%
Mart	1A and 2A	5	9 (1957, 1969, 1986, 1999–2000, 2006, 2008, 2010, 2012)		55.6%
Sealy	3A	5	6 (1978, 1994–97, 1999)	Four-peat (1994–97)	83.3%
Sonora	1A and 2A	5	6 (1966, 1968–71, 2000)	Back-to-back (1970–71)	83.3%
Lake Travis	4A	5	5 (2007–11)	Five-peat (2007–11)	100%
Stephenville	4A and 3A	5	5 (1993–94, 1998–99, 2012)	Two back-to-back (1993–94, 1998–99)	100%
Amarillo	5A	4	6 (1930, 1934–36, 1940, 1948)	Three-peat (1934–36)	66.7%
Ennis	4A	4	4 (1975, 2000–01, 2004)	Back-to-back (2000–01)	100%
Garland	4A and 5A	4	5 (1955–56, 1963–64, 1999)	Back-to-back (1963–64)	80.0%

High School	Conference	Titles	Appearances (by year)	Title Runs	Win Percentage
Goldthwaite	1A and 2A	4	6 (1985, 1992–94, 2009–10)	Back-to-back (1993–94)	66.7%
Aledo	3A and 4A	4	5 (1974, 1998, 2009–11)	Three-peat (2009–11)	80.0%
Stamford	3A and 1A	4	6 (1955–56, 1958–59, 2011–12) *stripped of 1959 title	Back-to-back three times	66.7%

INTRODUCTION

There is nothing like it anywhere else in America. In many Texas communities, high school football probably remains the most important male teenage rite of passage in the Lone Star State. It brings in its wake a groundswell of popular support, oftentimes leaving entire towns virtually vacant on any given football Friday. On game night, school administrators, faculty, school district staff, cheerleaders, dance teams, color guards, bands and adoring fans of every social strata, stripe and hue all unite as one.

Don Meredith, quarterback successively for Mount Vernon High School, Southern Methodist University and the Dallas Cowboys, once declared that Texas high school football embodies "something the state represents," something symbolic of a Texas peopled "by rugged individuals who would physically stand their ground." In the Lone Star State, football becomes "a communal thing…one town against another," "a great outlet for Texans, a way of saying this is what makes us best." It is "the first time that a young kid feels all the different responsibilities of belonging to a group, being a real member of his community."[1]

A chorus of authoritative voices affirms "Dandy" Don's declaration. Another All-Pro NFL quarterback, Joe Theismann—from New Jersey, no less—similarly assessed, "High school football over this country [Texas] is not just a game. It is a way of life."[2]

Jan Reid, the witty author, journalist, *Texas Monthly* writer-at-large and one-time "Rowdy" on the 1960–61 Wichita Falls High junior varsity, describes the sport as "a competition of towns, not just schools" in which "our boys can kick the tails of yours." He explains Texas high school football's magnetic appeal as a phenomenon found "in country pioneered little more than a century ago." The sport is a ritualistic, seasonal practice that "assimilates and refashions frontier traditions. Only in Texas [is football] so interwoven in a fabric of regional identity and chauvinism."[3] It's no wonder, then, that Boys Ranch ISD athletic director Paul Jones asserted, "People in Texas live high school football. People in other states just play high school football."[4]

In 1963, Rodney J. Kidd, the director of University Interscholastic League (UIL)—the governing body of the sport—described the high school football team as "potent a force in the community as the chamber of commerce."[5] Native New Yorker, *Philadelphia Inquirer* newspaper editor, lifelong sports fan and author of *Friday Night Lights* H.G. "Buzz" Bissinger suggested that the Odessa Permian football coach was more widely known than Odessa's mayor, police chief, city manager and county commissioners.[6] He was probably right. In a typical Texas town, these very public figures often lead the charge to Friday night's game.

They and hosts of townspeople congregate at stadiums—not quite cathedrals, churches or chapels, but somehow more sacrosanct than ordinary secular structures. Some, such as Odessa's Ratliff Stadium, San Antonio's Alamodome or Arlington's Cowboys Stadium, are spectacular and famous. Others are venerable, obviously past their prime yet exuding character, like Cleburne's Depression-era Public Works Administration stone edifice, Yellow Jacket Stadium (aka "The Rock"), completed in 1941 and noteworthy today for its English ivy–covered walls. A massive sign at the stadium's eastern end reminds visitors of Coach Fred Erney's 1920 Yellow Jackets co-state championship earned in the January 8, 1921 inaugural title game played in the mud and rain at Austin's Clark Field.

The best-loved stadiums take on the persona of temples or shrines. They are permeated with a palpable reverential aura. These playing fields are "great meeting places" for the "townsfolk." Jeff Wilson is author of *Home Field*, a wonderful pictorial trip preserving the view of the home-field stands as seen from the fifty-yard line at more than eighty of the most interesting Texas high school football stadiums. He describes these facilities as "cultural artifacts" offering "a window into the hearts of those responsible for them." Ranging in design from sparse and humble to the outright palatial, these community gathering places have "become a particularly special expression of how a community as a whole feels about the game and, oftentimes, how it feels about itself."[7]

In August 2011, Austin's Bob Bullock Texas State History Museum opened its exhibit "Texas High School Football: More Than the Game," reveling in this schoolboy sport as a unique sociocultural phenomenon. In his opening remarks at the August 5 All-Star Tailgate Party, exhibit curator, author and journalist Joe Nick Patoski declared, "If you want to understand Texas and Texans, watch high school football. There is nothing like Texas high school football." Keynote speaker at the gathering was Kenneth Hall, the "Sugar Land Express," who held the national record for career rushing yardage (11,232) from 1953 until November 16, 2012, when Yulee High School (Florida) running back Derrick Henry finally broke it. Hall aptly concluded his address, declaring, "And yes, Texas high school football is more than the game."

This very perception inspired Pulitzer Prize–winning journalist Buzz Bissinger's writing of the famous (or infamous—take your pick) *Friday Night Lights* (1989). His volume about Odessa Permian High School football sold 2 million copies. In a similar spirit, Jan Reid's *Vain Glory*, focusing on the Wichita Falls Coyotes, takes a penetrating look at schoolboy football's mixed side effects. Nevertheless, the lion's share of printer's ink goes to an uncritical celebration more reminiscent of *The Secret of Mojo*, a comprehensive history of the David-over-Goliath achievements of Odessa Permian football published by the late actress, teacher and television scriptwriter Regina Walker McCally only three years before *Friday Night Lights* appeared.

Two of the best volumes on Texas high school football comprehensively explore state champions, great teams, star players, successful coaches, most memorable games and human-interest stories. The first is *Texas High School Football* (1985), by *Houston Chronicle* sportswriter Bill McMurray. The other is *King Football: Greatest Moments in Texas High School Football History* (2003), a masterfully edited volume by Mike Bynum that captures the broad sweep of the sport from 1913 through 2002. Both books include thorough lists of state champions and vignettes about exciting title games. In contrast, the present work concentrates on one small facet of the larger story, specifically those few Texas high schools that have earned four or more state titles.

Many schools have played in the final. The roster of state finalists spans the whole of Texas, including unusual and exotic place names: Celeste, Copperas Cove, Electra, Idalou, Flatonia, Hondo, Poth, Teneha, Tomball, Thorndale, Throckmorton, Winthorst and Yoakum. Other teams reaching the championship round bear peculiar-sounding appellations: Motley County, Muleshoe, Petrolia, Prosper, Pharr-San Juan Alamo, Rosebud-Lott, Quanah, Rule, Shiner, Wink, Whitharrel and Zephyr. The names of still others bucolically resonate: Bushland, Brazoswood, Cotton Center, Coldspring, Fort Bend Willowridge, Sulfur Springs, Turkey Valley, White

Deer, Deer Park, West Orange-Stark and White Oak. Since UIL's Bureau of Football Results indirectly sanctioned an official 1920 state title competition, these and 355 others—391 high schools in all—have made it to "The Show."

Every state finalist has its story to tell, but not all have experienced the same success. A select few have been consistent winners, laying claim to the coveted moniker "dynasty." Which ones among the host most rightly deserve such distinction? In the political world, dynasties are successions of royal bloodlines exercising rule over a clearly delimited space and time. The distinctions are not always so clear in the pigskin kingdom. On the one hand, the metaphor of political dynasty suggests number of consecutive trips to the final. *Houston Chronicle* sportswriter David Barron offered a worthy definition of "dynasty" in Bynum's *King Football*: "Each school's performance over a minimum of four years and a maximum of ten years was considered in making the selection, and preference was given to postseason results over regular-season records." His list, which considered teams through 2001, included fourteen schools: Waco (1921–27), Amarillo (1930–36), Breckenridge (1951–59), Abilene (1954–57), Brownwood (1960–69), Plano (1965–71), Austin Reagan (1967–70), Big Sandy (1971–75), Odessa Permian (1980–89), La Marque (1993–98), Stephenville (1993–99), Sealy (1994–99), Celina (1995–2001) and Converse Judson (1990–98). There is merit to Barron's perspective, but the present work takes a slightly different tack.

Total number of wins in the championship game is a relevant measuring stick as well. In this regard, many schools deserve honorable mention. There is mighty Cuero, a ten-time finalist and back-to-back champion in 1973–74. Only Odessa Permian, Converse Judson and Katy, with eleven respective appearances, have been to the final more often. In the 1987 title game, Cuero's Robert Strait rushed for 291 yards and scored all of the Gobblers' points in their 47–0 win over Smithville. But the Gobblers have only three wins. Denison made three consecutive finals trips in 1995–97. None yielded a victory. In just four seasons, Coach Travis Raven's Austin Reagan Raiders earned three state championships (1967–68, 1970), all of them also National Sports News Service (NSNS) national titles. Over that short span, his team posted a magnificent 51–3 record. Midland Lee enjoyed a 1998–2000 three-peat. *USA Today* and the Dick Butkus Football Network gave the Rebels recognition as 1999 national high school champion. Lee's success was in no small way the product of the talented Cedric Benson, who became the first Texas high school football player ever to grace the cover of Dave Campbell's *Texas Football*. The list of worthy claimants could continue. But only twenty-six schools have replenished the trophy case four times or more.

History is written by the winners. This book is a history about those winners—the repeat performers. Over the past ninety-three years, only 204 teams have even made the final more than once. An even smaller elite among that group have consistently won. Since 1920, only twenty-six programs—6.6 percent of the 391 total finalists—have captured at least four titles. These programs are the focus of this volume.

The victories of this select twenty-six have come in various shapes and sizes. Some stretch across decades. Others were compressed into what Theodore Roosevelt called one's "crowded hour." There have been fifteen three-peats, four four-peats and one lone five-peat. Southlake Carroll packed four state titles into five short years (2002–06), losing only a single game, the 2003 state final versus Katy. Lake Travis won five straight titles (2007–11).

Top Consecutive State Final Wins

Conferences assigned according to relative placement by 2012 alignment standards

High School	Conference	Years	Wins
Lake Travis	4A	2007–11	5
Fort Hancock	Six-Man	1988–91	4
Sealy	3A	1994–97	4
Celina	2A	1998–2001	4
Waco	5A	1925–27	3
Amarillo	5A	1934–36	3
Abilene	5A	1954–56	3
Big Sandy	1A	1973–75	3 (1 co-title)
La Marque	4A	1995–97	3
Midland Lee	5A	1998–2000	3
Southlake Carroll	5A	2004–06	3
Carthage	3A	2008–10	3
Daingerfield	2A	2008–10	3
Aledo	4A	2009–11	3
Richland Springs	Six-Man	2010–12	3

Works like this book are, of course, but snapshots in time. Whatever criteria one uses to determine dynasties, over time, anyone's list has been, now is and forever will be kaleidoscopic. As in politics, football kingdoms rise and fall. Some schools drop from "the list," and other regents ascend the throne. In 1963, legendary Texas Associated Press sports editor Harold Ratliff published his seminal narrative history, *Autumn's Mightiest Legions*. The work was state-of-the-art in its time, the first comprehensive history on the topic. Today, his focus on the "great teams" of the 1920s through the 1950s seems almost otherworldly. A dramatic shift in power is seen by comparing Ratliff's "list" to longtime *Austin American-Statesman* sportswriter George Breazeale's *Tops in Texas: Records and Notes on UIL State Football Champions, 1920–1992*. Similarly, when compared to those works that have appeared before, the 2012 "Top 26" featured herein reveal a continually evolving landscape.

For now, these twenty-six are a cut above the remaining 1,144 football programs competing under the 2012 UIL umbrella. With four or more state titles, they have set themselves apart. Each school comes from specific respective locations tied to significant historical and socioeconomic circumstances. During the first four decades of Texas high school football—the 1920s through the 1950s—a substantial degree of success followed the oilfield. Later, desegregation of Texas schools in the 1960s often shaped the title trail. Championships earned by Corpus Christi Miller (1960), San Antonio Brackenridge (1962) and Lubbock Estacado (1968) are milestones along this pathway. Estacado's success was instant. Its 3A championship came with a 14–0 victory over Refugio in the Lubbock school's first year as a member of UIL. A third decisive factor was the dizzying post–World War II expansion of many Texas metropolitan suburbs. As postwar boom years fueled the growth and expansion of the Lone Star State, new school districts arose, and old ones took on different personalities. Consequently, UIL subdivided Texas high schools into a set of conferences based on size of enrollment. This democratic gesture greatly leveled the playing field among schools that ranged in student body size from several thousand to one hundred or fewer. It began in 1948 with the creation of multiple title opportunities (see the "UIL Conference Divisions" table below). This forward-thinking partition prompts football historians to divide Texas high school football into the "early" and "modern" eras, the latter dating from the mid-twentieth century. Still, many of the enduring features of the sport, both on and off the field, took shape and form during the critical early years.

Longtime UIL director Roy Bedichek (commonly considered the "father of Texas high school sports") identified the birthplace of Texas high school

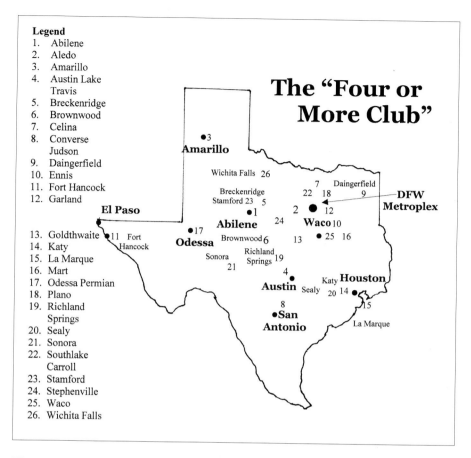

Legend

1. Abilene
2. Aledo
3. Amarillo
4. Austin Lake Travis
5. Breckenridge
6. Brownwood
7. Celina
8. Converse Judson
9. Daingerfield
10. Ennis
11. Fort Hancock
12. Garland
13. Goldthwaite
14. Katy
15. La Marque
16. Mart
17. Odessa Permian
18. Plano
19. Richland Springs
20. Sealy
21. Sonora
22. Southlake Carroll
23. Stamford
24. Stephenville
25. Waco
26. Wichita Falls

The "Four or More Club"

This map, while not precisely to scale, pinpoints the relative geographic locations of those twenty-six schools that have won four or more state titles. After ninety-three seasons of high school football under the supervision of UIL, the distribution of dynasties remains democratically spread across the Lone Star State. *Courtesy of the author.*

football as Dallas High School—"Dalhi." It happened in the fall of 1900.[8] Dalhi's captain, George Sergeant, later became Big D's mayor. In later years, Sergeant recalled that the new and sometimes violent sport survived in spite of early faculty skepticism and transparent student indifference. By 1905–06, Dalhi football players regularly received letter sweaters for their efforts. In 1912, Houston's Central High School (later rechristened Houston Sam Houston) unilaterally claimed football state champion status on the basis of winning nine straight games. The following year, the same Houston Tigers had opportunity to validate that claim in a quasi-official 1913 title match against Comanche, a contest that was the fourth Tiger game in a single week. Multiple games compressed into short spans were but one of the early challenges confronting the developing sport.

In the beginning, football was football—whether played by schools large or small. During the horse-and-buggy era, the latter often played the former. Coaches had to find opponents wherever they could. Predictably, schools with larger enrollments usually dominated the smaller ones. To fill a schedule, some coaches resorted to more than a single game each season against the same opponent. They often scheduled "town" or "community" teams or even the second-string, freshman or junior varsity team from a nearby college or university. Before 1920, Dallas High School played games against opponents as diverse as Dallas Social Club, Dallas Commercial College, the YMCA and Wesley College. Ninety miles south, Waco High School's schedule included games against the TCU "Lightweights," the Baylor "Lightweights," Hill's Business College and the TCU Reserves. Once UIL began establishing guidelines for participation and forming logical district and conference alignments, it became far easier for high schools to craft schedules matching their teams more evenly against regular-season opponents. But progress was initially slow. In the early 1900s, Texas school officials and administrators showed general ambivalence if not hostility toward what they largely considered a violent and brutal new sport. Early efforts to delineate a method of determining a state football champion evolved with wailing and gnashing of teeth.

Imbalanced schedules remained perhaps the greatest shortcoming of high school football prior to UIL's 1920 assumption of control and organization of the sport on a statewide basis. The problem reflected the difficulty of finding opponents, as well as the uneven nature of statewide competition. In 1913, Houston Sam Houston played Corpus Christi for the Southwest Texas title and the right to advance in the quasi-official playoff tournament. During the first twenty minutes of play, the Tigers scored sixty-two points to Corpus's none. That contest was the preamble to the 1913 championship game between Houston and Comanche that had but "a semblance of authority."[9]

UIL's tentative 1913 efforts to sponsor a state title contest proved embarrassing and disastrous. Great discontent fed by the newspaper press arose over a host of issues, including whether Comanche or Fort Worth should represent the North against the South's Houston Sam Houston Tigers. Following a December 6 playoff between Fort Worth and Comanche, UIL's State Executive Committee overturned the Cowtown victory, ruling that three Fort Worth players had been ineligible. In spite of lively (and possibly legitimate) Fort Worth protest, in an unofficial December 13 title contest, Houston played and defeated Comanche 20–0 on Austin's Clark Field. This problem-fraught experience was enough to put UIL off for another seven years before finally assuming direct, official regulatory power over high school football.

In subsequent seasons, Austin High School claimed unofficial back-to-back state titles (1914–15). Both years, Coach Bobby Whitaker's Maroons pitched opening-season shutouts against the Texas Deaf School, victories failing to equate to Austin's two title-game shutouts that the Maroons imposed on Fort Worth North Side in 1914 and 1915. Without some centralized supervision of the sport, title claims remained subjective if not suspect. Football's growing popularity, as well as UIL's evolving philosophy about the role of public education in general, ultimately demanded UIL supervision.

At the turn of the century, Texas public education was relatively new. There was uncertainty about what constituted legitimate "extracurricular activities." Temple Public Schools superintendent J.F. Kimball's 1912 appeal, "Athletics in the High School," declared that sports created "manly men" with "self-mastery and self-restraint"—that athletics shaped adults who became well prepared for real-world life. Roy Bedichek, UIL's director of athletics during the critically formative years of 1917 to 1922, explained that "the motivation of effort by awakening rivalry is one of the earliest devices adopted by man in the education of the young." He promoted "interscholastic competition as a means of using to advantage this competitive urge, impulse, or instinct." He drew inspiration from the ancient Greek "conception of life itself as tension" arising from a "conflict of opposites" and also, despite their limitations, "the monstrous competitions" that "dominated education in China for more than a thousand years." Bedichek declared that interscholastic athletic rivalry and the orchestration of "properly officiated contests" ultimately prepared the young for citizenship.[10] In particular, Bedichek "believed that the game of football was wholesome and beneficial, a necessary adjunct to a well-rounded education."[11] By 1921, the UIL Executive Committee officially decided that public education had the responsibility of training both body and mind. Thus, UIL embraced the notion that exploitation and benevolent direction of natural youthful and competitive urges would groom Texas teens for adulthood.

Bedichek and Roy Henderson, his 1922 successor as director of athletics, became the architects of the state playoff system that is the ancestor of today's modern playoff brackets. Based on 1920 team records, the duo independently selected schools they considered worthy of playoff berths. Armed with only

Roy Bedichek (1878–1959) appears circa 1928, some nine years after he and Roy Henderson brought Texas high school football under UIL auspices. The duo designed the ancestor of today's playoff bracket system leading to the state championship. Bedichek is commonly considered the "Father of Texas High School Sports." *Courtesy of Robert Bedichek and Alan Pipkin (top) and UIL (bottom).*

the haziest authority to act, the two men matched the state's six undefeated teams—Abilene, Bryan Street (Dallas), Cleburne, Corpus Christi, Clarkesville and Houston Heights—in an impromptu championship playoff resulting in a co-championship shared by Houston Heights and Cleburne. The durable UIL administration of Texas high school football had begun.

The December 1920 UIL publication *Leaguer* proudly informed readers that 239 teams played over six hundred games involving 4,302 young Texans. That same year, 2,432 Texas schools held membership in UIL. The number of schools leapt the following year to 3,345, making creation of logical football districts far less challenging for UIL administrators.[12] In 1922, sixteen such districts were organized by counties into a bracket system for postseason play, a configuration making geographic sense when long- and sometimes even short-distance transportation often presented significant obstacles. To resolve the related problem of large schools dominating smaller ones, UIL initially established two separate conferences. The "A" schools competed for state championships, while the playoff series for "B" schools extended only through the regional round. UIL made various refinements over the following decade. By 1934, UIL established an additional "C" conference. This group of smaller schools competed only for district titles.

In 1948, UIL tripled the number of state title opportunities, creating three conferences—City, 2A and 1A—all vying for separate state crowns. Three years later, a new configuration offered four football championships ranging from the largest conference, 4A, through the smallest, 1A. In 1972, three additional conferences joined the state title chase: B, Eight-Man and Six-Man. UIL dropped Eight-Man football in 1976. Four years later, the conference formerly designated as "B" became 1A, and remaining conferences were reclassified upward through the largest, today identified as 5A. In 1990, 5A programs began competing for two state titles, one for schools with larger enrollment in a "Division-1" (D-1), and the other smaller category classified as "Division-2" (D-2). Conference 4A received the same courtesy in 1996, raising the number of separate state titles to eight. Two years later, conferences 3A and 2A also received D-1 and D-2 distinctions. Finally, beginning in 2006, conferences 1A and Six-Man competed in two divisions as well.

UIL Conference Division, 1920–2012[13]

Year(s)	Conference(s)
1920	• All schools, regardless of size, competed for a single state title
1924	• Creation of an eight-division playoff bracket for larger Class A schools • Bi-district winners from sixteen Class B districts (smaller schools) advanced to play Class A district champions
1926	• Creation of Class A; competed for single state title • Creation of Class B; allowed to advance only through bi-district and regional rounds
1934	• Conference C added; could not advance beyond district title
1938	• Six-Man added; could not advance beyond district title
1939	• Conference AA (formerly A) went to state-title game • Conference A (formerly B) went to regional championship • Conference B went to bi-district
1941	• Six-Man teams competed for bi-district title
1946	• Conference A now competed for regional title
1948–50	City 2A 1A * Rows from this point forward indicate conferences offering annual state titles.

Year(s)	Conference(s)
1951–71	4A (845 and above enrollment) 3A (370–845 enrollment) 2A (200–370 enrollment) 1A (120–200 enrollment)
1972–75	4A 3A 2A 1A (100–119 enrollment) B (fewer than 100 enrollment) Eight-Man Six-Man
1976–79	4A 3A 2A 1A B Six-Man
1980–89	5A 4A 3A 2A 1A Six-Man * Beginning in 1982, both district champions and runners-up advanced to the playoffs.
1990–95	5A D-1 5A D-2 4A 3A 2A 1A Six-Man * Beginning in 1990, third-place 5A finishers also advanced to the playoffs.

Year(s)	Conference(s)
1996–98	5A D-1
	5A D-2
	4A D-1
	4A D-2
	3A
	2A
	1A
	Six-Man
	* Beginning in 1996, UIL instituted the sudden-death tie-breaker system.
1999–2005	5A D-1
	5A D-2
	4A D-1
	4A D-2
	3A D-1
	3A D-2
	2A D-1
	2A D-2
	1A
	Six-Man
2006–12	5A D-1, 5A D-2 → 245 5A schools
	4A D-1, 4A D-2 → 242 4A schools
	3A D-1, 3A D-2 → 184 3A schools
	2A D-1, 2A D-2 → 204 2A schools
	1A D-1, 1A D-2 → 165 1A schools
	Six-Man D-1, Six-Man D-2 → 130 Six-Man schools

Certainly, a chasm separates Six-Man football in schools with enrollment of fewer than 100 from the 5A or 4A conference eleven-man teams that draw players from student bodies of 1,000 to 4,500. Nevertheless, if enrollments differ drastically, enthusiasm remains uniform across conference divides. With twelve annual title games for six different conferences, regardless of conference, Texans old and young are no less passionate about bringing home a title. In that pursuit, a few Texas schools have established themselves, at least for now and according to the definition proposed in the present work, as high school football dynasties.

CHAPTER 1

IT'S GOOD TO BE KING

B y any objective measure, Waco owned Texas high school football in the 1920s. During that decade, the Tigers reached the final six times, winning it four times. Waco High School's football history began, however, at the turn of the century.

The school's monthly journal, *Daisy Chain*, mentions football as early as 1902. The yearbook editor of 1903–1904 wrote, "The record of our football team this year again shows that science has more to do with the game than sheer brute strength. Our team had no coach, no suits and were very much lighter" than their opponents. By November 1905, the yearbook proudly "notes that 'we have not lost a game [of football] in three years.'"[14] Regrettably, any specifics about the team's win-loss record during those seasons are lost to history.

Nevertheless, the sparse documentation of the program during the twentieth century's first decade does suggest that the Tigers did not have a losing season from 1907 through 1911. The team went 2–4–0 in 1912. The following season witnessed the arrival of the "Waco Wizard," Paul Leighton Tyson (1886–1950), the man who soon became a Texas football coaching legend. Tyson was born in Hope, Arkansas, the same town that later produced forty-second president Bill Clinton (1993–2001) and forty-fourth Arkansas governor Mike Huckabee (1996–2007). In 1890, Tyson moved with his family to Santa Anna, Texas. He earned his college degree at Texas Christian University (then located in Waco and called Addison-Randolph College).

Waco coach Paul Tyson in 1914, his first winning season as head coach of the Tigers. Tyson took his team to seven state finals (six of them consecutive), four state titles (1922, 1925–27) and one mythical national championship (1927).

With good reason, many today consider Tyson the "dominant figure of the first 50 years" in Texas high school football.[15] At age twenty-seven, Tyson took charge of the 1913 Waco High School Tigers. That team went 1–2–2. The following season, Tyson's players posted a 4–2–0 winning record, marking the beginning of a successful twenty-six-year run taking Waco High to seven state finals (six of them consecutive), four state championships (1922, 1925–27) and one mythical national title (1927). Predictably, Tyson received posthumous induction into both the Texas Sports Hall of Fame (1955) and the Texas High School Coaches Association Hall of Fame (1963). Tyson's Waco teams of 1921–22 and 1925–27 scored 3,006 points while allowing only 100. Their record against other high school teams was 66–0–2.

Like many of the great coaches that came after him, Tyson discovered and employed that delicate balance between discipline and calm, reasoned instruction that made his players respect him and want to perform well for him. He expected much from team members, but when they erred, he used gentle, clear direction about how to correct their mistakes—not derisive, explosive, emotional tirades. On the technical side, Tyson was an effective innovator. He borrowed and perfected the deceptive spin play from celebrated coach Glenn Scobey "Pop" Warner and then used it to leave defenses with little idea about which of his players on offense had the football. Tyson also took a leave of absence in 1931 to spend a season studying under Stanford University's Warner. That same school year, Tyson paid a visit to South Bend, Indiana, to observe Coach Knute Rockne's Notre

Dame spring practice. He returned to Central Texas, putting Warner's revolutionary single-wing offense to use at Waco High. Both Coach Rockne (1918–30) and Texas Christian University coach Leo R. "Dutch" Meyer (1934–52) considered Tyson one of the greatest coaches at any level of that particular era. (Fittingly, Meyer had been a guard on Tyson's Waco teams.) During Tyson's tenure at Waco High (1913–30, 1932–42), he coached his Tigers to more than two hundred wins.

But for the fact that Waco High School did not become a full-fledged member of UIL until 1922, Tyson might well have earned a fifth state title. With good cause, the 1921 Waco team claimed that it deserved that year's state championship. These Tigers beat Mexia 138–0 in the season opener, dispensed with nearby Marlin 97–0 in game two, shut out the Baylor freshmen 34–0, allowed only one of its nine opponents to cross the fifty-yard line all season long, scored 526 total points and averaged 53 points per regular-season contest. In their undefeated nine-game season (including wins over the junior varsities of Baylor and Southwestern University), Waco's defense did not allow a single score. Perhaps more importantly, that same Waco team posted a 28–0 victory over 1921 UIL state finalist Dallas Oak Cliff. Tyson unsuccessfully attempted to schedule a post-playoff matchup with that year's state champion, Bryan. The outcome remains forever uncertain since Bryan politely (and probably wisely) declined to play.

Waco's 1921 ambiguity toward UIL was manifest at the organization's November 26 Meeting of Delegates, hosted by the UIL Executive Committee in Dallas at the Oriental Hotel. Statewide representatives, including Waco principals E.T. Genheimer and E.D. Johnson, discussed the merits of an official UIL annual championship. Genheimer opposed a state title game because of the vast size of Texas, the expenses involved and the prospect of playoffs lengthening the season. Waco's reservations notwithstanding, delegates unanimously approved the plan. The following season, Waco High School put itself under the UIL umbrella and quickly made its presence felt.

The Tigers advanced to the championship round in each of the next six years (1922–27), winning four, including the 1922 matchup against Abilene High. The 1922 Tigers won the official UIL title, defeating Coach Pete Shotwell's Abilene High School Eagles 13–10. The Tiger victory in the finals capped an 11–0–1 season that began with five consecutive shutouts, including a 118–0 win over Waco State Home and a 100–0 victory over Corsicana. If the 1921 Tiger season is included, the latter victory marked Waco's fourteenth shutout in a row (at the time, second nationally only to a Los Angeles team that had posted fifteen from 1898 to 1899). Waco's

Page 16   CHAMBER OF COMMERCE NEWS   December, 1921

State Champions

WACO HIGH SCHOOL LINE-UP
First Row (left to right)—Meers, Walker, Sisco, Buchanan, Dutton, Nash (captain), Second Row—Naylor, Washam, Fall, Strickland, Coates, Rikard, Chambless, Brandon, Third Row—Rowell, Johnson, McCullough, Last Row—Crosthwait (manager), Gregory (trainer), Tucker (Morning News), Tyson (coach).

The 1921 Waco High football team has had a remarkable record and has turned in a string of victories seldom equaled, not only in high school circles, but among colleges as well. The team has scored a total of 526 points to its opponents' nothing during the year. This record has been achieved in eight games, during which the thirty-yard line of the Waco eleven was crossed only once. This distinction belongs to Oak Cliff (Dallas) High, which team had the oval on Waco's twenty-five-yard line during the first quarter of the game. Marshall High has the distinction of being the only eleven to hold Waco scoreless during the first period of the game. Marshall put up a game battle, but finally submerged to a 87-to-0 score. The other games have been walk-aways for the local crew.

Much credit for the splendor of Waco's season goes to Coach Paul Tyson, who has worked untiringly to give Waco a winning football team. He has rounded the material at hand into the most formidable high school aggregation in the state, a team that could give a good account of itself pitted against any high school eleven in the country. It is regretted that Waco could not meet some really strong out-of-the-state elevens this year.

The team is composed of eleven stars, all of whom have the ability to play "team" football. Individual stars are plentiful on the squad, but when it comes to team work the "Tigers", as the team is known locally, works like a well oiled machine. The average age of the team is 17.3 years, the oldest boy on the squad being 19 years old. Four are three-year men, the others are either first or second-year men. The average weight is 159 pounds. The Waco High School challenges any school in the state to show a higher scholastic standard than required by Waco of her athletics. In fact, a number of the boys have a remarkable scholastic record.

Waco did not see the wisdom of identifying herself with the Interscholastic League on the grounds that the schedule would be limited to a district, but at the same time the Waco High School observed eligibility and scholastic requirement more stringently than required by the League.

It is regretted that the Bryan High School, champions of the League, declined to meet Waco for the state championship. Waco High maintained training after its game with Marshall High on December 2 because of Bryan High to play the Waco team. On December 10 in Austin the Bryan authorities agreed to play Waco, but later backed out of this agreement and then a subsequent agreement. Waco's record being far superior to that of the Bryan High School and the fact that Bryan declined to play Waco after agreeing to do so, makes Bryan's claim to the state championship honors absurd in the minds of all fair-minded sportsmen. The Waco High School then is justly entitled to the title of State High School Champions of the football season of 1921.

The following is the record of the team:

Waco	138—Mexia 0.	Waco	63—Beaumont 0.
Waco	97—Marlin 0.	Waco	38—Austin 0.
Waco	34—Baylor Cubs 0.	Waco	41—Hillsboro 0.
Waco	28—Oak Cliff 0.	Waco	87—Marshall 0.

The 1921 Waco players, in their patented tiger-striped uniforms, pose on the Waco High School steps. As the newspaper article suggests, Tyson's Tigers believed they deserved that season's Texas state football championship whether their school was a member of the UIL or not.

State Champions 1922

The 1922 Waco Tigers became the first Waco team to win a state football championship sanctioned and authorized by the UIL.

winning streak ended at seventeen games when an undefeated Temple team tied the Tigers in the 1922 quarterfinals. In a football era long before today's overtime tie-breaking system, the Tigers and Wildcats reconvened a few days later, and Waco drubbed the opposition 30–0 in the rematch.

In the 1922 title game at Fort Worth's Panther Park, before a crowd of five thousand, Waco's John Drew "Boody" Johnson scored all thirteen Tiger points: a touchdown, the point after and two drop-kicked field goals, including the thirty-seven-yard game winner with only two minutes left in the contest. As late as 1968, "Mr. Schoolboy Football" Harold Ratliff declared, "Unhesitatingly, I would select Boody Johnson [1921–23] as the greatest high school football player in Texas history."[16] Waco's 1922 title bid was the first of Tyson's six consecutive finals appearances. Waco lost in 1923 and 1924. Before the 1923 Tigers-Eagles finals rematch, both Waco and Abilene had posted eleven shutouts during a single season, tying the then-national record set in 1907 by Berkeley, California. Shotwell's Abilene team won its first state title when Pete Hanna kicked a fourth-

The star of the 1922 state championship game was Waco's John Drew "Boody" Johnson, who scored all thirteen Tiger points. Harold Ratliff, "Mr. Schoolboy Football," considered Johnson the "greatest high school football player in Texas history."

quarter field goal. The final score was 3–0. It was the first loss by Tyson's Tigers since the 1922 finals.

The 1924 championship game took place in icy, eighteen-degree Dallas temperatures. Afterward, Waco fans complained that Coach Howard Allen's Dallas Oak Cliff (today's Adamson) Leopards enjoyed an unfair advantage using oil-burning stoves for warmth on the sidelines. Protestations notwithstanding, the Tiger's lost 31–0. The defeat was Waco's last until the 1928 loss to Corsicana. Over the next three seasons, Tyson teams secured the first title three-peat in Texas schoolboy history (1925–27), successively defeating Dallas Forest Avenue, Dallas Oak Cliff and Abilene.

Waco's 1925 team opened the season with ten straight shutouts. In the bi-district playoff round, it pounded poor Brady 122–0. Not until the quarterfinals did the Itasca Wampus Cats light up the scoreboard, but even then, their humble field goal paled alongside the 40 points posted by the Tigers. The season's only hiccup came the following week when Waco lost the semifinal "game on the field." Beaumont bested Waco 8–7 only to have its victory overturned by a postgame judgment that the winner was guilty of an eligibility infraction. In a rerun of the semifinal, Waco responded to its playoff resurrection by overrunning Robstown 32–0. At Dallas Fair Park on January 2, 1926, before 12,875 spectators, the 1925 Tigers beat Dallas Forest Avenue (today's James Madison) 20–7. At season's end, Tyson's mighty Tigers had scored 606 points while allowing a paltry 10. And 7 of those came in the title match.

The 1926 Tigers enjoyed a rematch against their 1924 finals adversary, Dallas Oak Cliff. They avenged Waco's earlier loss to the Leopards. On the way to that title win, the 1926 Tigers allowed only 7 points in their first ten contests, hanging 101 points on scoreless Corpus Christi in that year's district opener. Anticipating a 1926 title game against Oak Cliff, Tyson sent Assistant Coach Dusty Bogges to scout every regular-season Leopard game. Tyson's then-uncommon foresight paid off big. At the December 18, 1926 final in Waco's Cotton Palace Stadium before fifteen thousand (the largest title game crowd to date), Waco won 20–7, coming away from the contest with its third state championship in a mere five years. For their troubles, Tyson, whose 1926 salary was $2,250 (about $28,600 in today's economy), and his assistant coach, E.H. Bernhausen, received a trip to California's January 1, 1927 Rose Bowl, in which Alabama played Stanford to a 7–7 tie.

The 1927 Tigers duplicated their perfect 14–0–0 season of 1925, demonstrating far more offensive firepower. Waco won its first nine contests by shutting out the opposition, including a 93–0 season-opening win over Georgetown and a later 107–0 thrashing of Marlin. In the 1927 quarterfinals, the Tigers pounded Houston Davis 124–0. By season's end, Tyson's team had scored 782 points. The team averaged almost 56 points per game, setting a standard for single-season points scored that endured as the Texas record until the 1975 Class-B Big Sandy Wildcats broke it with 824. Defensively, Waco was as good as it was on offense. The Tigers did not even give up a touchdown until the tenth game of the season. Not only was the 1927 Tiger title win against Abilene the first-ever Texas three-peat, but that 21–14 victory also made Waco the first-ever team to secure four state titles.

Not content to let the glorious season end, Tyson took his team to its first interstate competition (something he had tried unsuccessfully to introduce in 1921 against teams from Oklahoma and Arkansas). Playing teams from out of state was not unprecedented. In 1922, Cleburne coach Fred G. Erney, whose 9–2 Yellow Jackets' season had ended in the state playoff semifinal,

The program from the 1927 state championship game between the Waco Tigers and the Abilene Eagles at Cotton Palace Park. Waco won the contest 21–14, thus securing the first-ever title three-peat in Texas schoolboy history and becoming the first Texas team to earn four UIL state titles.

The Tigers are in action before a huge Ohio crowd in the 1927 "national championship" matchup against Ohio's Latin School of Chardon. Waco decisively won the ballgame 44–12. The win marked the apogee of Paul Tyson's career as Waco High School head football coach.

took on a visiting Ohio team, Dayton's Steele High School. It was the first-ever intersectional game played in Texas. Steele met the Yellow Jackets behind the local high school building at Cleburne's Rhome Field, a facility opened only fifty-seven days before. On December 2, 1922, the Dayton team narrowly defeated Cleburne, 15–14. Steele returned to Texas in 1923. Before an eager overflow crowd, the home team lost again, posting only ten points to Dayton's thirty-seven. Undoubtedly, this experiment further fueled Tyson's growing interest in interstate competition.

On December 26, 1927, just nine days after his Tigers defeated Abilene for the 1927 Texas title, Waco did battle in Ohio before a crowd of eighteen thousand against Latin School of Chardon (twenty-five miles east-northeast of Cleveland). Contemporaries billed the contest as the high school national championship. Waco emerged the winner, defeating Latin 44–12. However mythical the national high school title is both then and now, Waco's convincing win at least confers some credence to the Tiger team's claim to the 1927 national championship. The honor would be the first of fifteen such titles received by nine different Texas schools—more schools than any other state in the nation through 2012. Only three other states—Ohio (twenty-five), California (seventeen) and Florida (fifteen)—can boast as many or more total national titles.

Meanwhile, the 1920s Waco win streak continued into the 1928 season. Corsicana ended it at twenty-five games. Harold Ratliff pinpoints that loss as the event leading to the succession of Coach Dewey Mayhew's Abilene High School Eagles to the high school football throne.[17] Abilene won the 1928 title 38–0 over Port Arthur.

While Tyson's 1929 team failed to reach the final, it won its first eleven games, losing only in the semifinal to that year's state co-champion, Breckenridge. The Tigers did not make the playoffs again until 1939. However, Waco ventured out of state once more in 1934, beating Grover Cleveland High of St. Louis, Missouri, 18–14. Four years later, Tyson's team fell 14–0 to Chicago Fenger from Illinois. When Waco finally returned to the Texas championship contest the following year, the team faced the Lubbock Westerners, the 1939 "team of destiny." This Cinderella squad's head coach, Weldon Chapman, had died in the middle of the season. Westerners assistant coach J.G. Keys successfully stepped in. The final was close, but a game-winning, fourth-quarter Lubbock touchdown stopped Tyson's Tigers from adding a fifth championship trophy to an already sizable collection.

Waco went a disappointing 3–6–1 in 1940. It was Tyson's first losing season since his inaugural year (1913), when his Tigers went 1–2–2. But Tyson rallied the troops again in 1941, posting a 7–2–0 season. Nevertheless, Temple stood between Waco and the District 10-2A title. The Wildcats advanced and continued undefeated until falling to Wichita Falls in the 1941 final. Waco's school board refused to renew the fifty-five-year-old Tyson's contract for 1942. Thus, a landmark era in Waco High School football came to an end. Thereafter, the Waco legend coached at Beaumont South Park and Dallas Jesuit High Schools. Tyson concluded his career in Brownwood at Daniel Baker College, going 2–6–2 for the 1949 football season. He died there during a faculty meeting in 1950 at age sixty-four.

Tyson's replacement was Coach Harry Stiteler, who had coached Corpus Christi to the 1938 championship. Stiteler took Waco to the 1942 playoffs but lost to Breckenridge in the bi-district round. The two teams met again in 1943, tying 13–13. This time, the Tigers advanced beyond bi-district to the quarterfinals, where Lufkin shut them out 25–0. In 1944, Stiteler's team reprised the previous year's performance, again defeating the Buckaroos but falling 33–6 to Lufkin. Finally, in 1945, Stiteler took the Tigers all the way. Waco won a share of a fifth state title that season, battling Coach Eck Curtis's Dallas Highland Park in front of a then-record crowd of 45,790 in the Dallas Cotton Bowl. The two teams had met early in the regular season, and Highland Park won 7–0. Waco gained a measure of retribution in the state final, as the teams tied 7–7 for a co-championship.

It was the first-ever Scottie finals title, coming after two previously frustrating seasons. Coach Rusty Russell (1942–44), Bobby Layne and Doak Walker came close in 1943, losing the semifinal 21–20 to the eventual state champion San Angelo Central Bobcats. Layne graduated the

Highland Park coach Rusty Russell counsels players Bobby Layne, Doak Walker and Douglas McDonald. During his three seasons there (1942–44), Russell's teams advanced successively to the quarterfinals, semifinals and finals. Before coming to Highland Park, Russell enjoyed a successful sixteen-year tenure as coach at Fort Worth Masonic Home, where his record was 33–4–2. In *Twelve Mighty Orphans,* Jim Dent christens Russell as the "Father of the Spread Offense."

following spring. Walker and his teammates lost the 1944 final at Austin's Memorial Stadium 20–7 to Port Arthur Jefferson. Layne and Walker later re-converged in Detroit, where they brought the Lions the 1952 NFL championship. In a recent echo of Highland Park's contribution to the Detroit franchise, 2005 state champion Scottie quarterback Matthew Stafford joined the Lions in 2009 and in 2011 helped make them a 2011 wildcard playoff team. The Lion's 10–6 regular-season record in the NFC North "Black and Blue" Division earned the team its first playoff appearance in twelve years.

Meanwhile, in 1946, Bill DuBose replaced Stiteler at Waco. After two seasons, yet another new coach, Carl Price, assumed the Waco helm. In his inaugural year, Waco posted a perfect 14–0–0 season. His Tigers scored 415 points and allowed only 89. The 1948 team delivered Waco's sixth state

By defeating Amarillo's Golden Sandies, the 1948 Tigers, led by Coach Carl Price (middle row, far right), earned Waco's sixth state title. The 1948 National Sports News Service anointed the Tigers as that season's unofficial national champion. It was Waco's second time to receive this honorable distinction.

championship. In Fort Worth before 16,000 fans, the Tigers shut out the Amarillo's Golden Sandies 21–0. At season's end, Waco received recognition from the 1948 NSNS as that year's unofficial national high school football champion (Waco's second such "title"). While the Tigers made it back to the semifinals in 1953 (a contest they lost 12–7 to Houston Lamar), Waco would not return to the championship round again until 2006.

In '48

During the fifty-eight-year interim between title appearances, many things changed, including the Waco mascot. The Tigers became the Lions in 1986 when "Old" Waco High merged with Jefferson Moore and Richfield High Schools. Leaving behind the ancient tiger-striped uniform and colors of the Tyson era, the "new" Lions returned to the state final twenty-one years after the tripartite merger. It was Waco's tenth state finals appearance. In the 2006 title game, Waco lost 34–14 to perennial 4A finalist La Marque. Today's Lions continue to field competitive playoff teams, hoping to better their admirable 6–4 record in the finals and carry forward their venerable tradition dating from the early twentieth century.

"Amicable #3" is drilled southwest of Waco in McLennan County's small South Bosque oil field. Discovery and development of this field roughly coincided with Waco's football heyday. Connection between Waco's petroleum production and football success is, of course, conjectural. But in the Oil Belt to Waco's west, the correlation between football and oil production is difficult to deny. *Courtesy of the Harry Ransom Center, University of Texas at Austin.*

It may be more than coincidence that the success of Tyson's 1920s Tigers followed the discovery of a small South Bosque oil field. The newly discovered petroleum reserves boosted McLennan County's early twentieth-century economy and brought Humble Oil tankers to Waco streets. Of course, no demonstrable connection exists between Waco's short-lived mini–oil boom and "personnel"—strapping, recently arrived young lads fueling local high school athletic fortunes. Not so 150 miles and more to the west, where a palpable link connects oil production and the rise of powerful "Petro-Dynasties."

CHAPTER 2

THE PETRO-DYNASTIES

The January 10, 1901 discovery of Spindletop oil in Beaumont made modern-day Texas. It opened an oil field producing 100,000 barrels of petroleum a day and defined the Texas economy for the rest of the twentieth century. It also defined the rise of several high school football programs. In fact, the rapid escalation of football's statewide popularity coincides with the ascendant Texas oil economy. From the 1920s through the 1980s, petroleum production powered not only the Lone Star State's economy but also many successful schoolboy football teams.

A generous 1920s UIL residence rule allowed boys to play as long as their parents lived in a school district by September 1. Ratliff remembers how "ambitious coaches," particularly in the Oil Belt, "began recruiting players and moving families from town to town. Ranger, Breckenridge and Cisco"—all highly successful programs—"were in the heart of the oil boom."[18] The proximity of these three towns, along with the nearby oil towns of Albany and Eastland, created an intense regional rivalry. Having petroleum reserves made a difference.

The example of Clyde is instructive. Located geographically in the Oil Belt but bereft of any significant oil deposits, Clyde was part of a seven-team district including the oil-rich powerhouse football communities of Ranger, Eastland and Albany. In 1961, coming off five consecutive losing seasons, Clyde's Bulldogs had a school record–tying nine-win season. In district play, Clyde even pitched three shutouts. This unprecedented Bulldog performance notwithstanding, in a day before multiple playoff berths coming out of

Odessa's Ratliff Stadium, built in 1982, is not merely a high school football field. It is a Texas football icon representative of the five Texas schoolboy Petro-Dynasties that rose to prominence in the Lone Star State. Appropriately, a pump jack stands in front of Ratliff, reminding fans of the connection between West Texas petroleum and Odessa Permian football success. *Courtesy of Mark Sterkel*, Odessa American.

district play, Clyde failed to advance beyond the regular season when the Bulldogs could not get past oil-rich district foe and defending state champion Albany. Albany's Lions, powered by multiple players who continued their football careers at the college level, went on that year to secure back-to-back titles with an 18–12 finals win over Hull-Daisetta. While concentration of petroleum reserves in a school district was no guarantee of victory, it often conferred decided advantage.

It is, of course, impossible to track all eligible move-ins whose families took oil-field jobs in locations with competitive programs with first-class

coaching and promising title chances. It is nevertheless naïve to dismiss the importance of such wily relocations and covert recruitment. Indeed, legend has it that the fabled "Slingin' Sammy" Baugh moved to Sweetwater only after someone purposely purchased an oil company, thus facilitating the Baugh family's transfer to this West Texas football town. This kind of practice became one of multiple factors prompting a 1950s tightening of UIL eligibility regulations.

Regarding the relationship between high school football and the petroleum industry, there is a reason that Al Reinert declares, "For years...[the] two most elite public high schools in the state, Highland Park in Dallas and Lamar in Houston, would meet in the state eliminations with teams from the oil boomtowns—places like Abilene, Stamford, and Wichita Falls—teams composed of roughnecks' sons and, often as not, of roughnecks themselves."[19] Whatever the role the oil field played in filling high school rosters, from the

1920s forward, there arose a remarkable number of successful programs in the oil patch. Among them were Amarillo, Abilene, Breckenridge, Wichita Falls and Odessa Permian, all schools that captured four or more state titles. All five locations have been basic Texas oil hubs for decades.

Amarillo Golden Sandstorms

The Amarillo Golden "Sandies," named after the sandstorms that turn Panhandle skies a yellowish hue, etched their name into the record books by making four trips to the state finals (1930, 1934–36) during the decade of the 1930s. In the process, they duplicated Waco's 1920s three-peat. Significantly, the discovery and exploitation of the massive Texas Panhandle oil field (with potential 1938 production of 1,178,796 barrels a day) overlapped Amarillo's three consecutive wins. Coach Blair Cherry (1901–66) directed the remarkable Sandies run through his skillful use of the double wingback formation and the careful choreographing of support from school district administrators, particularly the sports-minded high school principal R.B. Norman; the local newspaper's sports editor, who provided thorough game coverage; and community members who vicariously identified the Sandies successes as their own. Cherry used his gifts for football strategy, attention to detail and precision, motivation of players and unrelenting work to build a "Depression Dynasty" in the Texas Panhandle.

Cherry cut his teeth in the coaching profession at the Texas Oil Belt school of Ranger from 1926 to 1928. There, he compiled a 21–11–3 record that included a 1926 semifinal appearance against Dallas Adamson. After a one-year sojourn at Fort Worth North Side, Cherry headed for the Panhandle. He began his seven-year Amarillo tenure in 1930. The football gods smiled on him from the start. When he left Amarillo seven years later, his record was an impressive 81–7–1 (91 percent). The year Amarillo hired the twenty-six-year-old Cherry, some in the school district had hoped instead to hire Pete Shotwell, who already had two state titles to his credit—one at Abilene (1923) and the other at Breckenridge (1929). On their way to the 1929 title, Shotwell's Buckaroos had knocked the Sandies out of the playoffs in the quarterfinals. But Shotwell remained in Breckenridge, and Cherry came to Amarillo. Cherry's 1930 team quickly closed the mouths of naysayers, shutting out six of Amarillo's opponents and imposing humiliating defeats on Childress (52–13) and Wichita Falls (85–18). Shotwell's Buckaroos were among the victims of those shutouts, losing to Amarillo 13–0 in the bi-district playoff round.

The Sandies eventually advanced to the 1930 final, played in Fort Worth. They entered the game a prohibitive favorite over the unsung Tyler Lions. In spite of a 13–6 halftime lead, the Sandies faltered in the second half, and the Lions won their first state title 25–13. Cherry produced powerhouse teams the next three seasons, including a 1932 team that shut out Sammy Baugh's Sweetwater Mustangs 7–0 in the quarterfinal. The Sandies won that matchup in Amarillo on a snow-covered Butler Field. The next week, those same Sandies narrowly lost the semifinal, 7–6, to Coach Rusty Russell's boys from Fort Worth Masonic Home. Amarillo did not return to the final until 1934. To get there, the Sandies again faced Masonic Home in the semifinal, but this time they edged them out 3–0 on a Johnny "Red" Stidger field goal.

The 1934 Sandies won Amarillo's first state championship, upsetting the heavily favored Corpus Christi's Buccaneers 48–0. The two teams played before a then-record crowd of 21,986 at Fair Park Stadium in Dallas. Amarillo made five interceptions and limited Corpus to 86 yards of total offense. Amarillo offensive standouts Stidger and John Harlow (who became the first player ever to score four touchdowns in a final) contributed mightily to the 499 yards accumulated by the Sandies. Amarillo's forty-eight-point margin of victory remained the largest in a title game until 1962, when Chuck Curtis's Jacksboro Tigers beat Rockdale 52–0.

The 1934 Golden Sandstorms became the first Amarillo team to win the state title. After edging out Fort Worth Masonic Home in a closely fought 3–0 semifinal, the Sandies advanced to the championship game, where they hammered the Corpus Christi Buccaneers 48–0. Their shutout win remained the largest margin of victory in finals play for twenty-eight years.

The 1935 state-champion Sandies. Bob Cleeson contributed a pass and a run accounting for twelve of Amarillo's thirteen points. Coach Blair Cherry (upper left) took the Sandies to three consecutive state titles (1934–36), only the second three-peat in Texas schoolboy history. Upon Cherry's 1937 departure, Assistant Coach Howard Lynch (upper right) became head coach and led Amarillo to a fourth championship in 1940.

In spite of the loss of eight senior starters, the 1935 Sandies returned with a vengeance. In that year's playoffs, Cherry's Sandies successively defeated Breckenridge and San Angelo (both shutouts) and then Wichita Falls to return to the final. At the championship round in Dallas before fifteen thousand spectators, they earned a second consecutive title, winning by a slender 13–7 margin over Greenville.

Amarillo's three-peat came in 1936 over the Kerrville Antlers (future high school football home of "Johnny Football" Manziel, Texas A&M's 2012 Heisman trophy winner). The game was played before a crowd of seventeen thousand on Amarillo's Butler Field. The Sandies opened that season with three successive wins over out-of-state opponents Norman, Paul's Valley and Oklahoma City Capitol Hill—all from Oklahoma. They fared equally well against their Texas adversaries, shutting out six of the total ten. The Sandies won the championship 19–6 on the strength of an interception,

Blair Cherry appears during his later coaching years. Cherry became the only Texas football coach to lead his players to both a high school state title and a Southwest Conference championship. While head coach of the University of Texas Longhorns, Cherry guided his teams to wins over Alabama in the 1948 Sugar Bowl and Georgia in the 1949 Orange Bowl.

two blocked kicks by Mike Sweeney (one of which he recovered for a score) and a touchdown scored by "Wild Horse" Mayes. In seven glorious seasons—1930–36—Cherry had compiled eighty-one wins, including a remarkable forty-five shutouts. During Cherry's last three seasons at Amarillo, his Sandies had posted a fifty-four-game home winning streak and a 39–1 record. He left Amarillo in 1937, accepting a job under Head Coach Dana X. Bible at the University of Texas (UT). There, Cherry served first as offensive coordinator (1937–46) and later as head coach (1947–50). In the latter role, he compiled a four-year, 32–10–1 record that included postseason appearances in the Sugar Bowl, Orange Bowl and Cotton Bowl. In 1950, Cherry became the only coach to win a title at both the high school and Southwest Conference college level.

Upon Cherry's departure, his assistant of twenty-one years, Howard Lynch, took the top job at Amarillo High. Lynch served as head coach for the following fourteen seasons (1937–50). Over that span, the Sandies went 126–29–1 (80.8 percent). In 1940, Lynch also directed the Sandies to their fourth state title, a 20–7 win in Dallas over the Temple Wildcats. Temple barely made it out of bi-district, where the Wildcats tied the Stephenville Yellow Jackets 7–7. Based on the tie-breaking system at that time, Temple won 3–2 on penetrations beyond the opponent's twenty-yard line. Meanwhile, Amarillo, in the semifinal, met their old adversary, Masonic Home. It was the traditional close, low-scoring contest between the two, with the Sandies winning 14–7. In the final, Amarillo's Dub Wooten sealed the Sandies' victory with a fourth-quarter interception and eighty-seven-yard return for a score. The win marked the fourth Sandies championship in a short seven years.

Over the next seven seasons, Lynch's teams were consistent winners, missing the playoffs only in 1941 and 1943, but they never advanced beyond the semifinal (1942). A regular roadblock was another ascendant oil-field school, Wichita Falls, which took Amarillo out of the playoffs in 1945, 1946 and 1947. In 1948, the Sandies finally returned to the title game but bowed 21–0 to that year's state and national champion Waco Tigers. Lynch continued as head coach for two more seasons, never making it to the playoffs again. His coaching contract was not renewed after a 4–6–0 season in 1950. He ended his fourteen-year tenure as Sandies head coach but remained at Amarillo High School, where he worked in school administration. Such are the vicissitudes of life for Texas coaches, especially if they do not win. Buzz Bissinger knew whereof he spoke when he declared that there is "no profession in the state of Texas with worse job security than that of the high school football coach."[20]

In 1959, a new soon-to-be famous coach, Oail Andrew "Bum" Phillips, arrived in the Panhandle. He coached the Sandies for only three seasons (1959–61), compiling an 18–12–1 record that included one playoff appearance, in his inaugural season. Amarillo's bi-district opportunity resulted in a 34–6 loss to Wichita Falls. Ultimately, Phillips would ascend to the ranks of the NFL, coaching for three different franchises but enjoying his greatest success with the Houston Oilers (1974–80), which included appearances in the 1978 and 1979 AFC championship games. His career trajectory effectively illustrates a Jan Reid aphorism that "coaching is an occupation of gypsies." Another Reid assessment is amusingly close to the truth, as he describes high school coaches as "addicted former players." However true or false this assertion may be (unscientific observation suggests that Reid is on the mark), Phillips accurately represents the coach that "changed jobs often, trying to get ahead." As such, neither Phillips nor his kind ever gained "the dynastic reputation of [Wichita Falls's] Joe Golding, Abilene's Chuck Moser, or Brownwood's Gordon Wood."[21] Reid easily might have added to his list Emory Bellard, whose Breckenridge (1958–59) and San Angelo Central (1966) teams took state titles. If consideration is given to the two state championships Gordon Wood won while at Stamford before coming to Brownwood, all four coaching legends—Bellard, Wood, Golding and Moser—took teams from the Oil Belt to the title. The earliest of the Oil Belt schools to win a championship was Abilene.

ABILENE EAGLES

A bit more than a decade before the Sandies took their first state title, Abilene joined Waco as a titan of the 1920s. Leading the charge was Abilene coach Prince Elmer "Pete" Shotwell, who moved to Abilene in 1917 after coaching future Oil Belt powerhouse Cisco for two seasons (1916–17). His unlucky 1917 Loboes were a perfect 0–4, scoring only six points the entire season. Shotwell's luck in Abilene improved. In 1920, his third season as Abilene's head coach, Shotwell lost only the semifinal playoff game, to Cleburne, and that by only a single score. The following year looked much the same, with the Eagles losing only to Dallas Adamson, again in the semifinal. The 1922 Eagles took it one step further but fell 13–10 to Waco in that year's championship game. That defeat marked the third straight season during which Abilene lost only a single contest. Finally, in 1923, Shotwell's Eagles achieved back-to-back trips to the final. In Dallas, before 7,500 spectators, the Eagles defeated Tyson's Tigers 3–0. The winning score came on a thirty-two-yard field goal by Pete Hanna after Abilene recovered a fumble deep in Waco territory in the fourth quarter. It was a fitting end to a perfect 12–0 season during which Abilene surrendered only seven points, coincidentally to Cisco, with whom Shotwell had gotten his start in coaching.

Shotwell left Abilene High School in 1924 to coach at Abilene's Simmons College (today's Hardin-Simmons University). The Eagles nonetheless remained competitive, particularly under Dewey Mayhew, who coached at Abilene for twenty-four seasons (1927–40). Mayhew came to Abilene after a successful four-year tenure at Marlin (1923–26), where he coached the Bulldogs to a record of 13–4–1, including a 1926 Class B regional title appearance. Mayhew took the Eagles to the title game in his first season as Abilene's head coach. Although the 1927 Eagles entered the contest 12–0, they lost 21–14 to

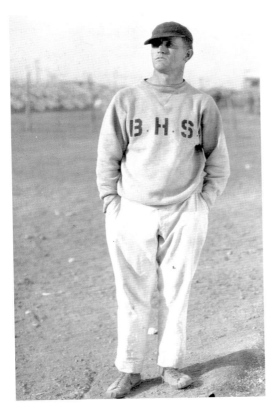

Pete Shotwell began his coaching career in the Oil Belt town of Cisco. After two years (1916–17), he came to Abilene, where he remained from 1918 through 1923. He and the Eagles won the state title his final season. Shotwell won a co–state title at Breckenridge in 1929. In 1937, while coaching at Longview (1935–45), he became the first coach to win three state titles at three different schools.

Tyson's Waco Tigers, who were putting the finishing touches on the first three-peat in Texas schoolboy history. A fourth-quarter Tiger interception set up the Waco win. Undaunted, Abilene, in its second back-to-back appearance in the finals, returned to the championship match in 1928. Entering the championship game, Abilene sported an 11–0–1 record (Ranger tied the Eagles 19–19 in a regular-season district contest). This time, Abilene would not be denied. On Mayhew's thirtieth birthday, his team gave him the gift of his first title, a 38–0 victory over Port Arthur that remained the most decisive finals win until 1934.

It took Mayhew just three years to return to the championship game. In spite of a regular-season 20–6 district loss to Oil Belt adversary Cisco, Abilene moved through its 1931 playoff run, giving up only six points to Sweetwater in the bi-district round. In a final played in Fort Worth, Abilene defeated Beaumont 13–0 for the school's third state championship in only nine years. In that title game, the sturdy Abilene defense allowed only two first downs.

Eagle prominence went into eclipse thereafter. Mayhew's last two seasons (0–9–0 and 4–6–1) were keen disappointments. He left Abilene High School in 1941 but eventually returned to coaching for nine more years, this time at the college level (Southwestern University and Texas A&I). Until 2007, when he was surpassed by Steve Warren, Mayhew remained Abilene's "winningest" coach (97–36–11).

Mayhew's replacement, Vernon Hilliard (1941–45), enjoyed only three winning seasons, none of which resulted in playoff trips. The venerated Pete Shotwell returned in to Abilene in 1946. Only four seasons during his seven-year tenure (1946–52) were winning ones, and only one of those, 1949, took Abilene back to the playoffs. Nevertheless, better times were about to come.

The 1950s witnessed an unparalleled Eagle resurgence, as Abilene realized its full potential as a one-school town with oil money. The exploitation of the Kelly-Snyder oilfield, where over 1,500 wells were drilled, probably contributed to the Abilene three-peat of 1954–56. As an oil center for Abilene's hinterland, the oil boom naturally would have brought a population increase to the city. The architect of the extraordinary impending Eagles

In 1928, Dewey Mayhew guided the Abilene Eagles to their second state championship. His Eagles won a second title in 1931. From Mayhew's retirement till 2007, his career record of 97–36–11 remained the best attained by any Abilene head football coach.

success was motivational mentor of high school athletes Chuck Moser (1918–95), who came from McAllen to Abilene in 1953 to replace Coach Shotwell. Today, a plaque on Abilene's Moser Field House appropriately commemorates the "Moser Era" (1953–59). In 1999, the *Dallas Morning News* christened Moser's Eagles as the "Team of the Century." Both honors came with good reason.

Born in 1918 in Chillicothe, Missouri, Moser was a 150-pound All-Conference lineman on the 1939 Big Six Conference champion University of Missouri team that played in that season's Orange Bowl. After graduation and coaching high school football for a year in Lexington, Missouri, Moser moved to the Rio Grande Valley, where he took his McAllen Bulldogs to the quarterfinals in his seventh and last season there. Before Abilene ISD Superintendent A.E. Wells persuaded him to come to Abilene, Moser had

Chuck Moser and his Abilene coaching staff. *Front row, left to right*: Wally Bullington, Moser, Hank Watkins and Bob Broseclose. *Back row, left to right*: Shorty Lawson, Tommy Morris, Blacky Blackburn and Nat Gleaton. In 1999, their handiwork inspired the *Dallas Morning News* to select Moser's Eagles as the "Team of the Century."

actually moved to Corpus Christi as new head coach at Miller High School. But as events soon proved, his fame and future would lie elsewhere.

An intense, highly organized, tough disciplinarian ahead of his time, Moser introduced multiple effective innovations: off-season training, "Scholarship Eligibility Report" forms (a precursor to the 1984 House Bill 72 "No Pass, No Play" provision), sophisticated scouting reports, a statistic-keeping book for making halftime adjustments and careful review of game film.

In seven seasons, Moser compiled a 78–7–2 record (89.7 percent), winning six consecutive titles in a district appropriately nicknamed the "Little Southwest Conference." He lost only once to perennial powers Breckenridge, Sweetwater, San Angelo, Odessa and Pampa and twice to Wichita Falls. Other respectable district opponents such Midland, Big Spring and Lubbock never defeated Moser's Eagles.

Abilene Reporter-News sportswriter and 1972 Texas High School Coaches Association Sportswriter of the Year Michael Grant was a fullback on Moser's 1958–59 Abilene teams. Reflecting on what made schools from Abilene's West Texas district the football juggernaut that they were in those years, Grant noted that all of these towns were "working-class cities with economies based on oil, agriculture and ranching, and the boys growing up to play football knew about work."[22] Moser's players applied that very knowledge to produce extraordinary success.

If Eagle fortunes had declined since the heyday of Shotwell and Mayhew, in 1953, the thirty-four-year-old Moser at least inherited an undefeated "B Team." He built a mighty program on that base, achieving the third-ever three-peat and a then–national record forty-nine-game win streak. The 1954 state champion Eagles started that streak. Ironically, that very season, the Eagles sustained a 35–13 drubbing at the hands of Breckenridge, a school whose enrollment was one-sixth that of Abilene's. The Buckaroos had, however, earned back-to-back 3A state titles in 1951 and 1952. Moser rallied his troops thereafter and set in motion the events that would make both him and his Eagles Texas football legends. The Eagles won every subsequent game until the Highland Park Scots tied them in the 1957 semifinal.

Following the 1954 season-opening loss to Breckenridge, the Eagles moved with seeming effortlessness through their pre-district and district schedule. In

Opposite, bottom: Chuck Moser (left) views game film in Denton with North Texas State College (today's University of North Texas) head football coach Odus Mitchell (1946–66). This novelty and many other innovative practices that Moser introduced at Abilene made him not only a coach ahead of his time but also one of the most successful coaches in Texas high school football history.

the playoffs, Abilene did not allow a single score until the final. That title game came in Houston against Houston's Stephen F. Austin Mustangs. In spite of five Eagle fumbles, the score was knotted at seven with only fifty-four seconds remaining. Eagle quarterback H.P. Hawkins hit Twyman "Old Glue Fingers" Ash for the winning score. *Abilene Reporter-News* photographer Don Hutcheson captured the magic moment in what reputedly is "the most reproduced photo in Abilene media history."[23]

Again in 1955, the Eagles had little trouble prior to the playoffs. They avenged their 1954 loss against Breckenridge, shutting out the Buckaroos 13–0. Their other district and non-district opponents felt the sting of Abilene's potent offense, which posted between thirty-five and sixty-two points in pre-playoff games. If Abilene had to pull a rabbit out of the hat in the closing seconds of the 1954 title game, their 1955 final at Fort Worth's TCU Amon Carter Stadium was far less challenging. With thirty thousand fans in attendance, the Eagles enjoyed a comfortable 20–0 halftime lead over East Texas's Tyler Lions. Glynn Gregory, Jim Welch and Henry Colwell combined for 351 Eagle yards on the ground. Gregory rushed for 171 of those yards, including two touchdowns (one of which came on a 40-yard "Statue of Liberty" play). Meanwhile, the Abilene "Warbird" defense limited Tyler to a paltry 72 yards of total offense. At game's end, the scoreboard read 33–13, and Moser's Eagles had won their twenty-third straight game.

Glynn Gregory did it all—rushed, passed, received and kicked. If his impressive career numbers for the first three were not enough, during the forty-nine-game "streak," Gregory kicked 122 points after touchdown.

Abilene's 1956 team won a school record fifteen games and earned distinction as the NSNS national high school champion. Through that stretch, the stingy Warbird defense surrendered only

trip to the state finals. Fifteen-year-old junior quarterback Ken Ford (who had replaced coach's son Ronald, whose play had ended with a late-season shoulder separation) led the Buckaroos into the playoffs. The team won an unshared 1951 state title, defeating Temple 20–14. Robbins exploited his success, taking a job offer from Texas A&M. His replacement, the energetic former U.S. marine Joe Kerbel, quickly discovered that expectations in Breckenridge were high. Kerbel courageously changed the Buckaroo offense from the single wing to the split T. He and his Bucks soon gave the city much to shout about.

In his three seasons at Breckenridge, Kerbel went 31–4–2 (83.8 percent), including two state championships. At Waco's Baylor Stadium, the 1952 championship team beat the same Temple Wildcats that Breckenridge's team under Robbins had bested the year before. The favored Wildcats fell 28–20. The fact that Kerbel had inherited the services of quarterback Ken Ford helped considerably. Kerbel also benefited from another returning veteran, center-linebacker Jerry Tubbs (1950–53). Tubbs continued on to become a 1956 Oklahoma University All-American center, a member of the 1955–56 OU national champion teams and an All-Pro Dallas Cowboy.

There was a 1953 interregnum for the Bucks, as opponent Big Spring took the district title and advanced to that year's final. Breckenridge returned with a vengeance in 1954, as Kerbel's 3A Bucks enjoyed a relatively smooth path on their way to the playoffs, auspiciously starting the season by successively knocking off three significantly larger schools: Wichita Falls (41–13), Brownwood (42–7) and that season's eventual 4A state champion, Abilene (35–13). In the semifinal, Lufkin battled the Bucks to a 14–14 tie, but Breckenridge

Jerry Tubbs played on the 1951–52, back-to-back Breckenridge state-champion teams. After high school, Tubbs played on Bud Wilkinson's 1955 AP national champion Oklahoma University Sooners team. He later became a Pro-Bowl Dallas Cowboy.

The 1954 state-champion Breckenridge Buckaroos. Coach Joe Kerbel, who took the Bucks to two state titles (1952 and 1954), stands at the far left on the back row.

still advanced. An auspicious coin flip allowed Breckenridge to host the final. Some 7,500 spectators crowded into its stadium, which offered seating for only 7,000. At the end of the day, Breckenridge outscored the Port Neches Indians 20–7. In spite of a pinched nerve in his hip, 1954 Buckaroo quarterback Bennett Watts played well, as did his teammate Jackie Sandefer. Watts, Sandefer and Dick Carpenter later followed former Breckenridge standout Jerry Tubbs to play football at OU.

The 1954 "Sixty-Mile Banquet" honored Oil Belt teams Abilene (4A champ who had lost to the Buckaroos 35–13 during that year's regular season), Breckenridge (3A champ) and Albany (1A runner-up). In 1955, Kerbel moved to four-time state champion Amarillo High School (1934–36, 1940), where he coached the Sandies from 1955 to 1957. Kerbel eventually

went to Lubbock as an assistant to Texas Tech's DeWitt Weaver (1957–59). Still later, he went to Canyon, where he became head coach at West Texas State University (1960–70). Dallas Cowboys coaching legend Tom Landry compared Kerbel to Vince Lombardi in his ability to inspire fear without loss of respect. Jerry Tubbs explained Kerbel's coaching philosophy, reflecting that he "figured as long as he outworked you, he could beat you."[26]

Kerbel's departure notwithstanding, Breckenridge soon made a second back-to-back appearance in the 3A final. Emory Bellard (1955–59) succeeded Kerbel. Bellard's predecessor had brought Breckenridge a state title in his first year directing the Bucks. Bellard, however, could get his 1955 team only to the quarterfinals, where they fell to Stamford, that year's eventual state champion. Nevertheless, greater successes lay ahead. During Bellard's four-year Breckenridge tenure, he developed the "Wishbone" triple-option offense that he later made famous as offensive coordinator for Darrell

The 1958 state-champion Breckenridge Buckaroos beat Kingsville 42–14 to win the title. Their coach, Emory Bellard (back row, far right) took his 1959 team back to the finals, where they met the Cleburne Yellow Jackets and battled to a 20–20 tie for a co-championship.

Royal at UT. A decade before, in his third season (1958), Bellard took the Bucks back to the title. The accomplishment was all the more impressive considering that his twenty-three-man squad was composed primarily of freshmen and sophomores.

In the second game of the 1958 regular season, Bellard's 3A squad defeated that year's eventual 4A champion, Wichita Falls, 26–22. In the 1958 final,

powered by the running of Joe Ed Pesch, who had 187 yards on fourteen carries for two touchdowns, the Bucks bested Kingsville 42–14. Fittingly, the *Fort Worth Star-Telegram* voted the 1958 Buckaroos the team of the twentieth century.

In an interesting way, the first UIL title game in 1920 foreshadowed the contest of 1959. In the latter year, Bellard's Bucks met the Cleburne Yellow Jackets, who had tied Houston Heights 0–0 for the 1920 co-title. The 1959 contest also ended in a tie, 20–20, giving both Cleburne and Breckenridge their second co-championships. Only a Cleburne two-point conversion in the last minute of play kept the Buckaroos from winning the championship

In today's downtown Breckenridge, one block off the courthouse square, a haunting *Spirit of the Buckaroos* mural evokes vivid memories of the football success of the town's beloved Buckaroos. *Photo by Annette Pierce Sherrod.*

outright. The 1959 contest marked the last of six Bucks appearances in the title round. In those six trips, Breckenridge never lost a title game. Four of the Bucks' championships—the first and last—were shared with opponents.

After the 1959 season, Bellard took the top job at San Angelo Central. His Bobcats won the 1966 title. In 1967, Bellard left for UT. While in Austin, his son Emory Jr. quarterbacked the 1968 Austin Reagan Raiders to a 17–11 title win over Oil Belt school Odessa Permian. Bellard eventually moved on to head coaching duties at Texas A&M (1972–78) and Mississippi State (1979–85) but completed his career back in Texas coaching at Spring Westfield High School (1988–93). At retirement, he had to his credit three schoolboy state titles at two different schools and a 177–59–9 (72.2 percent) career record in high school coaching.

In today's downtown Breckenridge, there is a *Spirit of the Buckaroos* mural on the west side of the Brickfield Marketplace building on the corner of South Court Street and US 180. It commemorates a community's special and enduring connection to its beloved Buckaroos and that team's magical power to master opponents often dwarfing them in physical size and school enrollment.

WICHITA FALLS COYOTES

Wichita Falls High School graduate and author Jan Reid once wrote of his high school's mascot, "The choice of a wiry and scrounging little predator… evoked the temper and promise of the surrounding farmland and mesquite-choked cattle range. Oilfield pump jacks, or lack of them, determined the worth of the terrain. And in the years following World War II, the team name reflected the style of football played in Wichita Falls." Iconic Coyote Stadium's location, "dug into a hillside near the edge of downtown," was a feature that "contributed acoustically to the Coyotes' home-field advantage." Coyote opponents dreaded road games there because the facility was user friendly to neither visiting players nor fans. Unofficially called "The Canyon," the stadium seated twelve thousand and was located on old Seymour Highway. Its glow "contained all the promise of bright lights [and] big city" in an otherwise "drab blue-collar town" with decidedly "scant aesthetics."[27]

The Coyotes came close to football glory as early as 1923. That season, they fell 25–0 in the semifinal to a Pete Shotwell Abilene team that one week later defeated Waco for the title. Over the next decade, the Coyotes experienced little success. The arrival of Ted Jeffries (1933–43) revived Wichita Falls football fortunes. The Coyotes returned to the semifinal in 1935, but that year's state champion Amarillo Sandies bested the Coyotes 27–13. Wichita Falls first appeared in the final in 1937. Going head to head against another Shotwell squad, the come-from-behind Longview Lobos, the Coyotes fell short by a touchdown, 19–12, and returned home without the title trophy.

In 1941, Wichita Falls fortunes finally turned. That season, the Coyote defense pitched eleven shutouts, three of which came against playoff opponents. For the championship, a Ted Jeffries Wichita Falls team met the 1940 finalist Temple Wildcats in Fort Worth. Before a crowd of eighteen thousand, Coyote quarterback Gene Hill threw for 286 yards and guided his teammates to a 13–0 victory. The 1941 title win heralded even greater things to come. Jeffries remained at Wichita Falls for two more seasons before leaving to pursue coaching at the college level, first at Lamar Junior College (1944–46) and later at Stephen F. Austin (1947–55).

Jeffries's replacement, Thurman Jones (1945–46), guided the Coyotes to a 1945 semifinal appearance against Highland Park, but it was Joe Golding (1947–61) who elevated Wichita Falls to dynastic status. With an overall record of 152–26–2, Golding took the team to six finals and four state titles (1949–50, 1958, 1961) in fifteen years. With good cause, he never had a losing season. Renowned as a tough disciplinarian and perfectionist, Golding drew on both his harsh experience as a child of the Great Depression in battered Oklahoma and, perhaps even more importantly, from his World War II experience as a physical training instructor for the U.S. Army Air Corps. In his four-hour football practice sessions at Wichita Falls, he applied the lessons drawn from both, demanding and receiving the best performance of the young men under his charge. Even the players who respected (or perhaps even liked) Golding often conceded that his coaching style was tyrannical.

As with many other great Texas teams before and after, Golding's players were often undersized and less athletic than their opponents. Moreover, while most schools were adopting new offensive formations like the T, Golding retained the anachronistic single wing. His "outdated" style and "average" players were no impediment to back-to-back Coyote titles in 1949–50. In his third season as head coach, Golding's "Little Iron Men," small in size but remarkable in endurance, posted a perfect 14–0 season record. The 1949 Coyotes featured the "Three Musketeers": Weldon Walker, Billy Bookout (who later played for the Green Bay Packers in 1955–56) and end/placekicker Jerry "Mr. Automatic" Fouts. In a title game played in Fort Worth before seventeen thousand, Wichita Falls won its second state title, defeating the Austin Maroons 14–13. The NSNS selected the Coyotes as the 1949 national champions.

The 1950 season began with high hopes but disastrous results. Golding's Coyotes lost four of their first five games. In three of the four—games against Breckenridge (18–0), Abilene (26–0) and Pampa (14–0)—Wichita Falls failed to score a single point. As the Coyotes entered district play, there was little hope for back-to-back championships. In the face of indignant community outrage, Golding steered a steady course. Knowing that the team's early poor performance had much to do with injuries to four key players—Ed Beach, Kermit Cummings, Tommy Fields and Everard Terrell—Golding got the team beyond its difficulties and to the district title. On the playoff trail, Wichita Falls avenged two of its early-season losses, defeating Pampa in the bi-district round by a whopping 44–7 and winning a 34–27 semifinal nail-biter against Dallas Highland Park. For their troubles, the Coyotes earned a rematch against the Austin Maroons in the Dallas Cotton Bowl. There the boys in red and black won handily, 34–13.

Over the next seven seasons, the best Coyote performance came in 1956, when Wichita Falls went undefeated until falling 20–6 to Chuck Moser's streaking Abilene Eagles in the semifinal. The 1957 Coyotes advanced to quarterfinals. In 1958, Golding's Coyotes began a remarkable run that took the team to the final in four consecutive seasons. That team sustained a surprising 26–22 early-season loss to small but mighty Breckenridge. From that point forward, however, the Coyotes imposed decisive defeats on all remaining opponents. Playoff wins over Borger, Abilene and Highland Park took Wichita Falls back to the final. Guided by quarterback Johnny Genung, who scored three touchdowns and rushed for 160 yards, the 1958 Coyotes bested Pasadena 48–6 at Austin's Memorial Stadium.

The only blemish on the 1959 Coyote pre-playoff record was an early-season 14–14 tie with Breckenridge. From there, Wichita Falls moved with relative ease through the remainder of the season. The Coyotes met Corpus Christi Ray in the final, where they lost 20–6. The 1960 Coyotes never saw defeat during the regular season. They advanced handily through the first three playoff rounds, giving up a meager eight points to Borger in bi-district. They were not so fortunate in the final, however, as Corpus Christi Miller, led by black Buccaneer running back Johnny Roland, beat the Coyotes 13–6. Roland's performance heralded changing times. School desegregation was coming of age in Texas.

Roland's 1959 success and, two years later, the magic of the swift and agile Warren McVea were examples of the unfolding impact of the 1960s

"Wondrous Warren" McVea catches the football during his days at 4A San Antonio Brackenridge. McVea's football skills made a monumental impact on Texas high school football, heralding coming changes in the way the game would soon be played throughout the state. After helping the Eagles to the 1962 4A title, McVea made history at the University of Houston, where he became the first black Cougar football player.

integration of Texas high school football. "Wondrous Warren" led 4A San Antonio Brackenridge over Borger to the 1962 state title. Al Reinert identified the Brackenridge championship as the pivotal event guaranteeing the "success of Texas school integration." He declared, "Within five years, the balance of prowess had shifted from the Oil Belt towns to East Texas."[28]

Prior to statewide integration and the incorporation of black schools into UIL, those all-black Texas schools fielded football programs under the supervision of the Prairie View Interscholastic League. Four schools in particular set themselves apart, each winning four state titles during the league's twenty-nine-year existence.

Prairie View League Dynasties, 1940–68

High School	Conference	Titles	Appearances	Title Runs	Win Percentage
Austin Anderson	2A/3A/4A	4	6 (1940, 1942, 1945, 1956–57, 1961)	Back-to-back (1956-1957)	67%
Dallas Washington	2A/3A	4 (1 co-title)	8 (1941, 1946, 1948, 1950, 1953, 1956–58)	3 consecutive appearances	50%
Houston Yates	2A/4A	4 (2 co-titles)	7 (1943, 1950–51, 1961–62, 1964–65)	3 back-to-back appearances	57%
Waco Moore	2A/3A/4A	4 (2 co-titles)	5 (1951–52, 1954, 1960, 1964)	Back-to-back titles (1 co-title)	80%

Houston Yates coach Andrew "Pat" Patterson (1939–42, 1946–67) was the architect of the so-called Negro League. Before integration and the 1969 dissolution of the league, Patterson would lead his Lions to four PVIL state titles. He had a career record at Yates of 200–64–9 (73.2 percent). In 1939, Patterson sought to bring order and organization to the games already being played by black schools in Texas. Reflecting on his motivation, Patterson remembered that he initiated the process "after we won the mythical state championship in 1939."[29] Working in concert with the Yates High School principal, William Holland, Patterson persuaded his boss to approach Prairie View A&M president E.B. Evans about establishing a league. The aim was to regulate black high school football, particularly regarding eligibility and attendance, in much the same way that UIL had done for white schools dating from 1920. Initially, twenty-one schools, all from urban areas, were part of the league. As time passed, membership expanded. By 1948, league administrators established 1A and 2A conferences based on the size of enrollment. By 1952, conference 3A was added, and in 1960, a 4A conference as well.

During the league's existence, most other teams under the UIL umbrella played a style of football well described by the old cliché "three yards and a cloud of dust." Brute strength, the running game and smash-mouth football were the norm. While PVIL teams were no less physical, their games were noted for exciting wide-open contests that stretched the field and capitalized on speed and passing—a style foreshadowing things to come in UIL football once integration began in earnest. Before that time, there were no "Friday night lights" for the black schools. Rather, there were Tuesday night lights. Games for black schools were typically held early in the week and, in an anachronistic *Plessy vs. Ferguson* trumping *Brown vs. Board of Education*, invariably at facilities that were decidedly sub-standard. Nevertheless, the games produced great players. To name only a few of the better-known stars who eventually played in the NFL, the roll call of PVIL standouts includes Jerry Levias (Beaumont Hebert), Dick "Night Train" Lane (Austin Anderson), Gene Upshaw (Robstown), Gene Washington (Baytown Carver), "Mean" Joe Green (Temple Dunbar) and Clifford Branch (Houston Worthing).

Once desegregation was underway, the question remained whether the process would unfold without racial tension—be it on the field, in the stands or worse still, both. *Houston Chronicle* sportswriter John P. Lopez pinpoints the October 12, 1967 Houston Sam Houston-Houston Kashmere game as a "critical turning point for integration." At stake was a district playoff berth. Fifty-four years earlier, the Sam Houston Tigers had won the 1913 "state title," such as it was, authoritatively defeating Comanche 20–0. On the playing field in 1967 was Sam Houston's D.W. Rutledge, the man who years later would turn Converse Judson into a greater San Antonio football dynasty. Many years later, reflecting on the contest, Rutledge recalled, "There was a lot of electricity as you went into the game, and it just got worse. There was no doubt there was prejudice for some people. There was tension." At halftime, Houston ISD athletic director Joe Tusa, who helped lead the process of integrating Texas high school football, spoke directly to both officials and coaches, admonishing them to clean things up in the second half and do it right. Thereafter, the tensions eased. Kashmere won the contest, beating the Tigers 14–6. Rutledge recalled, "We had a great ball club, but they just blew us away. You had to respect them. They were good."[30]

Ultimately, the PVIL dissolved, and desegregation spread across the Lone Star State. By the 1969–70 academic year, the PVIL was no more. And as the Sam Houston-Kashmere contest revealed, the multifaceted impact of integration was quickly felt in high school football. Nevertheless, notwithstanding the claim by Reinert about a shifting balance of power to the east, Oil Belt schools still retained vitality. Joe Golding's 1961 Coyotes dramatically demonstrated this truth by making their fourth straight trip to the title game. Wichita Falls shut out half of their pre-playoff opponents and allowed only twenty-four points before reaching postseason play. Although "recruiters never considered Wichita Falls a particular hotbed of blue-chip prospects," a major reason for the 1961 Coyotes success was high school All-American running back Larry Shields.[31] Indisputably, this six-foot, two-hundred-pound starting fullback was a major key to the three Coyote final appearances from 1959 to 1961. During those seasons, Wichita Falls went 39–2–1. Ironically, Sheilds's contribution to the 1961 state title had less to do with carrying the football and more with being the focus of Galena Park's defense.

Wichita Falls head coach Joe Golding meets with members of his Coyote team. Perhaps the most celebrated of them all was Larry Shields (#64), who played on three state finalist teams (1959–61). The 1961 Coyotes won a fifth Wichita Falls state championship.

The powerful running of versatile Coyote high school All-American fullback Larry Shields did much to fuel Wichita Falls success from 1959 through 1961. After high school, Shields headed for Norman, where he became a member of the Oklahoma Sooners football team.

While the Yellow Jackets keyed on Shields, Coyote tailback Mike Kelly ran for fifty-five- and fifty-nine-yard scores and passed for another. Still, Wichita Falls had to come from behind to win the ball game. The 21–14 victory was the fifth Coyotes state title and Joe Golding's final game as Wichita Falls head coach.

During his tenure, Golding captured eleven district titles, tied for one and posted an 86.5 win percentage. Always the disciplinarian, Golding's long, demanding, waterless practices were harder than those that many Coyote alumni endured in college. They toughened players, making them strong through all four quarters. For reasons similar to those of Abilene's Chuck Moser,

Joe Golding left coaching in 1961 to become the Wichita Falls ISD athletic director. The opening of Wichita Falls Rider High School in 1961 divided local talent and diminished the prospects of regular future playoff runs.

Nevertheless, the Coyotes, under former Golding assistant Donnell Crosslin (1965–79), won a sixth state championship in 1969 at Baylor Stadium. Running backs Joey Aboussie and Lawrence Williams combined for four touchdowns, two of them coming in the fourth quarter. The Coyotes won 28–20 over San Antonio Lee's Volunteers. Williams was one of four varsity Coyote football players who came to Wichita Falls in 1969 after the closing of Booker T. Washington

Top: Junior running back Joey Aboussie was a member of the 1969 state-champion Coyote team. After high school, Aboussie played in Austin for the Texas Longhorns.

Left: In 1971, Wichita Falls met San Antonio Lee for the 4A state title. The Coyotes lost the contest largely due to the effective passing of Lee quarterback Tommy Kramer. In 1971, Kramer was only getting started. He would go on to enjoy a highly successful career as signal caller for the Rice University Owls and thereafter for the NFL's Minnesota Vikings.

High. Its closure was an important milestone in North Texas desegregation, illustrative of the growing significance of black athletes in Texas high school football. The 1969 Coyote title is also novel in that it made Wichita Falls High the first school in Texas to win a championship after the creation of a second city high school. The opening of Rider had ended the one-and-only status formerly enjoyed by "Old High."

In 1970, Athletic Director Golding replaced "The Canyon" with Memorial Stadium, the first high school facility in Texas with Astroturf. In 1971, Coach Crosslin took the Coyotes to the state final, again playing against San Antonio Lee. Wichita Falls held Lee to negative ground yardage, but Lee's passing game won the day. In the first high school title game ever in Irving's Texas Stadium, future Rice University star and Minnesota Viking Tommy Kramer threw for 257 yards and three touchdowns and, with two minutes and twenty-one seconds remaining, kicked the game-winning point after, as Lee edged the Coyotes 28–27.

With ten finals appearances from 1937 through 1971, it is little wonder that Jan Reid observed that the "high school game in Wichita Falls, Texas, [became] an entrenched regime and envied institution."[32] Only three schools in Texas have visited the final round more times—one is Odessa Permian.

ODESSA PERMIAN PANTHERS

About Odessa Permian, *Friday Night Lights* author Buzz Bissinger concluded, "Football stood at the very core of what the town was about. It had nothing to do with entertainment and everything to do with how people felt about themselves." Stadium lights "become an addiction…the Friday night fix." High school sports become an "irresistible allure," and Odessa became a town whose "spirits crested and fell with each win and each loss." A state championship "became one of those events that was remembered in the psyche of the town forever."[33] Undoubtedly, Odessa's extreme geographic isolation, flat terrain and barren landscape dotted by thorny inhospitable mesquite trees all contributed to the powerful impact of football on the town. And so did the oil business. The Odessa oil boom came during the early and mid-1920s. Over succeeding decades, Odessa became a roughneck and service company town, a stark contrast to its more "sophisticated" eastern neighbor, Midland, which was the center for oil producers and finance. Odessa's oil wealth contributed mightily to the 1982 construction of Odessa's $56 million, 19,032-seat Ratliff Stadium. Regina McCally's *The Secret of Mojo* includes a poignant picture of this iconic facility. A pump jack appearing in the foreground of the image speaks volumes, illustrating the intimate connection between this remote West Texas oil town and high school football.

In the larger context of the 1980s oil depression, the period during which Bissinger spent his 1988 Odessa sojourn, Permian football gave Odessans a welcome weekly distraction from the economic woes that wracked the community during that difficult decade. Mojo Magic and the "Boys in Black" provided the languishing Odessa community with a certain vicarious fulfillment. Yet even before the oil glut turned the West Texas economy inside out, Odessans' football affections focused on the city's original secondary school, Odessa High.

Prior to 1946, other than a 1928 bi-district playoff appearance and a 1945 trip to the quarterfinals, the town of Odessa had experienced little postseason high school football success. During the 1946 season, locals were thrilled by Odessa High School's 21–14 finals win over San Antonio Jefferson at Austin's Memorial Stadium. Before thirty-eight thousand excited spectators, bruising Broncho running back Byron "Santone" Townsend and quarterback Haden Fry (later head coach at Southern Methodist University, North Texas State University and Iowa University) led teammates to victory over the Mustangs and their versatile running back Kyle Rote (subsequent Southern Methodist University All-American, 1947–50, and New York Giants star, 1951–61). But the future of West Texas football belonged to Odessa Permian, a school that opened its doors in 1959. The rapid ascent of the Panthers, not the Bronchos, inspired Bissinger to note in his now-famous volume that when he began searching for the best place to learn about American high school football, all roads led to Odessa.

Only seven short years after its creation, Permian High School ascended to the ultimate height, winning its first of its six state titles. The 1965 Panthers sustained only a single pre-playoff defeat—a 7–6 loss to Lubbock Monterey. They rectified that in the quarterfinals, settling old scores with the Plainsmen, and then in the semifinal dispensed with Texarkana. In a final played in San Angelo, Coach Gene Mayfield's Odessa team put on a defensive clinic, blocking two punts and recovering a fumble on the way to an 11–6 win over San Antonio Lee. Mayfield and the Panthers returned to the 1969 final, facing the defending 4A state champion Austin Reagan Raiders coached by Travis Raven and quarterbacked by Emory Bellard Jr. The Panthers fell 17–11. In 1970, the Panthers met the Raiders again, both teams playing for another title in just three years. Austin Reagan emerged victorious, defeating

Permian 21–14. During the five seasons that Mayfield coached the Panthers, he created a junior high feeder system that did much to build the durable Permian dynasty. Coaches across the state would model their own systems on Mayfield's design.

In 1972, the Panthers secured their second state title, as well as the NSNS national high school co-title. By that time, Gene Mayfield (1965–70) had moved on to the college ranks. He succeeded a fellow state-champion coach, Joe Kerbel, at West Texas A&M (formerly West Texas State University). Gil Bartosh, aka the "Granger Ghost" from his quarterback days at Granger High School (1945–48), took over at Permian in 1971. In that season, the Panthers posted a near-perfect 9–1 record, but their one and

Gene Mayfield was the first Odessa Permian coach to guide the Boys in Black to a state football title. Mayfield's Panthers returned to the finals in 1968 and 1970, playing Austin Reagan on both occasions.

only defeat, a 9–7 loss to district adversary Abilene Cooper, prevented them from advancing to the playoffs. The 1972 Panthers returned to the winner's circle, finishing the season 14–0 and defeating Baytown Sterling 37–7 in the final. Panther quarterback David Shipman contributed 270 yards in offense, while running back Ricky Sutherland scored three touchdowns. At season's end, Bartosh, now 23–1 at Permian over two seasons, took advantage of an offer to become an assistant coach under Emory Bellard Sr. at the University of Texas at El Paso. Two years later, Bartosh inherited the head coaching job with the Miners.

Meanwhile, back at Permian, Bartosh's assistant offensive coordinator, John Wilkins, began a thirteen-year tenure that produced a 148–16–6 record (89 percent), including fifty-five shutouts, ten district titles and two state championships (1980 and 1984). Wilkins, informally known by locals as "A.G." ("Almost God"), Darth Vader and other even less flattering monikers,

PERMIAN HIGH SCHOO

From Left To Right

1st Row—Gale Maxwell, Danny Edwards, Ricky White, David Routh, Larry Walsh, Ricky Jumper, Mike Cona...

2nd Row—Billy McDaniels, Ralph Blasi, Phil Fouche, Jack Freeman, Woodrow Dancer, J. C. Nickens, Paul ...
Collins, Jackie Moravcik.

3rd Row—Mike Jordan, Jeff St. John, Ricky McNurlen, James Garner, James Medley, Freddy Pugh, Dann...
Gary Payne.

4th Row—Richard Dennard, Glenn Habell, Mike Paddock, Don Carr, Tony Conley, Mike Ott, Stanley Woodw...

5th Row—Mike Campbell, David Byerly, John Roop, Ralph Sterle, Johnny Orr, Gary Horner, Jody Coleman...

STATE AAAA C

took the Panthers to four finals appearances. In Wilkins's third season (1975), he guided Permian to the title game only to lose 20–10 to Port Neches-Groves. Five years later, Wilkins took his undefeated Panthers to the final, where they faced the heavily favored Port Arthur Jefferson Yellow Jackets.

PANTHERS '65

MPIONS

The 1965 Permian Panthers brought home the school's first 4A football title. Their victory heralded even better things to come. Permian would return to the final ten more times and come home victorious on five of those occasions.

Regina McCally colorfully used this contest to begin her book *The Secret of Mojo*. A better example of the meaning of "Mojo" could not be found.

Permian's Boys in Black exploited their "Mojo Magic"—that "giant football spirit in the sky that neither slumbers nor sleeps and looks after

Permian's football fortunes."[34] Mojo turned ordinary schoolboys into all-state overachievers and made unsuspecting superstars of players such as Joe Bob Bizzell (1970–72), the five-foot-seven, 132-pound, three-time all-state "Big Little Warrior" also known as the "Paul Bunyan of Odessa." So it did as well in 1980 out of five-foot-eight, 136-pound state champion Panther quarterback Jerry Hix and his 155-pound fullback Phillip Crain. In one of the most exciting come-from-behind wins in finals history, in twenty-degree temperatures and whipping winds at Texas Stadium, the

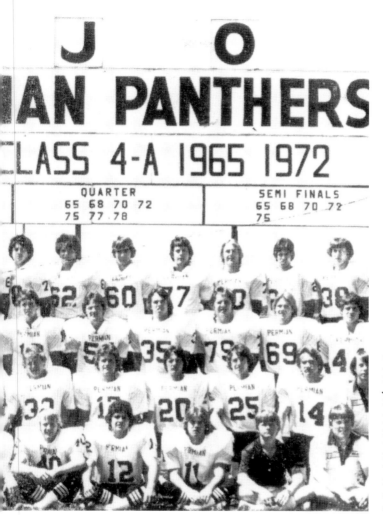

The 1980 Permian Panthers gave Coach John Wilkins his first 4A football championship. Before he became the Ector ISD athletic director in 1986, Wilkins would take his teams to the finals two more times, securing the co-championship in 1984.

1980 Panthers (behind 19–6 at halftime) beat highly touted Port Arthur 28–19. It was Wilkins's 100th career victory. Four years later, the Mojo met Beaumont French and tied 21–21 for the 1984 co-title. In 1985, Permian went undefeated all the way to the final, where it faced a Houston Yates school with a larger enrollment and bigger players. Permian had hoped to play the giant slayer yet again and win another title but was unable to rise to the occasion, as Yates won 37–0. Although this was the first Yates state championship under UIL auspices, within the PVIL (1940–69), Yates had appeared seven times in the title game, winning it four of those times. If the Yates championship of 1939 is also considered, the 1985 UIL title was the sixth Yates football championship in school history. Meanwhile, back in Odessa after the 1985 season, à la Moser and Golding, Wilkins left Permian to become the Ector Independent School District's athletic director.

In Wilkins's wake came Gary Gaines (1986–89), the man made famous first by Bissinger's book and later by Billy Bob Thornton in the movie *Friday Night Lights*. A more mild-mannered coach than his predecessor, some Odessans privately called Gaines "Luke Skywalker." The Panthers failed to make the playoffs in Gaines's first season. The next year, they rumbled through the regular-season schedule, losing only to Midland Lee in district play. In the playoffs, Permian went all the way to the semifinals, where 1987 state champion Plano beat them 29–21. The 1988 season lives forever in the various incarnations of *Friday Night Lights* (the 1990 book, the 2004 movie and the 2006–11 television series). The 1988 Panthers—in typical Permian

O CHAMPS '89

AN PANTHERS

5A 65 72 80 84 89

AL	QUARTER FINALS	SEMI FINALS
77 78 80	65 65 70 72 75 77 78 80 84 85 87 88 89	65 68 70 72 75 80 84 85 89

The 1989 Panthers, coached by Gary Gaines, defeated Houston Aldine 28–14 for the title. *USA Today* conferred the national high school title upon the team as well. The 1991 Panthers (left) returned to the title game and defeated San Antonio Marshall 27–14.

style, a group of fearless, undersized overachievers without particular athletic prowess—lost the semifinal to a Dallas Carter Cowboy team later declared in violation of eligibility regulations. Gaines continued one more year at Permian High.

In 1989, the undefeated Panthers enjoyed a clean, clear run to the 5A title, beating Houston Aldine 28–14. The stingy Mojo defense imposed shutouts on eight of that year's opponents. From season's beginning through the third round of the playoffs, only district rival Midland Lee even came close to threatening the Panthers. Instrumental in Permian's 1989 state victory was all-state wide receiver Lloyd Hill, who later played at Texas Tech (1990–93). As Gaines completed his first tour of duty at Permian, he looked back on a 47–6–1 record (87 percent) capped by a 1989 state title and an unofficial *USA Today* national championship. Thereafter, Gaines left Permian, coaching successively for Texas Tech University (1990–93), Abilene High (1994–95), San Angelo Central (1996–99), Abilene Christian University (2000–04) and

Permian receiver Lloyd Hill catches the ball as he sheds opponents. Hill was a member of the 1989 state and national champion Permian Panthers. Hill set Permian school records for career receptions (172), receiving yards (3,429) and touchdowns (34). He later continued his football career at Texas Tech University.

finally returning in 2009 to Permian, where he continued until the end of the 2012 season.

In the interim between the Gaines tenures, Permian made two more trips to the finals. Coach Tam Hollingshead (1990–93) took his 1991 team to a 27–14 championship win (a sixth Panther title) over San Antonio Marshall. His successor, Randy Mayes (1994–99), led the 1995 Panthers to the final, where they narrowly lost 31–28 to ascendant 5A football powerhouse Converse Judson. In some ways, Judson represented the wave of the future. As a thriving suburban community on San Antonio's northeast side, Converse was typical of the towns that increasingly produced state-champion high school football programs in the post–World War II period.

Permian football historian McCally accurately itemized the secrets of football success for Odessa or anywhere, be it in an oilfield town or a rapidly growing suburban region. They are the same secrets for succeeding in life: learning how to win; working hard; doing what you do with confidence; expecting success; practicing patience, teamwork, mental toughness, fair play, sportsmanship, determination and dedication; and, perhaps most important of all, learning how to beat the clock, win in the eleventh hour and come from behind to defeat a stronger opponent.

CHAPTER 3

THE METRO-DYNASTIES

In 1948, for the first time ever, UIL introduced more than one official Texas football state title. The new three-fold division brought at least some equity in a state where schools ranged in enrollment from hundreds to thousands. This three-year experiment created a "City" division exclusively for Dallas, Fort Worth, Houston and San Antonio, as well as separate classes 2A and 1A. In 1951, a four-fold conference division—4A through 1A—based strictly on student enrollment replaced the 1948 alignment. By 1980, UIL added conference 5A, the largest of the five.

These changes acknowledged that the larger schools in the biggest urban centers were likely to overwhelm competition from the hinterland. As decades passed and metropolitan areas continued to grow, the balance of high school football power has tipped decidedly toward the ever-expanding Sunbelt suburbs—that moving outward edge of the major "metro" areas, particularly greater Dallas–Fort Worth, Houston, San Antonio and Austin. Upwardly mobile families streaming into these locations characteristically have demanded nothing but the best academically and athletically for their overachieving children. Understanding the principle of "you get what you pay for," most such families have been quite willing to spend tax dollars in rapidly growing school districts on new athletic facilities and successful, well-paid coaches. Indeed, at the start of the 2011 football season, the average salary of head football coaches in the Dallas–Fort Worth Metroplex was $88,420. The two highest paid—Euless Trinity's Steve Lineweaver and Aledo's Tim Buchanan—received $114,413 and $109,240, respectively. And both have gotten great results.

Seven Texas high schools holding four or more state football titles perfectly fit the model described above; they are Garland, Katy, Plano, Southlake Carroll, Converse Judson, La Marque and Aledo. Relative community wealth in these locations is commonly high, and families below the poverty line are generally few. The success of Katy, Plano and Southlake predates their rise to 5A status. Early on, all three schools secured what today are considered 2A or 3A championships. Garland and Aledo earned both 3A and 4A titles. Championship pedigrees for 5A Converse Judson and 4A La Marque are more recent, but both similarly sprang from a steady stream of migrants putting down new roots at the periphery of the metropolis. This chapter tells the story of these seven "Metro-Dynasties."

Suburban Area	Median Household Income / Percentage Below Poverty Line	Population Breakdown
Southlake	$172,945 / 1.8%	95.0% white, 1.4% black, 1.7% Asian, 3.7% Hispanic
Plano	$84,492 / 4.3%	58.0% white, 8.0% black, 18.0% Asian, 14.7% Hispanic
Aledo	$54,327 / 1.4%	97.0% white, 0.3% black, 2.6% Hispanic
Katy	$51,111 / 8.4%	84.0% white, 4.3% black, 23.8% Hispanic
Garland	$49,156 / 8.9%	52.0% white, 14.0% black, 9.7% Asian, 37.0% Hispanic
Converse	$47,947 / 6.5%	69.0% white, 13.0% black, 2.2% Asian, 29.4% Hispanic
La Marque	$34,841 / 17.5%	56.0% white, 35.0% black, 15.4% Hispanic

GARLAND OWLS

The earliest metro area to establish its dynastic foothold was the Dallas suburb of Garland. Like suburban Metro-Dynasties that followed, Garland was a hinterland settlement that experienced steady population growth. Established in the early nineteenth century as a cotton-growing community on the northeast outskirts of today's Metroplex, Garland witnessed a postwar population boom—a four-fold increase in residents from 1950 to 1960.

Documentation exists for Garland football as early as 1906. The program experienced mixed success during the first few decades of UIL supervision. In the 1940s, the Owls went 78–19–8 (74.3 percent). The 1943 and 1944 teams advanced as far as UIL rules allowed at the time for Class A schools, winning regional titles both seasons. The 1954 Owls made it all the way to the quarterfinal, where they lost to 1954 state champion Breckenridge. The stage was set for Garland's first-ever state finals appearance.

The 1955 Owls, coached by Bill Ellington (1950–57), made it to the 3A final but lost 20–14 to Port Neches-Groves. This closely fought contest was tied until Indian receiver Nolan Adams caught the winning five-yard touchdown pass with only five seconds left in the game. In 1956, Garland returned to the final. A first-quarter, twenty-seven-yard Wayne Mullins field goal on a muddy field gave 3A Garland a 3–0 title win over a Nederland team that had fumbled six times. Undoubtedly, Garland residents perceived the 1956 football championship a welcome if indirect relief from the devastating drought that had crippled the recovering community from 1950 to 1954. But the best was yet to come. In 1963, a new coach, Chuck Curtis, came to town. He arrived with impeccable credentials. Curtis began his coaching career in 1958 at Holiday. The following year, he went to Jacksboro for a four-year head coaching stint. His 1962 Jacksboro Tigers won the 2A title, disassembling Rockdale 52–0. At season's end, Curtis had the opportunity to take the Garland job. The offer meant relocating to a larger, rapidly growing community whose population would expand from 38,500 to 81,500 during the 1960s.

In his inaugural season, Curtis took the 1963 Owls back to the title, defeating Corpus Christi Miller 17–0. The win made Curtis the first high school coach in Texas to win back-to-back titles at different schools in different conferences. But Curtis was not done. The following season, he joined Paul Tyson, Blair Cherry and Chuck Moser as the only coaches ever to three-peat. Curtis pinpoints the 1964 bi-district game against Coach Watty Myers's Texarkana Tigers as the contest in which his team

Above: Chuck Curtis (left, with his 2A Jacksboro staff) coached his first state-championship team, the Jacksboro Tigers, in 1962. When 4A Garland offered him the head coaching position for the following season, he took advantage and also took the 1963 and 1964 Owl football teams to Garland's second and third state championships. Curtis thus became the first Texas schoolboy coach to win back-to-back titles with schools in different conferences.

Left: The 1963 Garland Owls won their second state title in 1963. They met Corpus Christi Miller in Austin's Memorial Stadium, where Garland emerged victorious, 17–0.

"showed the most courage, confidence, poise and all the things you want."[35] The heavily favored Owls trailed 16–14 early in the second half. It took an unlikely niney-nine-yard Owl drive for a score with only fifteen seconds remaining to tip the balance in Garland's favor. In Houston's Rice Stadium before thirty-five thousand spectators, the Owls won the contest 20–16. In the 1964 final, Garland beat Galena Park 26–21 for a second consecutive Owl state title. It was the only championship game in which a Chuck Curtis defense allowed any points whatsoever. A third-quarter touchdown pass to Jimmy Adams gave the Owls the win. Garland's back-to-back 1963–64 football 4A championships opened new doors for Curtis. He left at season's end to assist one-time state champion Odessa Broncho quarterback and then–head coach at Southern Methodist University Haden Fry. Curtis made several subsequent high school stops—Grand Prairie, again to Jacksboro and Cleburne, where he defeated legendary Gordon Wood and the defending 4A state champion Brownwood Lions 9–3 in a 1982 district contest. Those nine points were the only ones the Lions gave up in district play that year. After a two-year stint at University of Texas at Arlington (1984–85), Curtis ended his career in 1987–88 at Aledo High School, where he took the Bearcats to back-to-back bi-district playoff games. His fifteen-year high school coaching record was 135–41–3 (79.4 percent).

Garland's population continued to grow during the 1970s (138,857), '80s (164,748) and '90s (215,768), but the Owls' next championship— their fourth—did not come until the end of 1990s. Playing in the Houston Astrodome before 39,102 spectators (at the time, the sixth-largest crowd

The 1964 Owl team returned to the final for a second consecutive season. There, Garland defeated Galena Park 26–21.

in Texas schoolboy history), Garland's 1999 team, coached by Joe Martin, won the title game 37–25 against Katy, a school making its fourth finals appearance. Like Garland, Katy was a suburban school that earned its place among the Metro-Dynasties of the modern era.

KATY TIGERS

Today's Houston suburb of Katy is named for the nineteenth-century Missouri-Kansas-Texas, or "K-T," railroad. In its earliest days, the Katy community existed as a sugar cane– and rice-growing settlement. By 1898, area residents founded a public school for their youth, but the full-fledged incorporation of Katy as a city did not come until 1945. In the 1950s, at the end of which the Katy Tigers won their first state football championship,

Katy High School's graduating classes numbered in the 40s and 50s. By the time the Tigers won their second title, in 1997, some 500 students a year were walking at Katy High School graduation ceremonies. Obviously, between 1959 and 1997, Katy grew like Topsy. Katy itself is located on Houston's western extremity along Interstate 10. During the 1970s, Houston's "Energy Corridor" moved west along the interstate. Katy and its hinterland grew in population, and upscale, planned communities began sprouting up. Today, 250,000 people live in the greater Katy area, which includes unincorporated portions of Harris and Fort Bend Counties, from which the Katy ISD draws. Katy's comfortable $51,111 median household income has nurtured high school football success.

Katy's 1959 Tigers were the first team to bring home a Katy High School state football title, beating the formidable Sundown Roughnecks 16–6. Although Katy did not return to the championship game for another thirty-five years, when it did, the Tigers began a run of finals appearances that averaged almost once every other year.

The first Tiger championship came in 1959 under Coach Gordon Brown (1955–63). Katy earned the 1A title with a 16–6 victory over favored West Texas powerhouse the Sundown Roughnecks, who throughout the season had averaged over forty points a game. Indeed, the Tigers had been underdogs in every one of their four previous playoff contests. Their victory in the final capped a perfect 15–0 season, heralding the kind of football success enveloping Katy in more recent years. The 1959 title game took place in Brownwood on December 19. The Roughnecks turned the ball over three times in the first half. In the second, Katy's 137-pound return man, Charlie Shafer, took back a kickoff eighty-two yards for the score.

Much later, compressed into a nineteen-year span (1994–2012), the Katy Tigers have added six more titles out of ten total finals appearances. From

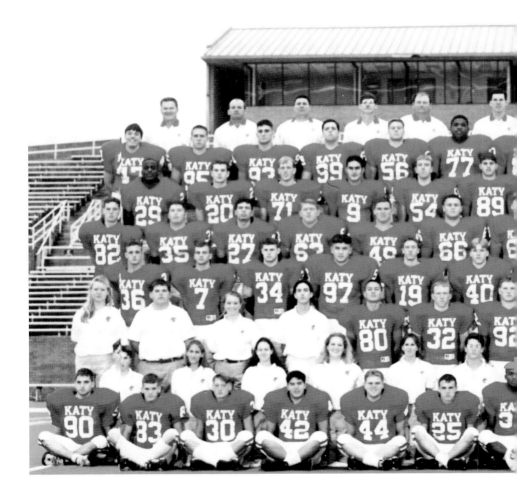

the 1939 founding of the Katy football program, the high school boasts twenty-seven district titles and thirteen regional championships. Since 2000, the Tigers have posted a remarkable 160–20 record (88.9 percent). Coach Mike Johnston was the principal architect of Katy's modern dynasty. In spite of going 4–26 his first three seasons, over twenty-two years (1982–2003), Johnston compiled a 200–76 record at Katy, including thirteen district titles, five state final appearances and three state championships. Through force of will; emphasis on leadership, work ethic and strength training; and the

The 1997 Katy Tigers brought Katy its second state championship. It was the first title for Coach Mike Johnston (back row, eighth from left). Before Johnston stepped down as Katy's head coach in 2003, he took his team to five finals appearances and won three titles (1997, 2000, 2003). *Courtesy of Visual Services of Texas.*

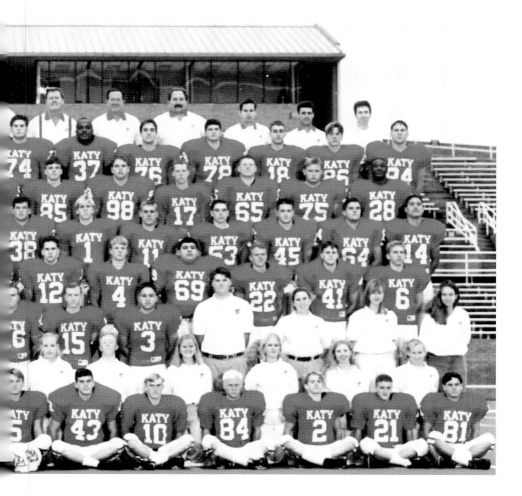

creation of a brand-new winning tradition, Johnston built a dynasty where the memory of 1959 had long since dimmed and faded. During his Katy tenure, he became recognized statewide almost as much for his trademark red suspenders as his coaching success. The suspenders were a gift from one of his players, Jason DeBusk, who had shortly before been diagnosed with leukemia. Johnston remembered DeBusk telling him, "Our coaching clothes were too plain. We needed to dress up some."[36] From that point forward during his Katy career, Johnston wore the suspenders each game day.

Johnston's first trip to the final came in 1994, when his Tigers fell 28–7 to a Plano Wildcat team making its ninth finals appearance. Three years later, the 1997 Tigers returned to the championship round, facing the Longview Lobos in Houston's Astrodome. Katy won the contest 24–3. All-State Tiger linebacker and 1997 Texas Sportswriter Player of the Year Rusty Bucy later

declared, "We didn't win because of talent; we won it with heart. The 1997 Katy Tigers dared to dream."[37]

The 1998 season held great promise for the Tigers. After finishing the regular season undefeated, Katy powerfully moved through the playoffs, securing a berth for that year's final against Midland Lee. During the week separating the semifinal from the final, an eligibility violation came to light, undercutting Katy's opportunity for back-to-back championships. The Tigers forthwith forfeited their previous two playoff wins and stayed at home on the weekend of the finals.

The following season, the Tigers played the 1999 final against Garland, losing 37–25. They had better luck in 2000. In a battle of the big cats at Houston's Astrodome, an undefeated Katy took on Tyler's John Tyler Lions in the final. Katy quarterback Jared Kaspar had a banner day with 153 yards through the

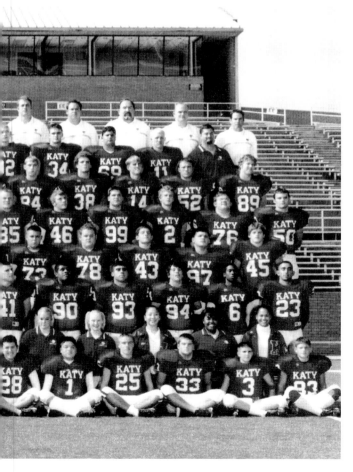

The 2003 Katy Tigers defeated the Southlake Carroll Dragons in what proved to be Coach Mike Johnston's last game of his twenty-two-year career as Katy head coach. The title win was Johnston's 200th victory. *Courtesy of Visual Services of Texas.*

air and 79 on the ground. Running back Jamal Branch complemented Kaspar's stellar performance with 147 rushing yards and two touchdowns of his own. At game's end, the Tigers had outscored the Lions 35–20.

Perhaps Johnston's most gratifying win at Katy was his last. Capping his twenty-two-year tenure, Johnston's 2003 Tigers derailed Southlake Carroll's "Todd Dodge Express," which had a run of 79–1 from 2002 to 2006. Katy defeated the defending 5A state champion Dragons 16–15 in the Alamodome. Johnston's game plan was to establish a Tiger running game early and control the tempo of the contest. That strategy worked, as Katy running back James Aston finished the game with thirty-one carries for 163 yards. With two and a half minutes left in the game, Katy trailed 15–9. A play-action fake to Aston set up a 51-yard game-winning touchdown reception by Ryan Mouton. Although Carroll got the ball back with ample time to win the game, Will Thompson's fourth-quarter interception with one minute and twenty-seconds left sealed the Tiger win. The Katy victory ended Southlake Carroll's thirty-one-game winning streak and was Johnston's 200th career victory. Johnston left Katy at the end of the 2003 season, taking a coaching position at Houston Christian, then a member of the Texas Alliance of Accredited Private Schools.

Johnston's replacement, Gary Joseph (2004–present), perpetuated the winning tradition, taking the Tigers to five finals in eight seasons (2005–12). The son of a coach himself, Joseph did not take long to get the Tigers back to the championship game. In his first trip there, 2005, Katy fell 34–20 to Southlake. The Tiger quarterback that season was Andy Dalton, who continued his post–high school football career at Texas Christian University. At TCU, Dalton was a record-setting, four-year starting quarterback and the acknowledged leader of the 2010 number-two-ranked Horned Frogs that beat the Wisconsin Badgers in the Rose Bowl. The following year, Dalton moved on to the NFL's Cincinnati Bengals, where, as starting rookie quarterback, he led the team to a 9–7 regular-season record and a spot in the AFC playoffs. The first-year Dalton was also a 2011 Pro Bowl selection. In that contest, played in Honolulu, he completed seven of nine passes for ninety-nine yards and two touchdowns. In 2012, the Bengals and Dalton returned to the playoffs as a wildcard team out of the AFC North.

Back in greater Houston, the only 2006 Katy Tigers loss came to Cypress Falls in the quarterfinals. The 2007 and 2008 teams set the stage for a possible three-peat in 2009. Successively beating Pflugerville 28–7 and Wylie 17–3 in the championship rounds, the nationally ranked and heavily favored Tigers fell to Abilene's 2009 Eagles, powered by cousins Herschel and Ronnell Sims.

In 2012, after a two-year absence, Katy returned to the finals for the eleventh time. In a contest against 2006 champion Cedar Hill, the number-three-ranked Tigers were favored but hampered by a number of injuries. Gimpy Tiger quarterback Kiley Huddleston was among the "wounded." He nevertheless persevered, playing well throughout the contest. In a match featuring multiple momentum shifts, Joey McGuire's Longhorns remained in the game well into the mid-fourth quarter, at which point they led 24–21. But Cedar Hill could not hold on. Coach Gary Joseph explained in his postgame interview, "We made one more play than they did." With six minutes and forty-six seconds left to play, on fourth and short, Tiger running back Adam Taylor traversed 56 yards to put Katy ahead 28–24. Subsequently, the stiff Tiger defense denied the Longhorns. Katy's defense, led by Defensive MVP Matt Dimon, chalked up eight quarterback sacks. With one minute and fifty-five seconds to play, Taylor put the game on ice with a 45-yard touchdown dash that gave the Tigers a comfortable 35–24 lead. With thirty carries for a whopping 275 yards and five rushing touchdowns, Taylor was the unquestioned Offensive MVP, a particularly gratifying recognition considering that he had sustained a season-ending knee injury in the first game of the 2011 season. At game's end, a smiling Coach Joseph declared that title wins "never get old." The championship victory was Joseph's third (2007, 2008 and 2012) and Katy's seventh, placing the Tiger juggernaut behind only Celina and Southlake Carroll. On December 26, *USA Today* moved Katy into the number-two spot nationally behind only John Curtis Christian High of River Ridge, Louisiana.

Coach Joseph articulates part of Katy's formula for success, observing, "Kids going through the program now expect to win. Their coaches expect them to win."[38] As Katy presses forward into the twenty-first century, its football program continues to live up to the inscription affixed to the field house foyer: "When excellence becomes tradition, greatness has no limits."

Plano Wildcats

Katy is part of metropolitan Houston, and Plano is part of the North Texas Metroplex. The suburban evolution of both locales is similar. Plano's first European-descended settlers arrived in the 1840s. The farming and cotton community that they established grew slowly, its population reaching only 500 by 1874. By the turn of the twentieth century, some 1,300 residents lived in the vicinity. When the 1965 Wildcats under Coach Thomas Gray

The Plano Wildcats earned their first state title in 1965. In that year, Plano was a class-2A high school. As Plano grew and school enrollment increased, the high school frequently moved up in realignments. Consequently, Plano High School holds the unique distinction of winning state football titles in conferences 2A, 3A, 4A and 5A.

(1959–65) won the 2A football title in rain-soaked Austin, fewer than 4,000 people called Plano's flatland farming community home. Thus began a 6–3 run in finals appearances stretching across the next thirty years. During the same three decades, Plano's population veritably exploded.

Much as McCally explains the Odessa Permian Mojo, Wildcat team historian Bart Benne describes "Plano Mystique" as victory "against strong odds. Either the other team was highly favored, dominated in the statistics, or was ahead late in the game—but Plano won anyway."[39] Benne documents Wildcat football excellence dating from the 1920s, when the 1925 team went 8–0–0. The 11–7 Wildcat victory over the Celeste Blue Devils capped the end to that year's perfect Plano season. Under the UIL playoff system of the time, the Wildcats were too small to advance beyond the regular season. The Plano community nonetheless rewarded its hometown heroes with

a celebratory end-of-season banquet at the local Lions Club. The school retired the number thirteen, worn by 1925 team captain Johnny Dunn. For many years, his jersey remained on display in the Plano trophy case.

The 1934 Wildcats became the first of a host of Plano teams that advanced to the playoffs. They fell 44–13 in the regional final against Crowell. In succeeding decades, Plano football experienced periodic success, but the Plano dynasty began in earnest with the 1965 Wildcat 20–17 win over 2A Edna. Coach Tom Gray's Wildcats put an early-season pre-district loss to Bonham behind them and moved through the remainder of their schedule with relative ease. In that year's playoffs, Plano shut out two of its first four opponents—West and DeKalb—and subsequently allowed only fourteen combined points to Lake Worth and Iowa Park. The December 18 championship game in Austin could not be played at Memorial Stadium, which was under renovation. Nelson Field—a venue without a scoreboard— became the site of the final. Amusingly, to keep spectators abreast of the score, officials had to borrow a basketball scoreboard (held in place by a forklift) from the University of Texas.

Two years later, Plano, now a growing town of fourteen thousand, returned to the final. By that time, Coach Gray had moved on, taking a new position at Amarillo Palo Duro. The 1965 Wildcat line coach, John Clark, was in the process of relocating to Henderson when Plano ISD offered him the head football coach/athletic director position. Clark changed his plans and coached the Wildcats the next ten seasons (1966–75). He hit pay dirt his second year. To get to the 1967 final, Plano played a semifinal matchup against the Phillips Blackhawks. The game took place in Vernon on a blustery, bitter-cold night with a sub-zero wind-chill factor. In a hard-fought contest, Plano emerged victorious, 15–13, and headed to the final for the second time in three years. The Wildcats faced San Antonio Randolph in a championship played in Waco's Baylor University Stadium. Black senior Wildcat running back John Griggs made a sixty-six-yard touchdown run at the very start of the contest. The Randolph Ro-Hawks quickly rallied to an 8–7 advantage, but San Antonio would not score again that day. Alex "Jackie" Williams and Griggs combined for two more Plano touchdowns, and the Wildcats won the 2A title game 27–8. Four years later, Plano enjoyed more of the same.

When the 1971 team took the 3A title, Plano's residents numbered about eighteen thousand. That season, prior to the playoffs, only Greenville scored double-digit points on Plano. Six of Plano's regular season wins were shutouts. After dominating Azle in the bi-district round, the Wildcats fought their way to narrow victories against Jacksonville in the quarterfinals and two-time defending state champion Brownwood in the semifinal. In the latter game at Fort Worth's Amon Carter Stadium, Plano took revenge on the Lions, who had knocked an 11–1 Wildcat team out of the playoffs in the 1970 semis. A Pat Thomas field goal with twenty-one seconds left to play gave the Wildcats a come-from-behind, 10–8 victory that sent them to the title game and dealt Gordon Wood's invincible Lions their only playoff loss ever in a game beyond bi-district. One week later in Austin, Plano's margin of victory was even slimmer. Again, Pat Thomas (future All-American at Texas A&M) became the hero. He had touchdown runs of one and forty-five yards and kicked all three Wildcat points after touchdowns (PAT). His final PAT was Plano's margin of victory, the difference being a missed extra point by Gregory-Portland after a third-quarter score. With only fourteen seconds left in the game, Gregory-Portland quarterback Marty Akins (the Gregory-Portland coach's son, as well as future UT wishbone option quarterback) missed a twenty-five-yard field goal that would have won the game. At the end of the day, Plano savored the 21–20 victory that brought the Wildcats their third state title.

The Plano teams of 1971 (above) and 1977 (below) won the third and fourth Wildcat state titles. The 1971 team won the championship in Conference 3A. Six years later, the growth of Plano moved the Wildcats into the larger 4A classification. As would be the case with other rapidly growing Metro-Dynasties, competing in the larger conferences seemed to nurture championship-caliber performances rather than obstruct them.

John Clark continued coaching the Wildcats for four more years, after which he became solely the Plano ISD athletic director. He looked back on a 107–17–0 career record (86.3 percent). Clark passed the football program into the very capable hands of Tommy Kimbrough (1976–91), who began coaching in Plano ISD his first year out of college. At the time of Clark's departure, Kimbrough served as Wildcat offensive coordinator. When he completed his tenure as head coach, he boasted a 171–28–7 career record (83.0 percent), four finals appearances and three state titles (more than any Plano coach to date).

The first championship came in 1977. The road to the final was challenging, particularly the quarterfinal "Miracle Game" against Highland

Park. A crowd of 35,000 witnessed the Wildcats surmount a 21–0 halftime deficit, as well as a Scottie touchdown that stretched their third-quarter lead to 28–0. Thereafter, the Wildcat defense came to life, and Plano's offense posted twenty-nine unanswered points. With a scant thirty-three seconds remaining in the contest, a thirty-three-yard flea-flicker pass from Stevie Haynes to Perry Haynes put the Wildcats within one. Plano erased the deficit when Steve Ulmer found the end zone on a two-point conversion, giving the Wildcats a 29–28 victory. Things were no easier in the semifinal the following week when Plano met Odessa Permian at Texas Tech's Jones Stadium. In the end, a first-quarter thirty-three-yard field goal by Stevie Haynes made all the difference. A stiff Wildcat defense turned back all Panther attempts to score, and Plano punched its ticket to the final with a 3–0 shutout. One week later, before a national record crowd of 49,953 in Texas Stadium, Coach Kimbrough guided Plano to its third state title. The "Cardiac Cats" defeated perennial finalist and 1975 state champion Port Neches-Groves 13–10.

Plano returned to the 1978 final but lost 29–10 to Houston Stratford. Wildcat fans quickly noted that the three most recent Plano finals appearances coincided with Dallas Cowboy appearances in Super Bowls VI, XII and XIII. The outcomes were even the same. Both Cowboys and Wildcats won in 1971 and 1977. Both lost in 1978. While the Cowboys succumbed to a Pittsburgh Steelers team powered by Terry Bradshaw, Franco Harris, Rocky Bleier, Lynn Swann and John Stallworth, Plano was unable to control a Houston Stratford Spartans team led by running back Craig James, who set a then–state single-season rushing record of 2,411 yards. The Spartans won the contest 29–13, with James scoring nineteen of the Stratford points. James later became part of the legendary SMU "Pony Express" (1979–82) alongside Sealy's Eric Dickerson. Curiously, the same year that James and his Stratford Spartan teammates beat Plano for the 1978 4A title, in Conference 3A, Dickerson led Sealy to what became the first of five Tiger state championships. After successful college careers, both Dickerson and James went to the NFL. The latter played in Super Bowl XX for the New England Patriots. After retiring from professional football in 1989, James became a widely recognized radio/television sports analyst. More recently, James left ESPN after announcing on December 19, 2011, his intention to vie for the 2012 Republican Party nomination to take Kay Bailey Hutchison's U.S. Senate seat. One of nine political hopefuls, James garnered 4 percent of the primary votes.

Between 1980 and 2000, during which Plano went 3–1 in 4A or 5A finals, the city's population leapt from 72,000 to 222,030. In 1986–87,

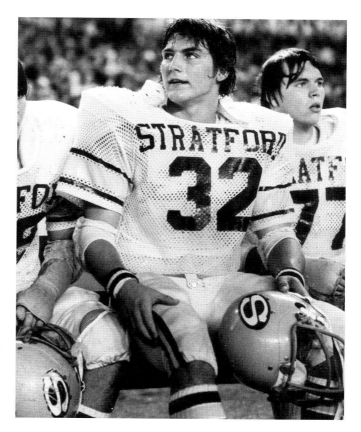

Craig James played high school football on the Houston Stratford team that defeated Plano for the 1978 state championship. James continued his football career at Southern Methodist University and later with the New England Patriots who played in Super Bowl XX.

Kimbrough's Wildcats made another back-to-back finals appearance, this time winning both contests. The 1986 team defeated La Marque 24–7. These Wildcats got off to a disappointing 2–2 season start, losing to both Duncanville and Richardson. From that point forward, however, Plano moved effectively and efficiently, decisively defeating all opposition on its path to the playoffs. The Wildcat quarterfinal against Longview (17–12) and semifinal against Hurst L.D. Bell (28–21) were both tighter contests, but neither prevented Plano from moving on to secure a seventeen-point win over La Marque in the finals.

The 1987 Wildcats posted a perfect 16–0 season. To so do, they came back from a 21–14 halftime semifinal deficit to take a 29–21 win over powerful Odessa Permian. The following week, the squad avenged Plano's 1978 loss to Houston Stratford, beating the Spartans 28–21. Six members of the 1987 team—more than any other school in the nation—received Division 1A scholarships, and Plano laid claim to the mythical 1987 national high school

In 1987, Plano again met Houston Stratford in the state final matchup. The Wildcats (above) won the contest 28–21 and received acclaim from the National Sports News Service as the mythical 1987 high school national champions.

title. Plano's Kimbrough Stadium, completed in 2004, is named in honor of the venerable Plano coach with the most state titles. Kimbrough's successor, Gerald Brence (1992–2007), took Plano to back-to-back title games in 1993–94. The Wildcats played both against fellow Metro-Dynasties. They lost to Converse Judson, 36–13, but defeated Katy 28–7. Plano continues to grow and prosper and is one of America's safest cities. Its 2007 median income was an affluent $84,490. With more than 250,000 residents, it is the ninth-largest city in Texas, as well as the corporate headquarters for eleven major businesses.

SOUTHLAKE CARROLL DRAGONS

Plano's affluent neighbor on the north-northwest edge of the Metroplex is Southlake Carroll. Southlake residents did not always enjoy the $172,945 median income of today. Originally settled in the 1840s as a rural community,

it remained exactly that for the next 130 years. Southlake was not even officially incorporated until 1956. The area became a rapidly growing "boom-burg" after the 1973 completion of DFW International Airport. As the city of Southlake quickly expanded during the 1980s, the Carroll High School football program became one of the best in the Lone Star State. Under Coach Bob Ledbetter (1979–95), from 1986 through 1994, Southlake won a state-record seventy-two consecutive regular-season football games (breaking the 1970–76 Big Sandy standard of fifty-three). During the streak, the Dragons scored 3,136 points while allowing a mere 441. Included in the run were thirty-four shutouts. In 1994, Carroll moved from the smaller 3A conference into 4A. Most of the veterans from the 1992–93 title teams were gone, significantly reducing the prospects of moving through yet another undefeated regular season. In the second contest of the 1994 season, the streak ended when the Dragons fell 43–21 to a talented group of Gainesville Leopards.

Four years before that transition, Ledbetter's undefeated 3A 1988 Dragons gave Southlake a football program fit for a community on the rise. That season, only two of Carroll's opponents scored in double digits. Carroll offensive coordinator Steve Lineweaver (who later found great head coaching success at Commerce and Euless Trinity) used his multi-bone option formation, directed by quarterback Mike Uldrich and running back David Blanchard, to power Carroll's way to a perfect 15–0 record. Meanwhile, defensive coordinator Ken Cook muted opposition, allowing only Gainesville among all Dragons' 1988 opponents to score more than ten points. The Dragons handily rolled through bi-district to the final, even pitching shutouts in the quarterfinal and semifinal games. Southlake won its first state football 3A title by decisively defeating Navasota 42–8. The 1988 team's sophomore placekicker was Jason Fernandez, who went on to set a new high school national record of 212 successful extra-point kicks by the 1990 end of his schoolboy football career.

After 1988, Ledbetter's Dragons did not return to the final for another four years, but during the next three seasons, Southlake went to the quarterfinal (1989) and then back-to-back semifinals (1990–91). The 1992 and 1993 teams took the process one step further. In a 32–0 run, SLC earned back-to-back 3A championships, first beating Coldspring 48–0 in a game in which running back Dane Johnson rushed for five touchdowns. Signal caller for that team was the five-foot-nine, 150-pound Will Mantooth, who received recognition as the 3A 1992 Player of the Year. At season's end, Southlake's 803 total points placed the Dragons fourth on the all-time single-season scoring list behind then–national record holder Big Sandy (with 824), and teams from Maxton, North Carolina, and Sheridan, Indiana. In the 1993 final, Carroll shut down perennial playoff contender Cuero 14–6. Tom Rapp succeeded Ledbetter in 1996. While Carroll had several respectable seasons in the years that followed, nothing compared to the 2000 arrival of Todd Dodge.

The Dodge story begins at Port Arthur Jefferson, where he played from 1978 to 1980 for the pass-happy coach Ronnie Thompson. Dodge's high school career overlapped that of teammate and schoolboy All-American Brent Duhon, one of the best and fastest receivers of his era. Dodge quarterbacked a 14–0 Port Arthur Yellow Jacket team going into the 1980 final against Odessa Permian. On the way, he became the first Texas high school quarterback to pass for over 3,000 yards in a single season. He also set new state standards for single-season (221) and career completion marks (393). In the 1980 title game, Dodge surpassed Tommy Kramer's career passing record, compiling 5,642 yards. At the turn of the twenty-first century, when Dodge arrived at Carroll with his "Air Raid Offense," one heard a discernible echo of 1980.

Opposite, bottom: Dodge quarterbacks his Port Arthur Jefferson Yellow Jackets in the 1980 final played against Petro-Dynasty Odessa Permian.

Todd Dodge (left) appears with pass-happy Port Arthur Jefferson coach Ronnie Thompson (middle). Dodge enjoyed the services of speedy All-American receiver Brent Duhon (right) as one of his favorite targets.

Before that monumental moment, Dodge became a record-setting quarterback for the Texas Longhorns. In 1987, he began his coaching career at Rockwall and subsequently went to McKinney (1988–91). Two years after that, Dodge coached quarterbacks and wide receivers at the University of North Texas in Denton. In 1996, he returned to the high school ranks, coaching successively in the Metroplex at Newman Smith (1996–97) and Fossil Ridge (1998–99).

In 2000, Dodge brought his patented passing attack to Southlake Carroll. In the image of his Port Arthur Jefferson high school years, Dodge turned Southlake into a veritable quarterback factory. Over the next seven seasons, he posted a 98–11 record (89.9 percent), including five consecutive trips to the finals with four state championships. From 2002–06, the Dragons were 79–1. During Dodge's last three seasons, his teams were 46–0. Either *USA Today* or the National Prep Poll (or both) acknowledged SLC as mythical national champions all three years. In his first two seasons at Southlake, Dodge's Dragons made the quarterfinals and the semifinals, setting the stage for one of the most extraordinary runs ever witnessed in Texas high school football. Today's visitors and fans entering Southlake's magnificent Dragon Stadium, completed in 2001, are truly entering the "House that Dodge Built."

The wide-open 2002 Dragon offense made a 16–0 run through the title game. On the way, in eleven of those contests, the pass-crazy Carroll offense posted forty points or more. Dragon quarterback Chase Wasson enjoyed a banner year, throwing for single-season state records of 4,800 yards and fifty-four touchdowns. Three of his targets had more than 1,000 receiving yards each. In the 2002 title contest, Southlake routed Smithson Valley 45–14. Katy imposed a 2003 championship interregnum, but the game went down to the wire, and the margin of victory was but a single point. Perhaps more importantly, junior Dragon quarterback Chase Daniel gained valuable experience that he would exploit the following season.

The 2004 Dragons reasserted 5A dominance, as ten of their sixteen wins came by forty or more points. On three occasions, the Carroll offense posted between sixty-one and seventy points. Carroll won that year's final over Smithson Valley 27–24. Chase Daniel contributed more than his fair share. In his two seasons as signal caller, he posted a 65.2 percent completion rate, 8,298 yards in the air and ninety-one touchdown passes. For good measure, he also rushed for another 2,954 yards and scored thirty-nine touchdowns. It came as no surprise when Daniel won 5A Player of the Year. EA Sports even named him the National Player of the Year.

After high school, Daniel went to Missouri, alma mater of the mighty Chuck Moser. There, Daniel enjoyed a highly successful college career. He

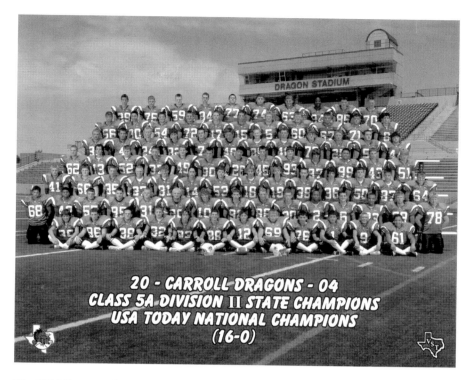

The 2004 Dragons played Smithson Valley for that year's 5A title. The game program for that contest declared, "Protect the Tradition," suggesting Southlake's keen self-awareness of the championship football tradition that had grown since 1988. The mantra remains with the team today. The Dragons of 2004 performed their custodial duty and won the contest 27–24. *Courtesy of Jake and Mike Truitt of Visual Services of Texas.*

became Mizzou's 2006 starter and threw for 3,527 yards and twenty-eight touchdowns. Those numbers improved in 2007, rising to 4,306 yards and thirty-three touchdowns. Missouri's 12–2 mark that season was also a school record, earning the Tigers a successful trip to the Cotton Bowl, played on January 1, 2008. The Tigers ended their season with a best-ever AP ranking of fourth. Daniel became the only Missouri Tiger ever to receive recognition as Big 12 Offensive Player of the Year. He was fourth in the 2007 Heisman Trophy voting. With 13,256 total offensive yards, Daniel ended his 2008 senior season as Missouri's career leader. During the 2009–12 NFL seasons, including Super Bowl XLIV, Daniel was on the active roster of the NFL's New Orleans Saints. Curiously, in New Orleans, Daniel reunited with an SLC teammate, placekicker Garrett Hartley, who has been a Saint since 2008.

Meanwhile, back at Southlake, Daniel's successor, Greg McElroy, continued the winning Dragon tradition. In leading his teammates to another perfect

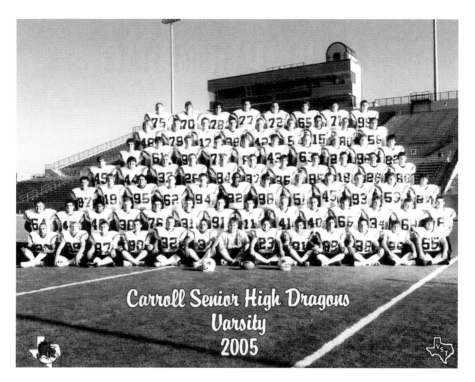

The expertise of one of the best high school quarterbacks in Texas enabled the 2005 Dragons to continue Southlake's championship run. Greg McElroy (sixth row, third from left) quarterbacked his team to the 2005 Texas 5A high school title and a national high school championship. Five years later, he took Alabama's Crimson Tide to the national crown. *Courtesy of Jake and Mike Truitt of Visual Services of Texas.*

16–0 record, McElroy passed for 4,687 yards and a new state record fifty-six touchdowns. In the 2005 title game, Southlake extracted a measure of revenge for its 2003 loss to the Katy Tigers. At game's end, McElroy and his teammates savored a 34–20 victory over Katy and a third Dragon championship in just four years. McElroy earned game MVP honors for his twenty-one completions that netted 328 yards and four touchdowns. Like his predecessor Daniel, McElroy received recognition as 5A Player of the Year.

And also much like Daniel, McElroy moved directly into a storied college career. In his junior season at Alabama (2009), he set school records for single-game consecutive completions (fourteen) and passing efficiency (thirteen of fifteen for 86.7 percent). Ironically, the latter record came in a game against the University of North Texas, by then under McElroy's old high school coach, Todd Dodge. That same season, McElroy guided Alabama to the SEC Championship as the Crimson Tide overran the

Florida Gators 35–13. The win punched Alabama's ticket to the 2010 BCS National Championship game against Texas. The Tide decisively beat the Longhorns 37–21. Following his senior season, McElroy was drafted by the same NFL franchise that had made good use of another former celebrated Alabama quarterback, Joe Namath. The New York Jets took McElroy as the 208th pick in the 2011 draft.

During McElroy's 2005 senior high school season, one of his targets was sophomore receiver Riley Dodge, son of the Carroll coach. Like Chase Daniel in his junior year, Riley moved from receiver to quarterback. Junior Riley Dodge picked apart otherwise respectable defenses with his deadly no-huddle offense spread. In a pattern that had become familiar at Carroll, Dodge passed for 4,184 yards and fifty-four touchdowns, quarterbacked the Dragons to a perfect 16–0 season and took the 2006 5A crown. Carroll won that year's title, defeating Austin Westlake (making its sixth finals appearance) 43–29.

The following season, Todd Dodge took a University of North Texas offer to become head football coach. There, he served from 2007–10. In 2011, Dodge moved to the University of Pittsburgh, where he coached (what else?) quarterbacks. After one season in Pennsylvania, Dodge returned to Texas to direct the 4A Marble Falls Mustangs. Under Dodge's tutelage, Mustang quarterback Mike Richardson set a new Texas schoolboy standard of 715 passing yards in a single contest. Richardson's mark also ranked second best ever nationally. Meanwhile, from 2007 to 2012, Southlake's Dragons continued to be a playoff-making machine, now under the mentorship of Hal Wasson (father of the former Carroll quarterback, Chase).

After a four-year absence from the final, Wasson took his undefeated 2011 Dragons back to the championship round. At Arlington's Cowboys Stadium, Carroll faced Fort Bend Hightower. Amidst an ocean of Carroll green in the stands (some two-thirds of the spectators were Dragon fans), 42,896 watched Southlake in its ninth finals appearance. The long preamble to what became the eighth Dragon title is worth mention. Carroll sustained an unexpected setback in the 2010 season when a UIL ruling denied the use of a transfer student who otherwise would have been Southlake's starting quarterback. That judgment accelerated the development of then-sophomore Kenny Hill, who found himself suddenly in the starter's role. Hill came to the new responsibilities with an impressive pedigree. The son of Ken Hill, former All-Star pitcher for the 1995 American League champion Cleveland Indians, Kenny inherited his fair share of athletic ability. His underclassman status notwithstanding, he and the Dragons advanced to the 2010 quarterfinals, a prelude to a perfect upcoming Dragon season.

In 2011, Southlake moved undefeated into the playoffs, where the Dragons successively bested challenging 5A opponents, including Plano East, Cedar Hill, Arlington Bowie and Arlington Martin. The semifinal against Dallas Skyline, however, appeared to be the end of the line, as the Dragons trailed by two scores with just sixty-seven seconds left to play. Miraculously, in that short span, Hill scored two touchdowns, bringing the Dragons back to win the contest 28–24. Hill's performance in the final was no less spectacular, as he threw for 229 yards, including two touchdowns, and ran for another 117. Baylor commit Sabian Holmes hauled in eleven of Hill's tosses for 138 yards. The Dragons won 36–29 at the end of the day. The victory tied Southlake with Celina for a state record eight state titles. As the dust from the 2011 season settled, the Dragons found themselves ranked sixth nationally as part of the annual "Fab 50."

Veteran quarterback Kenny Hill entered the 2012 season with a 23–3 record as a starter for a program with the motto "Protect the Tradition," pointing to the Dragon hope of surpassing Celina's Bobcats for most-ever Texas state football titles. Upon that sturdy base, the Dragons advanced in 2012 to the quarterfinals, where they lost a closely fought contest to the talented DeSoto Eagles. Today, with a population of twenty-five thousand (95.0 percent white), a median household income of almost $180,000 and only 1.8 percent of its population below the poverty line, Southlake may have reached its geographic limits, but its football program's future remains as bright as ever.

CONVERSE JUDSON ROCKETS

Some three hundred miles south-southwest of Southlake, in the upscale northeast San Antonio suburb of Converse, another football dynasty arose. The Converse Judson Rockets resemble the Oil Belt champion Odessa Permian in two respects: both schools were established in 1959, and both have played in a record-tying eleven finals contests. Before Judson won its first state title in 1983, other San Antonio schools had made their mark on Texas football history. Brackenridge, Churchill, Jefferson, Lee and Randolph all had made it to the final. But none of these high schools nor any of the other six that have made it to the final since—Alamo Heights, Cibolo Steele, MacArthur, Marshall, Roosevelt and Taft—have made the monumental impact that their northeastern neighbor has. From 1983 through 2007, Judson brought home six state championship trophies.

The 1983 Judson Rockets were the first of six Converse Judson state-champion football teams. That year's Rocket team defeated Midland Lee 25–21 for the title.

In 1962, when the small rural community of Converse fielded its first high school football team, the early results were disastrous. Wins were few and far between. The Rockets finally enjoyed liftoff under Coach Jerry Sanders (1977–79), who made Judson a late-1970s regional power. During his three seasons at Judson, Sanders posted three ten-win seasons. Coach Frank Arnold took the 1983 team to the pinnacle, defeating Midland Lee 25–21 in that year's championship game. In this televised contest at Irving's Texas Stadium, Judson's Chris Pryor (who broke the 5A single-season rushing record with 2,800 yards) scored four touchdowns and set Judson's future trajectory. Like other successful Texas coaches before him, Arnold immediately moved to the athletic director's office. His celebrated successor was Judson's defensive coordinator, D.W. Rutledge.

A native of Houston, the intense and passionate Rutledge brought an impressive football resume to the task. During his college playing days, Rutledge was linebacker and captain for the 1974 Texas Lutheran University team that won that year's NAIA Division II national title. Rutledge found a way to get the most out of all who played for him. Before his 1984–2000 tenure was done, he compiled a 197–32–5 record (84.2 percent) that included a dozen district titles, seven finals appearances and four state championships.

Rutledge's 1988 Rockets made the final, facing the highly touted Dallas Carter Cowboys. Carter won the game on the field, 31–14. However, Carter was stripped of the title in 1991 in an early manifestations of controversial 1984 House Bill 72, aka "No Pass, No Play." The architects of the provision were Texas businessman H. Ross Perot and the Texas Education Committee. The regulation itself was the most recent in a long line of measures aimed

D.W. Rutledge (center) was the architect of the Converse Judson Metro-Dynasty. Although Judson earned its first title five years before Rutledge coached his 1988 title team, from 1988 through 1998, he led the Rockets to seven finals appearances, four of which were Judson wins.

at setting practical and reasonable eligibility standards. Regulations during the early days of UIL supervision sound outright alien compared to more modern parameters. In the early decades, it was not uncommon for former players aged twenty or older to return home to play in the occasional contest. "Encores" even became a euphemism for the use of such ineligible players. Indeed, in a decade predating birth certificates, documentation of actual age often proved highly subjective.

In 1923, UIL actually instituted a rule forbidding teachers from playing in the games—something that seems a redundant articulation of plain old common sense until one sees coaches fully suited out and ready to compete in 1920s-era yearbooks. That same year, UIL introduced measures to undercut "tramp" athletes, including the requirement that each player must have officially recorded credit in three classes during the semester prior to the current season. Also instituted was a "half-year rule" mandating that athletes must "have been in attendance half of the year he was last in school."[40] A

1926 regulation reduced the age limit for players from twenty-one to twenty. As the decades passed, rules became more stringent.

The 1984 no-pass, no-play provision required classroom accountability of student athletes. They had to have at least a 70 average each grading period in all the classes in which they were enrolled. Three years after the fact, the UIL Executive Committee unanimously voted to overturn Carter's 1988 victory over Judson. Other than Carter, only Stamford's 1959 team (which had won what would have been the fourth Bulldogs title in five years) has been stripped of a championship for eligibility violations.

A month before the 1991 UIL decision awarding Judson the 1988 title, Rutledge had returned with the Rockets to the 1990 final. Judson narrowly lost 21–19 to Marshall. Next season, the 11–3 Rockets made it to the 1991 semifinal, which they lost to Fort Bend Dulles. During the next two years, Judson went 27–1–2, including back-to-back state titles. Both championship wins were classic blowouts. Star Judson running back Jerod Douglas rushed for over 200 yards in both title contests (as well as 6,189 for his high school career before later starring at Baylor University). In Austin's Memorial Stadium, Rutledge's 1992 team met first-time finalist Euless Trinity (which has since made four finals appearances to earn three state titles). Thanks to a 1990 UIL provision allowing third-place 5A district finishers to enter the playoffs, Trinity advanced to the final that year in spite of a record-high five regular-season losses. Predictably, the Rockets bested the Trojans, 52–0, tying Jacksboro's 1962 mark for largest margin of victory in a title game. That standard stood until Midland Lee's 54–0 rout of San Antonio-MacArthur in 1998. The 1992 Trojans did not even run a play on Judson's side of the field until the fourth quarter.

The Rockets returned in 1993, earning the second of back-to-back titles with a 36–13 win over fellow suburban juggernaut Plano. In a battle waged in Waco's Floyd Casey Stadium, that year's Rocket signal caller was Clint Rutledge—none other than the coach's son. Bruised ribs sustained in the semifinal notwithstanding, Clint donned a flak jacket for the final and persevered. Remarking on his son's determination, Coach Rutledge observed, "He's a tough kid and wanted to be a part of this, too. It would have been tough to keep him out of the lineup." In the game's aftermath, the coach continued, "I was probably more intense and excited than for any game we've had. It's hard not to be excited when you have a state championship game and your son is playing on your team." Clint himself declared, "I guess this is a once-in-a-lifetime situation for both of us. Winning a state championship with your father is something you dream

about from an early age."[41] Thus, the pair was an early addition to a small, elite fraternity of Texas high school father-and-son/coach-and-quarterback combinations that grabbed the brass ring together. Later additions included Art and Kendal Briles, Todd and Riley Dodge, Sam and Graham Harrell, G.A. and Gary Don Moore and Wayne and Hagen Hutchinson.

Judson's 42–19 loss to Katy in the 1994 semifinal prevented a Rocket three-peat. However, the defeat did not stop a back-to-back 1995–96 title appearance. The 1995 Rocket win was gratifying to Rutledge on several

The 1992 Judson Rockets overwhelmed the Euless Trinity Trojans 52–0, tying a 1962 state final record for the widest margin of victory in any title game. *Courtesy of Visual Sports of San Antonio.*

levels. The victory was Judson's fifth state title. It came against the oft-appearing championship contender Odessa Permian Panthers. The narrow three-point margin of victory—31–28—likely made the win all the sweeter. In the contest played at Texas Stadium, the Rockets overcame a 21–17 deficit at the end of the third quarter. Two fourth-quarter touchdown passes from Judson quarterback Guy Anderson to Wilmer Wade and Teddy Carrier were enough to cement the Rocket win. The following season, an undefeated 1996 team from Lewisville undercut Rocket hopes of a second

The 1993 Rockets made it back-to-back championships with the coach's son, quarterback Clint Rutledge, leading the team to a 36–13 win over the Plano Wildcats. *Courtesy of Visual Sports of San Antonio.*

set of back-to-back wins. In fact, the Rockets' road to the 1996 final was near miraculous in the first place. In the bi-district round against Austin Bowie, Judson overcame a 31–0 deficit with just over eight minutes left in the third quarter. Thirty-two unanswered Judson points opened the door for a Rocket run to the championship round. Judson took advantage and advanced to the December 14 final, a shootout before 17,200 at Baylor's Floyd Casey Stadium. As time expired in the opening half, a Richard Mendoza–to–Darryl McKnight touchdown pass put the Rockets within striking distance. Lewisville held a 34–27 halftime lead. But the Fighting Farmers proved too much for Judson. In the second half, Lewisville took the 1996 title, winning by a score of 58–34.

Rutledge's Rockets returned in 1998 for his last finals appearance. In Houston's Astrodome, the Rockets took a 14–7 halftime lead against Duncanville. They extended their advantage by another seven with five minutes and forty-two seconds left in the third. Subsequently, the Panthers posted seventeen unanswered points, securing the win with a field goal late in the final quarter. Judson received the ensuing kickoff and drove down the field but was unable to score. Duncanville emerged the winner, 24–21.

Rutledge left coaching in 2000, taking a position as executive director of the Texas High School Coaches Association. His influence extended well

1995
JUDSON ROCKETS

The 1995 Rockets earned Judson's fifth state title, defeating perennial petro powerhouse Odessa Permian 31–28 in Irving's Texas Stadium. Judson quarterback Guy Anderson's two fourth-quarter passes secured the Converse win. *Courtesy of Visual Sports of San Antonio.*

beyond Judson's high school setting, even before he left for the THSCA. In a 1998 interview with AP sportswriter Kelley Shannon, Rutledge eloquently explained his coaching philosophy, declaring, "I think coaching is a ministry. We've got a platform to be around hundreds of young people on a daily basis. You can change lives through this profession." Not surprisingly, he coauthored the binder book *Coaching to Change Lives* with his one-time Judson offensive coordinator Dennis Parker. In one of the ironies of state finals history, Rutledge met Parker (by then the head coach at Marshall) in the 1990 championship game in which the Mavericks narrowly bested the Rockets 21–19. In 2006, Judson acknowledged Rutledge's immense contribution to the school district by renaming the local stadium in his honor.

Rutledge's longtime assistant head coach and successor, Jim Rackley, nurtured the winning Rocket tradition. He has taken Converse back to the final three times, winning it in 2002. In San Antonio's Alamodome before a crowd of twenty thousand, the 2002 Rockets met Midland High in the Bulldogs' first-ever trip to the finals (and their first trip to the playoffs since 1951). Rocket running back Chancy Campbell had a banner day, rushing for 185 yards and three first-half touchdowns. However, the contest became a nail-biter going down to the wire. With one minute and ten seconds left to play, Judson retook the lead on a Dustin Quinney field goal. The "Dawgs" answered with a touchdown pass with only twenty-two seconds left in the game, putting Midland ahead 32–27. With seven seconds left, Quinney hit senior running back Andre Williams with a 76-yard touchdown pass. The Bulldogs received the ensuing kickoff, but Jason Castillo intercepted a Midland pass at the Rocket 3-yard line, thus securing a 33–32 Rocket victory. Subsequently, two other Rackley teams made the championship game. Both lost to "Haka-powered" Euless Trinity. The 2005 contest ended 28–14, while the score in the 2007 match-up was 13–10.

Judson's competitive performance in early twenty-first-century football is much the product of one of the largest student bodies in the Texas public schools. As of late, Judson's enrollment runs from 3,800 to 4,000. Academic excellence complements the high school's athletic achievement. In 1999–2000, Judson received National Blue Ribbon School distinction. In 2000, Converse's population climbed to over 11,000, with a $47,947 median household income. With impressive resources, an outstanding school district both academically and athletically, a robust football tradition and six state titles in eleven finals appearances, the Rockets promise to remain a perennial contender.

La Marque Cougars

With a population today of some fourteen thousand, La Marque is significantly smaller than its aforementioned suburban counterparts. However, like Katy, La Marque is part of greater Houston. It is the childhood home of longtime Texas Republican senator Kay Bailey Hutchison (1993–2012). Lying near the Gulf Coast and about forty miles southeast of downtown Houston, La Marque is the least affluent among suburban football powerhouse high schools. The city has a median household income of $34,841, and 17.5 percent of its population is below the poverty line. From 1986 to 2010, Cougar football teams reached ten finals. Long before that era, La Marque running back Norm Bulaich (1963–64, when the school mascot was the Tiger) enjoyed a successful high school career after which he starred for the TCU Horned Frogs. From 1970 to 1979, Bulaich played in the NFL for the Baltimore Colts, Philadelphia Eagles and Miami Dolphins. Before those days, Bulaich's running powered La Marque to 1963's semifinal and a 9–7 fourth-quarter Tiger loss to Pharr-San Juan-Alamo.

La Marque made its first trip to the finals twenty-three years later, when the Cougars met mighty Plano. While today's Plano has the largest ethnic diversity of the Metro-Dynasties, La Marque has more than double the black population (35 percent of the town's total) of any of its suburban champion counterparts. The prelude to the 1986 state final was perhaps more dramatic than the title game itself. Only two days before that year's quarterfinals, Cougar coach Hugh Massey died. His team, with its high-scoring, run-and-shoot offense now guided by Larry Nowotny, persevered

Before the 1990s, when La Marque became synonymous with championship high school football, Norman Bulaich (above) put La Marque's football program on the Texas map. His powerful running did much to get his team to the 1963 semifinal, where La Marque fell 9–7 to Pharr-San Juan-Alamo.

and successively defeated quarterfinalist Aldine MacArthur and semifinalist Austin Reagan. In the final, the Cougars were not so fortunate. In Plano's sixth state title game appearance, the Wildcats bested the Cougars 24–7. Thereafter, the La Marque program entered a period of decline.

The 1993 season marked the start of a remarkable Cougar run under Coach Alan Weddell (1990–97) with his multiple-I offensive scheme and a sturdy La Marque defense. Weddell had a wealth of football experience. Before becoming an offensive lineman and backup center for the 1970 Texas Longhorns national championship team, Weddell had played high school football in Brazosport. His first head coaching job came in Victoria (1982–89) at the same school from which legendary Gordon Wood had come immediately before establishing a Brownwood dynasty that won seven state championships. Weddell had good success reinvigorating the Stingaree

COUGAR Magazine

1986 TEXAS 5-A
STATE CHAMPIONSHIP
FOOTBALL GAME

DECEMBER 20, 1986
KYLE STADIUM
COLLEGE STATION

OFFICIAL PROGRAM

"I believe if a coaches first job is to build and lead young men morally and spiritually, the teaching of football techniques will fall quickly into place."

"Young people are crying today for guideline. They want to be told what is right and what is wrong. True, they want freedom on one hand, but on the other hand, they want, and desperately need a centerline to set the sights of their lives upon."

Hugh Massey
1947-1986
Head Coach - La Marque Cougars

LA MARQUE COUGARS
VS.
PLANO WILDCATS

Although the Cougars did not win the 1986 final, the game marked La Marque's first-ever appearance in the title round. The commemorative program above features Cougar head coach Hugh Massey, who died just two days before the 1986 quarterfinal against Aldine MacArthur. La Marque continued to advance but fell 24–7 to a 1986 Plano team that took its fifth state title.

program, bringing Victoria High School its first-ever district 26-5A title (1986). The Stingarees lost the bi-district matchup with Converse Judson, after which Weddell began carefully watching the Rocket program. Learning from the opposition, he began developing his own unique style à la D.W. Rutledge.

Weddell arrived at La Marque in 1990. His success was instant. Over eight seasons, he never missed the playoffs. During Weddell's first two years, the Cougars made back-to-back round-two appearances. In 1992, they advanced to the quarterfinals. The team was 31–6 during Weddell's first three years. The stage was set. Under his subsequent mentorship, La Marque made five straight trips to the title game. The Cougars lost the first two—1993–94—to a Stephenville program revitalized by Art Briles and en route to dynasty status in its own right. The next three years, La Marque dispensed with a less challenging Yellow Jacket team—the Denison variety—winning each and every final to become the state's seventh Eleven-Man team to three-peat. Over these three consecutive seasons, the stingy Cougar defense allowed Denison a meager eleven total points while the La Marque offense scored eighty-two. The 1995 Cougars beat Denison 31–8. The 1996 team bested the Yellow Jackets again, this time 34–3. In 1997, La Marque won 31–0. Weddell left La Marque at the end of the 1997 season to take a job as linebacker coach for R.C. Slocum at Texas A&M. He looked back upon an impressive seven-year 103–13 record (88.8 percent). More recently, Weddell served as University of Houston's defensive coordinator.

After Weddell departed, his one-time assistant head coach and offensive coordinator Larry Walker took the reins (1998–2002). Over the next four seasons, Walker took the Cougars back to the finals once (1998), completing La Marque's remarkable six consecutive trips to the finals. The Cougars were the first team since Tyson's 1920s Waco Tigers to accomplish such a feat. In the 1998 championship contest, Stephenville again defeated the Cougars. In 2002, Walker moved from coaching to a La Marque ISD administrative position, becoming the director of personnel and operations. His replacement was Bryan Erwin, a new head coach who during his five-year tenure (2002–2006) brought the Cougars two additional state titles.

As La Marque mentor, Erwin compiled a record of 65–8 (89 percent). At the Alamodome in 2003, Erwin's Cougars took on the defending 4A state

University Interscholastic League
Texas High School Football
2003 Class 4-A Division II
State Championship

LA MARQUE COUGARS

District, Bi-District, Area, Regional
Semi-Final, Regional & State
Semi-Final Champions
15-0 Season Record
Region 3 District 23-4A

VS.

Denton Ryan Raiders

District, Bi-District, Area, Regional
Semi-Final, Regional & State
Semi-Final Champions
14-1 Season Record
Region 1 District 6-4A

Saturday, December 20, 2003 • 4:00 PM
San Antonio Alamodome

The 2003 Cougars won La Marque's fourth state championship in an exciting first-ever triple overtime finals contest played in San Antonio's Alamodome (see program above). They bested a formidable Denton Ryan team making its fourth consecutive finals appearance.

champion Denton Ryan Raiders, a team making its fourth consecutive finals appearance (2000–2003). The undefeated Cougars found themselves in *terra incognita*, especially after disassembling San Antonio Alamo Heights 66–14 in the previous weekend's semifinal. In the final at the Alamodome, Ryan posted fourteen unanswered first-quarter points. Late in the third quarter, it remained a two-possession game with Ryan leading 21–10. By the end of regulation, the game was deadlocked at 28–28. In the end, La Marque emerged victorious, winning 43–35 in a thrilling first-ever finals triple overtime.

The next two seasons, La Marque made quarterfinal appearances, succumbing first to 2004 state champion Kilgore and then to 2005 semifinalist Brenham. Erwin's 2006 Cougars returned to San Antonio, the site of the fourth Cougar state title, to add a fifth. The contest pitted La Marque against Waco—a championship matchup with old football royalty playing new. In what *Daily News* sportswriter Corey Roepken described as

2006 LaMarque High Varsity Cougars

The 2006 Cougar team secured La Marque's fifth title, defeating Waco High School 34–14.

"one of the most dominant final-quarter performances in the history of the Texas state football championships," the Cougars ran away with what had been a 14–14 tie. The Cougar performance was all the more remarkable since La Marque, no doubt hearing an echo from 2003, had trailed 14–0 late in the first quarter. The Cougars scored on all three of their fourth-quarter possessions and took the title 34–14. After his 2006 state championship, Erwin accepted the head coaching position at Flower Mound Marcus, a move that placed him much closer to his native Hillsboro.

When the Cougars returned for their tenth title appearance, they were under the direction of Darrell Jordan. Before coming to La Marque, Jordan had coached the Kimball Knights to a 52–29 record and playoff appearances in all seven of his seasons there (2001–07). In his first year at La Marque, 2008, the Cougars won only three games and missed the playoffs for the first time since 1989. The startling downturn was at least partly the blame of Hurricane Ike, which did tremendous damage to the Texas Gulf Coast in 2008. The 2009 season was little better, with the team going 4–6. Bluer skies returned in 2010. Although the Cougars failed to win their sixth state title, they made the final, losing 69–21 to undefeated Aledo and record-breaking Bearcat running back Johnathan Gray, who scored a title-game record eight touchdowns. Today's Cougars, now in Conference 3A and under Coach Mike Jackson, continue to maintain their winning tradition.

ALEDO BEARCATS

Aledo High School is located in Parker County about thirty miles from downtown Fort Worth. At first glance, little suggests that Aledo should be included among the Metro-Dynasties. Its official 2000 population of 1,726 is not even large enough for inclusion as one of the Micro-Dynasties examined in Chapter Four. In fact, the westward expansion of Fort Worth has already begun to swallow Aledo in much the same way that Metroplex growth in earlier decades absorbed Garland, Plano and Southlake. A 2010 Susan MacKeague Karnes and Homer Norris history, *Around Aledo*, accurately describes today's community as an idyllic place with "a pastoral lifestyle minutes from the urban amenities of the Fort Worth-Dallas Metroplex." At the time of the Bearcats' 2011 championship, enrollment at Aledo High School was 1,469—only 257 fewer than the city's official population. The conundrum is resolved when one realizes that 4A Aledo ISD draws from a twenty-by-ten-mile area. Occasionally, the finest Bearcat athletes reside well beyond the city's corporate limits yet within the school district's quasi-rectangular boundaries straddling Interstate 20.

From the mid-twentieth-century origins of the Bearcat football program, early pigskin success came slowly. The 1970s brought better days. By 1974, Aledo enjoyed fourteen consecutive wins that took the Bearcats to that year's 1A championship contest. Through Aledo's ten regular-season games, seven of which were shutouts, the Bearcats hung 435 points on all opponents while allowing a meager 31. The *pièce de résistance* was a 94–0 victory over district opponent Millsap. In the first four playoff contests against China Spring, DeLeon, Princeton and Tuscola Jim Ned, Aledo posted 130 points while giving up only 6 in the bi-district contest. In the 1A final, the number-one-ranked Bearcats met an undefeated Grapeland team that had struggled to get to the championship round. Had the Sandies failed to stop a 2-point conversion attempt at the end of the semifinal, Falls City would have advanced instead. The final in Temple's Wildcat Stadium was no less dramatic. A crowd of 3,500 watched a game that went down to the wire. In the second quarter, Bearcat quarterback Leland Hughes hit Chuck Green for Aledo's first score. Mike Wedgeworth ran the ball in for a second score with eight minutes left in the game. Still, the Sandies led 19–12. The Bearcats scored one last time on a Steve Lacefield–to–Joey Jackson pass, narrowing the margin to 19–18. Aledo went for two and the win, giving the ball to that year's star Bearcat running back Darryl Lowe, but the Sandie defense rose to the task and carried home the title trophy.

The Bearcats periodically enjoyed winning seasons through the remainder of the decade, as well as under coaching legend Chuck Curtis, who directed the program in 1987–88. But the real resurrection of the Bearcat program came with the 1993 arrival of Tim Buchanan. Like most winning high school coaches in Texas, Buchanan brought a wealth of football experience. During his own high school days, he played linebacker for the Killeen Kangaroos and thereafter for Abilene Christian University. After learning his trade as an assistant coach under Ross Rogers at College Station A&M Consolidated, Buchanan assumed head coaching duties at Aledo. Undaunted by a program in decline and a 2–8 record his first year there, he rapidly revived the Aledo program.

In 1998, Buchanan took the Bearcats to their first state title, a 3A D-1 crown won over the Cuero Gobblers. In spite of beginning the season without a single returning starter on offense, the Bearcats moved through the regular season with only a single loss. In the final itself, the offense sputtered during the first half, accumulating a total of minus-seven yards. The game remained a scoreless tie at intermission. The skies brightened in the second half as Aledo mounted two successful drives, one for sixty-two yards and the other for seventy-three. Both drives resulted in scores. Bearcat quarterback Joel Laminack's thirty-four-yard third-quarter touchdown run, followed by a two-yard Matt Saunders score with two minutes and forty-five seconds left to play, proved enough to earn a 14–7 championship win.

Aledo's success continued. From 2002 through 2011, Buchanan took the Bearcats to the quarterfinals nine out of ten seasons. Three of those nine (2004, 2006–07) resulted in trips to the semifinal. The last two semifinal losses were to a state-bound Copperas Cove Bulldog team directed by future 2011 Heisman Trophy winner Robert Griffin III. During the 2009–11 seasons, Aledo won the trifecta, elevating the Bearcat program to dynastic status. During its back-to-back-to-back state title run, Aledo became the fourteenth team in Texas to win three consecutive championships.

A big reason for the Aledo three-peat was record-setting running back Johnathan Gray, the 2011 Gatorade National Player of the Year. In his

Johnathan Gray receives congratulations on the Aledo sideline after breaking the national high school touchdown record in the fourth quarter of Aledo's December 17, 2011 win over Manvel for the 4A D-2 state championship. The score put Gray past Mike Hart of Nedrow, New York's Onondaga Central High School. Gray also set new state standards for touchdowns in a season (sixty-five), career games of one hundred or more rushing yards (fifty-one), and career scoring (1,232).

Bearcat seasons, Gray set a new national record for career touchdowns (205), as well as new state records for touchdowns in a season (65), career games of 100 or more rushing yards (51) and career scoring (1,232—only 14 points off the national record). In the Texas record book, Gray's 10,889 career rushing yards ranks him behind only the legendary "Sugar Land Express," Kenneth Hall.

Aledo's 4A D-2 2009 title win over Brenham was only the beginning of even better things. The Bearcats entered that year's final at Austin's Darrell K. Royal-Texas Memorial Stadium with only a single early-season loss. Aledo's sophomore running back Gray carried the ball thirty-two times for 252 yards and four touchdowns. Senior Bearcat quarterback Trey Ozee contributed to the scoring with a 34-yard touchdown run. At the end of the day, Aledo took the championship over the Cubs, 35–21, and added a second trophy to the Bearcat display case.

In 2010, on the way to a perfect 16–0 season, Aledo's only real regular-season challenge came from defending 4A D-1 state champion Lake Travis. Although shorthanded due to early-season injuries, the Cavaliers put up a valiant fight, narrowly losing the contest 14–10. The Bearcats glided through the first three playoff rounds, outscoring opponents 166–56. Aledo met stiffer resistance in the quarterfinal against Erath County rival Stephenville, which led in the contest 10–6 late in the third quarter. The Bearcats rallied to win 18–10 but encountered another challenge from a feisty Mesquite Poteet team that lost the semifinal 29–27. The following weekend, Aledo took on perennial 4A Metro-Dynasty La Marque at Cowboys Stadium. Johnathan Gray again ran wild, crossing the goal line eight times for a record-setting finals performance. His remarkable accomplishment brought his season touchdown total to fifty-nine, breaking a fifty-seven-year-old mark of fifty-seven (albeit in only twelve games) held by Kenneth Hall. In front of a crowd of 27,330, Gray romped for 325 yards. On the other side of the ball, junior Cougar running back Tim Wright also posted impressive numbers—201 yards rushing and three touchdowns—but not nearly enough to bring La Marque its sixth state title. The game was within Cougar reach at halftime with Aledo leading 34–27, but critical La Marque turnovers—five in all and three in the second half—undermined any potential shift in momentum. In addition to Gray's overwhelming performance, junior Bearcat quarterback Matthew Bishop contributed to the cause, completing nine of twelve passes for 209 yards and two scores to receiver Michael Mann. The Bearcats proved too much for the Cougars, as their 69–34 victory made it back-to-back Bearcat titles. The sixty-nine Bearcat points in the title game matched a state Eleven-Man finals record set in 2008 by Sulfur Springs.

With a returning veteran running back and quarterback, as well as six other starters on offense and five on defense, Aledo began thinking three-peat even in the afterglow of the 2010 title win. Along with Texas A&M running back Cyrus Gray, Johnathan Gray graced the cover of Dave Campbell's 2011 *Texas Football*, cleverly titled "Amazing Grays." But the season began inauspiciously. Stephenville's Yellow Jackets shocked the Bearcats in the season opener, winning the contest 48–47. Two games later, Lake Travis avenged their 2010 loss, pounding Aledo 62–35. The defeat was only the second Bearcat home loss since the 2006 opening of its palatial Bearcat Stadium. The remaining seven regular-season opponents felt Bearcat wrath as Aledo summarily dispensed with them all, averaging over sixty-three points scored against a stingy nineteen points allowed per game. Aledo's playoff run was hardly less successful. The Bearcats drubbed Fort Worth

Dunbar 59–10 in bi-district and then beat Mansfield Summit 59–23 in the second round. In round three, Canyon Randall came within twenty-eight points of the Aledo, and in the quarterfinals, Stephenville's Yellow Jackets came within thirty-three. Aledo continued to roll in the semifinal, devastating Corsicana 68–28. Only the undefeated Manvel Mavericks stood between the Bearcats and a third consecutive title. On December 17, 2011, at Cowboys Stadium, Aledo realized that goal.

Some 43,369 spectators watched the Bearcats battle the Mavericks. As other teams had discovered over the past three seasons, Johnathan Gray might be slowed by defenses that keyed on him, but he could not be stopped. More importantly, concentration on Gray opened opportunities for Bearcat quarterback Matthew Bishop. In the title match, Bishop passed for 186 yards and 3 touchdowns. He also ran for an additional 36 yards and two more scores. Bishop's performance earned him Offensive MVP honors. Meanwhile, Gray posted 241 yards rushing and a fourth-quarter score with

With just over three minutes left in the state 4A D-2 final at Arlington's Cowboys Stadium, Johnathan Gray (#32) and Matthew Bishop (#4) line up one more time during their final high school game together. In their three seasons as Aledo Bearcats, Gray and Bishop helped their team to a 45–3 record and three consecutive state titles. Bishop earned Offensive MVP honors in the 2011 final.

just under seven minutes left in the game. That touchdown—a 37-yard romp on a draw play—not only increased the Aledo lead to fourteen, but it was also Gray's 205th career touchdown, breaking the eight-year-old national standard set by Michael Hart from Nedrow, New York (2000–03). (Hart later set the University of Michigan rushing record and enjoyed a three-year NFL career with the Indianapolis Colts.) Gray's touchdown was his sixty-fifth of that season, setting the state single-season record. Aledo distanced itself from the Mavericks after that score. At the final gun, the Bearcats had a comfortable 49–28 win and their fourth state trophy.

The three-peat for Coach Tim Buchanan elevated him into that elite group of coaches who have four career state title wins. He became only

In an oft-repeated playoff scene of recent date, Aledo head coach Tim Buchanan holds a championship trophy during his postgame speech to the Bearcats. Since the start of the playoffs in 2009, Aledo has notched nineteen consecutive postseason wins and is the most recent Texas program to secure a 4A three-peat. *Courtesy of James Albritton, Salt Fork Images.*

the twelfth Texas schoolboy coach to reach this high-water mark. The win was undoubtedly all the sweeter since it was something of a family affair. Buchanan's eldest son, sophomore Caleb, played backup linebacker on the 2011 title team. His daughter Madeline, an Aledo High School senior, contributed to the championship by working as team filmer, videotaping both Bearcat practices and games. In a curious echo from the past, starting strong safety on the 2011 team was Clayton Lowe, the son of Darryl, who played on the 1974 Aledo finalist team. Clayton was the fourth Lowe brother to play for Buchanan. Bearcat senior Ty Lowe was a starting linebacker on the 1997 semifinalist Aledo team that went 14–1, Cody Lowe was a starting sophomore fullback on the 1998 state champion Bearcats (Buchanan's first title team) and senior Kyle Lowe played on the 2003 team that made the quarterfinals. Collectively, the Lowe siblings have contributed to 119 of the 211 (56.4 percent) career wins that Buchanan has gathered thus far as Aledo head coach. In his 2011 post–title game interview with Fox Sports Southwest, Buchanan reflected on the impending loss of Gray, Bishop and their fellow seniors. Smiling broadly, he joked about the upcoming 2012 season, musing, "I'm gonna have to go back to coachin' football again."

CHAPTER 4

THE MICRO-DYNASTIES

Today's Metro-Dynasty urban centers provide a smorgasbord of cultural, recreational and entertainment opportunities suitable to satisfy citizens of every taste and interest. In more rural Texas, "micropolitan" hubs (defined by the Office of Management and Budget as population centers of ten thousand to fifty thousand) offer fewer recreational options. From Palo Duro in the Panhandle to Pharr in the Rio Grande Valley, from San Elizario in the west to Marshall in the east, such limitations help explain the devoted, passionate interest universally commanded by football in small- to mid-sized Texas towns.

Brownwood, Stephenville and Ennis, with populations from fifteen thousand to twenty thousand and median household incomes from $27,000 to $38,000, all established micropolitan football dynasties. Predictably, the identity of high school football team and community merge each fall. On football Friday nights, towns turn maroon and white or navy blue and gold, depending on whether the home folks are supporting the local Lions or Yellow Jackets.

Suburban Area	Median Household Income / Percentage Below Poverty Line	Population Breakdown
Brownwood	$27,325 / 21.4%	82.7% white, 5.5% black, 21.3% Hispanic
Stephenville	$27,489 / 8.0%	91.0% white, 1.5% black, 11.6% Hispanic
Ennis	$38,923 / 10.4%	66.5% white, / 14.7% black, 33.2% Hispanic

Three coaches transformed these schools into dynasties: Gordon Wood, Art Briles and Sam Harrell. Over forty-three seasons, Wood achieved football immortality. In Brownwood from 1960 to 1985, he accumulated fifteen district titles, two district co-championships, a career record of 256–53–7 (82 percent) and seven state championships (1960, 1965, 1967, 1969–70, 1978, 1981). Over his twenty-six years at Brownwood, his Lions outscored opponents 8,160–2,865. If his two titles at Stamford (1955–56) are included, Wood earned a career- and state-record nine championships. The next closest competitor, G.A. Moore, has eight.

The "Four or More" Coaches Club[42]

Coach	Schools Where Titles Were Won	Career High School Record	State Titles
Gordon Wood	Stamford Bulldogs and Brownwood Lions	396–91–15 (80–6–0 at Stamford, and 257–52–7 at Brownwood)	9 (1955–56, 1960, 1965, 1967, 1969–70, 1978, 1981)

Coach	Schools Where Titles Were Won	Career High School Record	State Titles
G.A. Moore	Celina Bobcats and Pilot Point Bearcats	423*–97–9 (215–27–3 at Celina, and 180–43–6 at Pilot Point; also coached two seasons at Sherman and three at Aubrey) *If Moore's forfeited eight wins in 2004 at Pilot Point are included, he has 431 victories on the field.	8 (1974, 1980–81, 1995, 1998–2001) *two co-titles
Jerry Burkhart	Richland Springs	139–11 (also coached at Lohn)	6 (2004, 2006–07, 2010–12)
Danny Medina	Fort Hancock Mustangs (Six-Man)	121–12	5 (1986, 1988–91)
Paul Tyson	Waco Tigers	224–63–18	4 (1922, 1925–27)
Joe Golding	Wichita Falls Coyotes	152–26–2	4 (1949–50, 1958, 1961)
D.W. Rutledge	Converse Judson Rockets	197–32–5	4 (1988, 1992–93, 1995)
T.J. Mills	Sealy Tigers	195–78 (148–38 at Sealy)	4 (1994–97)

Texas High School Football Dynasties

Coach	Schools Where Titles Were Won	Career High School Record	State Titles
Art Briles	Stephenville Yellow Jackets	167–45–4 (136–29–2 at Stephenville; also coached at Hamlin and Georgetown)	4 (1993–94, 1998–99)
Todd Dodge	Southlake Carroll Dragons	128–52 (including SLC, Cameron Yoe, Carrollton Newman Smith, Keller Fossil Ridge and Marble Falls)	4 (2002, 2004–06)
Steve Lineweaver	Commerce Tigers and Euless Trinity Trojans (Lineweaver was also offensive coordinator for the SLC state champion teams of 1988 and 1992.)	236–38–2 (including 3 state finals at Commerce and 4 at Trinity)	4 (1999, 2005, 2007, 2009)
Tim Buchanan	Aledo Bearcats	211–53–3	4 (1998, 2009–11)

Also worthy of honorable mention are Pete Shotwell, Chuck Curtis and Terry Cron. While none have won four titles, Shotwell is the only Texas high school coach to win three state titles at three different schools: Abilene (1923), Breckenridge (co-title, 1929) and Longview (1937). Shotwell's career high school record was 247–83–16 (71.4 percent) at four different high schools. Chuck Curtis, who won three consecutive titles, was the first Texas high school coach to win back-to-back championships at different schools in different conferences: 2A Jacksboro (1962) and 4A Garland (1963–64).

Curtis had a career record at six different high schools of 135–41–3 (75.4 percent). In 2001, Terry Cron became the first coach to win state titles at three schools all in different conferences: Bartlett (1A, 1992), Mart (2A, 1999) and Commerce (3A, 2001).

BROWNWOOD LIONS

The Town of Brownwood was not incorporated until 1884. Like most Central Texas settlements of the period, it was small and agricultural. At one point in its history, Brownwood boasted a population of more than eighty thousand, but that figure was the ephemeral product of World War II, as Camp Bowie, a mile and a half southeast of the city, provided residence for a host of soldiers. At conflict's end, the size of the community predictably contracted. Brownwood had enjoyed sparing football success both before and after the war. Prior to 1960, little suggested that the local high school was destined to usurp the mantle of mighty Breckenridge, which even in Brownwood's better years consistently undermined Lion hopes of advancing further than regular-season district play. Between 1945 and 1959, only once in seven truly successful seasons (1953, when the Lions won their only district title prior to 1960) did Brownwood get to the playoffs. Gordon Wood's arrival in 1960 began a brand-new era in both the history of the high school and the town.

Perhaps it was the football gods—perhaps the ghost of legendary Paul Tyson hovering over Brownwood. After all, Tyson's final coaching duties were at Brownwood's Daniel Baker College. But something certainly helped Brownwood take seven state championships in eight title appearances from 1960 to 1981. More likely, it was Gordon Wood (1914–2003), who came to town with seventeen years of head coaching experience, including two state titles in the Oil Belt city of Stamford. Stamford's small size notwithstanding, in an era prior to UIL supervision, the Bulldogs had beaten all comers for the 1916 West Texas championship. Wood's 1955 Stamford team beat Hillsboro 34–7 for that year's 2A state title. Their undefeated season on the way to the final included a round-two playoff shutout over the highly favored defending Conference 2A champion Panhandle powerhouse Phillips Blackhawks. It also featured a 13–7 round-three, away-game win over Emory Bellard's defending

A year before leaving Victoria, Gordon Wood (right) posed with "Mr. Schoolboy Football," journalist Harold Ratliff. At this 1959 Coaches Banquet in Dallas, Ratliff presented Wood with the Texas High School Coaches Award.

state champion Breckenridge Buckaroos (who in 1955 had moved from 3A to 2A). The Bulldogs returned to the championship game in 1956, defeating Brady 26–13. Over seven seasons at Stamford, Wood averaged less than one loss per year. In addition to his two state titles, his teams made the semifinal in 1952 and the second round in 1953. Savoring a 9–2 Bulldog season in 1957, Wood had every intention of remaining at Stamford, but an old friend, Dr. Andrew Tomb, persuaded him to at least make a trip to Victoria and consider taking the head coaching position for the Stingarees. Describing himself as "a fish who needed a bigger pond,"[43]

Wood ultimately relented and took the position. He remained in Victoria for two seasons. By 1960, Brown was on the move again.

That year, 4A San Angelo Central passed over Wood for Emory Bellard. By his own admission, Wood was both surprised and disappointed when he failed to get the San Angelo job. He had long been interested in moving into the competitive West Texas district known statewide as the Little Southwest Conference. In fact, seven years earlier, Wood had also been among the 1953 applicants beaten out by Chuck Moser for the Abilene coaching job. Meanwhile, Bellard went on to lead the 4A Bobcats to the 1966 state title. It took Wood far less time to take Brownwood to the top. Indeed, his 3A Lions administered a convincing 34–6 drubbing to 4A San Angelo Central during the 1960 regular season.

More importantly, in his initial season, Wood guided his 1960 Lions to their first-ever championship and created a dynasty that largely owned conference 3A football for the next quarter-century. Even before Wood took the Brownwood

At career's end, Gordon Wood's record at seven different schools was 396–91–15. His nine state championships are the most collected by any Texas high school football coach. Wood appears above (third from left) with fellow coaching icons Pete Shotwell (far left) and Chuck Moser (second from left).

position, he clearly understood that his work would be cut out for him there. He described the Lion program of the late 1950s as "a civic disgrace. The Lions didn't play good football, and their fan support was pathetic."[44] In short order, the new Lion coach remedied all three problems. In his first season at Brownwood, he lost only a single game—a closely fought contest in which Temple's Wildcats came out on top 26–22. From there, Brownwood showed all comers a clean pair of heels on their run to the title finish line. The 26–6 Lion win over Port Lavaca Calhoun in 1960 initiated a palpable championship mystique that continues to cloak Brownwood to this very day. In the final, Lion quarterback Ben Elledge threw for three touchdowns, including one strike to Lawrence Elkins, who later became a two-time All-American flanker at Baylor University. Elkins continued his football career with the American Football League's Houston Oilers (1965–68).

Brownwood failed to advance to the playoffs in 1961, but in the 1962 season, the Lions went undefeated until the quarterfinal. They again stayed

at home for the postseason in 1963 and 1964. In 1965, Wood took the Lions to their second state title (and his fourth). Fast out of the gate that season, Brownwood shut out ten of its opponents and allowed only one team—Breckenridge—to score in double digits. The Lions completed the season undefeated. Perhaps the most satisfying of all the shutouts came in that year's final against a high-octane Bridge City Cardinal team powered by future Longhorn great Steve Worster. Wood's autobiography, co-written with popular sports author John Carver, preserves the delightful story of

The 1960 state-champion Brownwood Lions pose for a team picture. These Lions brought Brownwood the first of seven state championships, marking the beginning of the Brownwood football dynasty.

how Wood creatively secured Cardinal game film from a Galveston coach. Evidently, Wood's strategy worked, as the Brownwood defense limited Worster to eighty-seven yards on twenty-four carries. The game itself took place at College Station during a steady, uncomfortable drizzle on a muddy, rain-soaked Kyle Field. Brownwood won the contest 14–0.

Brownwood's next title came in 1967, as the Lions won their third championship in just eight years. Reflecting much later on the character and dedication of this squad, Wood expressed great satisfaction in describing the

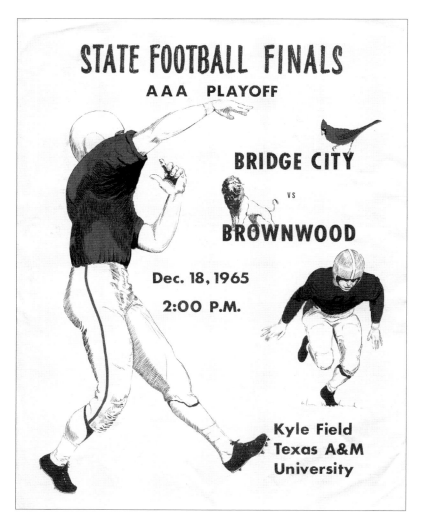

The 1965 title-game program. The 1965 Lions secured the second Brownwood state championship by shutting out the Bridge City Cardinals, powered by future Longhorn running back Steve Worster.

1967 championship as perhaps the purest championship that Brownwood ever earned. Those Lions were without a stable of superstars. They were, however, specialists in the come-from-behind win. Their never-say-die attitude proved the difference time and again throughout the season. At the final in Austin's Memorial Stadium, the Lions won 36–12, decisively dealing the El Campo Ricebirds their only loss of the season. David Wallace and Wayne Fenton each scored twice. Lion quarterback Si Southall threw

The 1970 state-champion Lions pose for their annual team picture. Their 14–0 defeat of the Cuero Gobblers brought Brownwood its only back-to-back state titles.

Shae Southall, the 1970 championship Lion quarterback, with his father, Morris. Morris Southall was Gordon Wood's longtime trusted assistant during Wood's lengthy career at Brownwood.

for 162 yards and three touchdowns. Thus, Gordon Wood became the first Texas high school football coach to win five state titles.

The Southall family was almost as integral to Brownwood's football success as Gordon Wood. Morris Southall was Wood's assistant at Seminole (1947–49) and again in Victoria. He followed Wood to Brownwood. Three of Southall's sons—Terry (who later played at Baylor), Si and Shae—all quarterbacked the Lions. If "only" an assistant coach, Morris Southall is the only assistant ever chosen as head of the Texas High School Coaches Association. In 1985, he and Wood fittingly retired together. Over their twenty-six years at Brownwood, the dynamic duo took the Lions to the playoffs eighteen times.

Brownwood lost to Lubbock Estacado in the 1968 bi-district playoff round. The 1969 Lions began their season inauspiciously, decisively losing their first three games to Abilene Cooper, Woodrow Wilson and Abilene High. In district play, Brownwood turned the season completely around. Avenging their bi-district loss of 1968, Brownwood dispensed with Estacado 29–13. With equal dispatch, the Lions defeated Monahans (28–13) and Bonham (28–12), advancing to the final, played against West Columbia. In spite of an enormous size differential between the Roughneck defensive line and the two Brownwood running backs, 146-pound Kenny Ephraim and 142-pound James "Squirt" Thompson, the Lion backfield rose to the challenge. Brownwood quarterback Jimmy "The Rifleman" Carmichael completed fourteen of twenty passes, three of which were to Perry Young for scores. Accolades accumulated for Carmichael. He received all-state and all-American recognition, as well as selection by *Texas Football* magazine as the most outstanding high school quarterback of the 1960s. As for the 1969 title game, the Lions bested West Columbia 34–16.

The following season, most football pundits believed that Brownwood would have to rebuild, as twenty seniors from the 1969 championship team were gone. Lion fans need not have worried. After losing the season opener to 4A Abilene Cooper, Brownwood moved successfully and easily through the remainder of the regular season as well as the bi-district round (again, against Lubbock Estacado). Round two against Monahans proved a much greater challenge. The game ended locked in a 10–10 tie, but the Lions advanced 5–3 on penetrations. In the semifinal, Brownwood met ascendant Plano, a team that had won 2A state titles as recently as 1965 and 1967. At the end of the day, Lions quarterback Shae Southall and his teammates punched their ticket to the final as Brownwood won 35–21. The following week, Gordon Wood's team met that year's 3A Cinderella squad, Buster

Gilbreth's Cuero Gobblers, who were making the first of what would become ten Gobbler championship-round appearances. Cuero and Brownwood collided in Austin's Memorial Stadium, where the two teams fought through a scoreless first half. During the final twenty-four minutes, the balance tipped in Brownwood's favor. At the end of the day, fourteen points proved enough to defeat the scoreless Gobblers. Brownwood coaches and players savored their fifth 3A title and their first back-to-back championship run.

Over the following six years, Wood teams traveled to semifinal appearances against Plano (1971) and Gainesville (1974, a 20–20 tie) and the 1976 quarterfinal. In 1977, the undefeated Lions breezed through their playoff opponents, making it back to the 3A final, where they met Dickinson in Austin's Memorial Stadium. The Brownwood defense proved no match for Gator quarterback Donnie Little, who rushed for 254 yards and three touchdowns. Little's teammate and running back Jeff LaFleur scored three times as well. By the third quarter, the Gators sported a 33–8 advantage. The Lions fought back, but in the end, Dickinson prevailed 40–28. It would be the only Brownwood loss ever in a title contest.

The 1978 Lions rebounded from their 1977 defeat in spite of dropping their season opener. The number-four-ranked 5A Abilene Cooper Cougars bested number-one-ranked 3A Brownwood 38–22. The Lions did not lose again the rest of the season. Perhaps the biggest Lion challenge came in the semifinal in Austin against the undefeated Bay City Black Cats and their talented running back Billy Booker. Coach Wood later described the Lion victory as "the greatest comeback in Brownwood history."[45]

Both teams scored throughout the first three quarters, but the Cats took a 21–17 lead early in the fourth. Soon thereafter, Bay City exploited a fumble recovery to extend their lead to 28–17. In what had become a two-possession contest, seven minutes and seventeen seconds remained. Brownwood quarterback Scott Lancaster then led his team down the field, capping the drive with a twenty-three-yard touchdown pass to Kevin Taylor. The score came on a fourth-and-eighteen play. Lancaster then hit Gerald James for a two-point conversion. It was now 28–25, a one-possession, three-point game. Subsequently, the Brownwood defense held. Lancaster then engineered another scoring drive that put the Lions on top 33–28 with twenty-six seconds left to play. The Cats fought back, but Brownwood intercepted a Bay City pass with only six ticks left on the clock.

The heart-stopping win earned Wood's 1978 Lions a trip to Irving's Texas Stadium, where they met the Gainesville Leopards. In a clash of the big cats in front of 13,446 fans, Brownwood established a 21–0 halftime lead.

Thereafter, the Lions played control football, securing their sixth state title with a 21–12 victory. It was Wood's eighth state championship. On top of the 1978 accolades laid upon his team, the National High School Athletic Coaches Association named Gordon Wood the High School Football Coach of the Year.

Wood took both his 1979 and 1980 teams to the quarterfinals. His final championship came in 1981 courtesy of a talent-laden team on both sides of the ball. In a start reminiscent of 1978, 5A Abilene Cooper beat the 4A Lions 14–13. This contest went down to the wire, however. The Cougars scored with forty-one seconds left to take a 14–7 lead. Brownwood returned the favor, scoring quickly as well. Rather than settling for a tie, Wood elected to go for two. Brownwood's attempt fell one foot short, and the season began with a 0–1 Lion record. The Lions did not taste loss again that season. With the exception of close wins against Weatherford (19–17) and San Angelo Central (15–10), Brownwood pounded all opponents from the second week of the season through the bi-district playoff round. Even more impressive, the stiff Lions defense allowed only twenty-two points throughout their entire four-game playoff run. The semifinal at Baylor Stadium against Rockwall was a close-fought contest but ended in a 19–13 Brownwood win.

The following week, ten thousand spectators gathered in Austin's Memorial Stadium to watch Brownwood take on the Fort Bend Willowridge Eagles. Thanks to the athleticism and toughness of Lion quarterback Tyler Tabor (who had sustained a significant shoulder injury in the semifinal), Brownwood would win the game. With five minutes left to play, the Lions broke a 7–7 deadlock. A Gene Gibson score put Brownwood ahead, 14–7. As time slipped away, a Willowridge punt pinned the Lions on their own eight-yard line. Brownwood went three and out, leaving an eternity—one minute and six seconds—on the clock. Coach Wood instructed his punter, Jimmy Morris, to take a safety, making the score 14–9. Instead, Morris booted a free kick fifty-seven yards into the wind. With only seconds left in the game, Wood put the injured Tabor into the game to play defense for the first time all season. Tabor intercepted the last Eagle pass of the contest, securing for Brownwood a then–state record seven titles. It was Wood's ninth and final title overall. He would coach four more seasons, during which his Lions made two trips to bi-districts and one to round two.

Gordon Wood died in 2003, but he lives forever in the annals of Texas high school football. Today's Brownwood High School students are reminded daily of his extraordinary career by the seven Texas-shaped monuments in front of the school commemorating each state title. Brownwood's football

Above in Gordon Wood Stadium is the November 10, 1989 dedication marker and statue of Wood kneeling in front of helmets commemorating Brownwood's seven state titles. Left to right, the author and family members Jess, Cindy and Doug Sherrod stand prior to the 2010 Brownwood-Stephenville rivalry game. In that year, the Lions made it to the 3A semifinals, their deepest post-Wood playoff penetration to date. *Photo by Annette Pierce Sherrod.*

stadium is also named in his honor, and within it is a tangible aura of an apotheosized Wood still upon the premises. Over his forty-three-year career as a high school head coach, Wood averaged 9.4 victories a season. More significantly, he left an enduring legacy through his coaching philosophy and the life lessons that prepared his players for the future and endured long beyond their football careers. The 1999 *Dallas Morning News* conferred upon Wood the moniker "Coach of the Century." Wood selected it as the title of his 2001 autobiography.

The Gordon Wood legacy continues in Brownwood today. That special era in Brownwood's history is commemorated in the Brownwood Hall of Champions. While the coaching staff has evolved across the subsequent quarter-century, many of Wood's younger colleagues and peers—men like home game announcer Larry Mathis and radio broadcaster for the past four decades Dallas Huston—perpetuate the venerable Brownwood football tradition. And so do the Lions, who lately remain competitive under current coach Bob Shipley, the father of celebrated Longhorn receivers Jordan and Jaxon. Most recently, Shipley took Brownwood to the 2010 semifinal, round three in 2011 and round one in 2012. Meanwhile, sixty miles northeast, a new power had long been on the rise.

During the 1990s, Stephenville's Yellow Jackets assumed the championship role long the personal, private province of its Brown County neighbor. Coincidentally, Gordon Wood's first head coaching duties were at Rule (1940–41). It was Rule's 1973 Class B state finalist quarterback who crafted Stephenville's 1990s "Decade of Dominance."

STEPHENVILLE YELLOW JACKETS

An hour's drive north up Highway 377 from Brownwood, Stephenville became successor to its longtime district nemesis. Colonists from Waco, future seat of the earliest Texas schoolboy football dynasty, originally laid out the Stephenville city square on July 4, 1855. Twentieth-century residents of both locales followed a similar football pathway, although Waco got there first. By 1927, Waco's schoolboys had captured their fourth state title. It was more than seven decades before the Yellow Jackets reached the same benchmark.

Known today variously as the "Cowboy Capital of the World," the "Dairy Capital of Texas," the home of Tarleton State University and the playground of early twenty-first century UFOs, Stephenville rose to pigskin prominence in the 1990s when Coach Art Briles transformed the 'Ville into the "City of Champions." Hired in 1988, Briles rapidly revitalized the Yellow Jackets. In a dozen seasons at Stephenville, he compiled a 136–29–2 record (81 percent) and earned six district titles and two back-to-back state championships (1993–94, 1998–99). His 1998 team set the national high school record for total season offense with 8,664 yards.

Similar to Chuck Moser, who was hired in 1953 by Abilene out from under Corpus Christi Miller, Stephenville ISD Superintendent Ben Gilbert persuaded Briles to forego exploring a new job opportunity at Snyder and come to Stephenville instead. The hire opened a new era in Stephenville football history, one that far outstripped anything Erath County had ever seen before.

During 1920s and '30s, the Yellow Jacket program had been highly competitive. Its first playoff run came in 1924 when Dr. Verne Scott took the

Above: In the late 1980s and 1990s, Art Briles breathed life into a moribund Stephenville Yellow Jacket football program. Above on the sidelines at the 1999 quarterfinal are, left to right, Randy Clements (who went with Briles to the University of Houston and Baylor University), Briles, Joseph Gillespie (Yellow Jacket head coach since 2008) and Randall Edwards (who holds eight state rings—four from Stephenville and four from Lake Travis). *Courtesy of Ellen Skipper.*

Right: Briles is currently the head coach at Baylor University. In this photo, he appears in New York City with his co–offensive coordinators, Philip Montgomery and Randy Clements, and Baylor Director of Football Operations Colin Shillinglaw. These four former Yellow Jacket coaches rest their hands on the 2011 Heisman Trophy, won by their Baylor Bear quarterback Robert Griffin III. *Courtesy of Colin Shillinglaw.*

team two deep in the playoffs, losing to the Cisco Loboes. In the mid-1920s and 1930s, teams coached by Joe Brown (1926–33) and Jim Mobley (1936–37) racked up five district titles. Mobley's undefeated 1936 Jackets went as far as the regional, the deepest that the Class B playoff system allowed in that day and time. That year's Jacket superstar Derace Moser continued his football career at Texas A&M, where he became an All-American and played on the undefeated 1939 Aggie national championship team. Coach Jimmy Marshall's 1940 Yellow Jackets won the District 9-2A title and went undefeated into the bi-district round, where they played that season's state finalist, Temple High School. At game's end, the teams were deadlocked 7–7, but Temple won 3–2 on penetrations. The Wildcats advanced, and the Jackets went back home.

A dozen years passed before Stephenville earned another district title. Little wonder, since the Jackets regularly faced the Breckenridge Buckaroos in district play. During those same years, this little Oil Belt city dominated high school play. In 1952, Coach Mike Murphy finally broke the cycle. The Jackets won the District 10-2A crown and made the deepest playoff run in Stephenville history, advancing to the third round before succumbing to a Terrell Tiger team that completed its perfect season by winning the 2A 1952 state title.

After 1952, the Stephenville program entered a thirty-seven-year playoff drought. Quality teams occasionally came and went, but none ever advanced to postseason play. If Stephenville eventually escaped the bane of being in Breckenridge's district, the Jacket plight became no easier with Brownwood on the rise. Even after the 1985 departure of Gordon Wood, the Lion program continued to block Stephenville's pathway to the playoffs. But when Briles arrived in 1988, the Jackets finally made a breakthrough. Modest though it may have been, and in the context of a humble 4–5–1 season record, Stephenville tied Brownwood 7–7. At game's end, Jacket fans poured onto the field with an excitement and enthusiasm suggesting Stephenville's time at long last had arrived. To the untrained eye, this humble Yellow Jacket-Lion stalemate was nothing other than more of the same. In retrospect, it is better viewed as a major step toward a dynasty in the making.

The 1989 Jackets lost to Brownwood, 63–21. But that was their only district loss. With a 10–2 record, Stephenville went two rounds deep into the 1989 playoffs. The following season, both Briles and his Jackets broke new ground. Prior to the playoffs, the only 1990 Jacket loss was in pre-district play to Sweetwater (where Briles had coached from 1980 to 1983). From that defeat to the semifinal, Stephenville did not look back. At season's end, the Jackets had come just one game away—a loss in Texas Stadium to 1990 state champion Wilmer-Hutchins—from making it to the show. It was not long before the Jackets had their second chance. The 1991 team went two deep. In 1992, Stephenville made the quarterfinals. The stage was set—the time had come.

Stephenville's first state title came in 1993. Between 1993 and 1999, the Jackets gathered four 4A championships. The story of the route to these four titles is often as good as the story of the finals themselves. Several pre-final playoff contests—semifinals in particular—were fraught with drama. By reaching the 1993 semifinal, the Stephenville squad equaled the performance of its 1990 predecessors. In Waco's Floyd Casey Stadium, the upstart undefeated Jackets met the number-one-ranked defending state champion Waxahachie Indians. In that contest, Waxahachie hung more points on Stephenville than any team during that year's regular season. Late in the game, the Jackets scored on a fifty-yard Branndon Stewart touchdown pass to Jason Bragg. Stephenville was within a point of tying the game. The tie-breaking system at the time still advanced the team with the most penetrations beyond their opponent's twenty-yard line, and the Indians had more penetrations than the Jackets. Instead of kicking the extra point, Coach Briles decided to go for two. Stewart again hit Bragg, this time in the end zone for the two-point conversion. Over the remaining five minutes of play, the Jacket defense confuted Waxahachie's efforts to score. One week later, Stephenville played La Marque, making its first of four trips in seven years to the finals. The two teams met at Austin's Memorial Stadium. Despite a 13–3 halftime deficit, the Jackets rallied. A Stephenville defense that had allowed less than five points per game during the regular season held the Cougars scoreless in the second half. Meanwhile, the Jacket offense came alive, giving Stephenville a 26–13 win. Stephenville had its first state title, as well as a new national record for most offensive plays (1,037) in a single season.

Stephenville rode the momentum from the previous season into 1994. A stingy Jacket defense allowed just ten points per game through the ten-game regular season. On the playoff trail, the Jackets met determined resistance in the quarterfinal, as the Sherman Bearcats jumped out to a 17–7 second-quarter lead. The Stephenville defense held thereafter, while the Jacket offense posted seventeen unanswered points. The 24–17 Jacket win advanced Stephenville to its second final in two straight seasons. Riding a thirty-one-game win streak, Stephenville again met La Marque, this time in Houston's Astrodome. The 14–0 Cougar halftime lead dimmed the prospect of a Yellow Jacket repeat. During the halftime intermission, Defensive

The 1993 Stephenville team was the first to win a 4A football championship. Yellow Jacket quarterback Branndon Stewart (above) led Stephenville to that year's state final. His combination of passing and determined running helped secure a 26–13 victory over the La Marque Cougars.

Coordinator Mike Copeland circulated through the locker room, telling every player, "If you don't think we can win this game, don't go outside that door; stay in here." As the second half began, Copeland repeated his admonition as the players made their locker room exit. Stephenville rallied on the field, scoring thirty-two points while allowing only three. Two Glenn Odell touchdown passes to Jeffrey Thompson did much to turn the tide. Thompson's second reception put the Jackets ahead, and they never looked back, winning by a final score of 32–17. At season's end, Stephenville had scored more rushing touchdowns (96) than any high school team in history other than Big Sandy's 1975 Wildcats (114).

During the next three seasons, the Jackets could not get past three-time state finalist Denison High School. But 1998 proved to be a banner year. An early-season district loss to Brownwood dampened spirits, but only briefly. In their next game, Stephenville overcame a daunting halftime deficit against district opponent Cleburne. From that point forward, the Jackets posted between fifty-five and sixty-five points in four remaining district games. Perhaps the biggest challenge came in the bi-district round when the Jackets met a highly touted group of Andrews Mustangs led by future NFL Buffalo Bill running

The 1998 Yellow Jackets not only brought Stephenville its third state title, but their 8,664 yards of total offense broke a national record that had existed since 1925. When Briles moved on to coach at the university level in 2000, he left behind four state championships and local passion for high school football that resembled what Gordon Wood's twenty-six-year coaching tenure had done for Brownwood.

back Shaud Williams. Williams rushed for five touchdowns and 275 yards, but the potent Yellow Jacket offense would not be denied. Stephenville overcame a 21–17 Andrews halftime lead and won the contest 41–35.

The next three playoff opponents posed far fewer problems. Not so with Southlake Carroll, which the Jackets faced in a semifinal match played in Irving's Texas Stadium before 16,209 excited fans. This thrilling contest featured nine lead changes, taking a fifty-two-yard Kelan Luker–to–Cody Cardwell touchdown pass with just over a minute to play to give Stephenville the final lead. In the time remaining, the Jacket defense held, and Stephenville emerged victorious, 31–28. The following week, Stephenville returned to Texas Stadium, where they met La Marque in the final for the third time in six seasons. The Cougars scored first, but they never found the end zone again. At the end of the day, the Jackets led 34–7 and savored their third state title. And there was more. In the final game, the Jackets rewrote the national standard for offense, accumulating 8,664 season yards. Jacket quarterback Kelan Luker set new state records for single-season (4,697) and career passing yards (8,297), while his favorite target, Cody Cardwell, rewrote the national single-season receiving record (2,427) and the then–state career mark (4,241).

The 1999 Jackets reprised their '98 performance, experiencing far less difficulty through their regular season. The first two playoff rounds seemed *pro forma* as well. Stephenville met unexpected resistance in round three against a tenacious Wolfforth Frenship team that would not go away. The Jackets nonetheless emerged with a hard-fought 31–28 win. The Tiger challenge was not nearly as unsettling as the semifinal round against the Ennis Lions. Stephenville amassed 541 yards in total offense, but as the game neared completion, Ennis put together two fourth-quarter drives that knotted the score at 31. On the final Yellow Jacket drive, Stephenville kicker Eben Nelson put the ball through the uprights with a scant eight seconds left on the clock. His end-of-the-game field goal secured the win.

The following weekend, the Jackets convened in the Astrodome to meet Port Neches-Groves. It was the sixth Indian appearance in the finals. The largest crowd ever to attend a Stephenville game—39,102—watched as "Briles & Briles" became architects of the fourth Yellow Jacket title in seven seasons. Jacket coach's son Kendal Briles ran wild across the Astroturf. He rushed for three touchdowns and 95 yards on eighteen carries, and passed for thirteen of eighteen, adding another 125 yards to team offense. For good measure, he picked off two errant Indian passes. Stephenville's 28–18 victory secured a second back-to-back championship, as well as the Jackets' third undefeated season.

During its four title runs, the duo of Art Briles and Mike Copeland was Stephenville's answer to Brownwood's "Wood-and-Southall" coaching combination. A seasoned defensive coordinator, Copeland (who began his Stephenville coaching career in 1969) was the perfect counterpart to Briles's wide-open offensive play—the perfect yin and yang of Stephenville football. From 1988 through 1999, their combined labor produced eleven trips to the playoffs, six district titles, seven quarterfinal appearances and four state 4A titles. Together, they put many Jacket points on the scoreboard and allowed the opposition very few. In 2000, Briles moved on to the college coaching ranks. He is presently head coach at Baylor University, where he and 2011 Heisman Trophy–winning quarterback Robert Griffin III led the Bears to a record-setting 67–56 shootout victory over Washington at the Valero Alamo Bowl and a final BCS ranking of thirteen (Baylor's first Top 25 recognition since 1986).

In 2012, Griffin was drafted number two overall by the Washington Redskins. His stellar play in his rookie season made him a 2012 NFC Pro Bowl selection along with Aaron Rodgers and Matt Ryan. More significantly, in November, Griffin's teammates elected him team captain for the second half of the season. In that role, he led the Redskins to seven consecutive wins to secure the NFC East title and a first-round playoff berth. No wonder

Joseph Gillespie, Art Briles and Mike Copeland reunited in Waco on May 19, 2012, for Copeland's receipt of the Tom Landry Award. The honor placed Copeland in the illustrious company of fellow coaching greats and previous recipients of the award D.W. Rutledge (2000), Jim Rackley (2011) and G.A. Moore (2001). *Photograph by author.*

"RG3" received selection as the AP 2012 NFL Offensive Rookie of the Year, again beating out Andrew Luck, the athlete who finished second to Griffin for the 2011 Heisman (also a Texan who played his high school football at Houston Stratford). Meanwhile, Baylor played in the December 27, 2012 Bridgepoint Education Holiday Bowl in San Diego, where they disassembled UCLA's seventeenth-ranked Bruins 49–26.

In 2000, Briles departed Stephenville, but Copeland remained, assuming head coaching duties for the next three seasons. Preserving the winning tradition, Copeland took all of his teams to the playoffs. Kevin Kolb was Jacket quarterback all three years of the Copeland era. After high school, Kolb followed Briles to the University of Houston, where he enjoyed a four-year record-setting career as starting Cougar quarterback (2003–06). Kolb was the thirty-sixth pick in the 2007 NFL draft. He played for the Philadelphia Eagles from 2007 to 2010 and in 2011 became the starter for the Arizona Cardinals. In 2012, Kolb led the Cardinals to four consecutive wins before sustaining a season-ending injury in game six.

Back in Stephenville, Mike Copeland's replacement, Chad Morris, came to town with impressive credentials: four trips to the finals with 2A Elysian Fields (1998–99) and 4A Bay City (2000–01). When Morris left in 2008 to take over Austin's Lake Travis program, Joseph Gillespie assumed the Stephenville reins. Gillespie's Jackets produced playoff-caliber teams, including three reaching the quarterfinals (2008, 2010–11). Gillespie's first-year performance earned him honors as All-Big Country Coach of the Year. His 2009 Yellow Jackets won the 8-4A district title, and the 2011 team earned the district co-championship. The biennial realignment in 2012 moved Stephenville into Conference 3A, but the pre-district Jacket schedule remained rigorous. Stephenville rose to the occasion, beating ranked opponents including 4A Aledo, 3A Waco La Vega, 4A Amarillo and then in district play 3A Glen Rose and 3A Alvarado. After winning District 7-3A outright and ending the regular season as the AP number-three-ranked 3A Texas team, Stephenville moved with a high hand into the playoffs. There, the Jacket offense averaged a whopping 56.7 points per game.

In the quarterfinals, Stephenville authoritatively overcame number-two-ranked Abilene Wylie, 59–28. Thereafter, *Abilene Reporter-News* sportswriter Evan Ren captured the character of the 2012 Yellow Jackets in his December 3 article "2010 Brownwood vs. 2012 Stephenville? A Tough Pick." Musing over his previous "contention that the 2010 Brownwood Lions were the most talented Class 3A football team" he had ever seen, Ren intimated that perhaps the 2012 Jackets might be even better. Noting the extraordinary talent of Stephenville's Division 1 college recruits, the versatile All-State Jacket signal caller Tyler Jones and his favorite target, two-time All-State wide receiver Brice Gunter, Ren also drew attention to the other "quality receivers" in the Jacket offensive arsenal: Alex Sanchez, Jarrett Stidham and Brock Morrison. Four days after Ren's article appeared, Stephenville's 3A D-1 semifinal win over Kilgore gave Gillespie his fiftieth career victory and the Jackets their fifth trip to the finals. Before a crowd of 17,655, Stephenville met the undefeated El Campo Ricebirds in Arlington's Cowboys Stadium.

All season long, the Jacket offensive line ("The Wall")—fortified by six-foot-four, 295-pound two-time All-State Bryan Manley—and teammates Max Jones (All-State), Matt Diaz, Tyler Ferguson and Dayton Laxon provided ample opportunities for the offense to shine. Going into the final, Jacket running back Witt Westbrook already had 1,111 rushing yards (he would end the season with 1,187). The nimble, speedy Jones had accounted for another 885. Throughout the season, Westbrook did double duty on defense, administering punishing hits as a Jacket linebacker. Closer to the line of scrimmage, All-State and MaxPreps

The 2012 Yellow Jackets won Stephenville's fifth state title in record-setting fashion. Quarterback Tyler Jones (top center) contributed a state record nine touchdowns (five through the air and four on the ground), while the 70 points Stephenville scored bested the previous state record in an Eleven-Man title game. Moreover, the 283 points scored by the Jackets during their five-game postseason run was one of the highest point counts in playoff history. *Courtesy of Debbie Cashell.*

All-American defensive end Chase Varnado (who also scored two touchdowns in spot play on offense as fullback and tight end) regularly ran rampant in opponents' backfields. Two-time All-State junior safety Mookie Carlile and All-State senior speedster Preston Brown, along with outside linebacker Tyler Isham, delighted fans with hard hits, smothering coverage and interceptions in the Stephenville secondary.

On game night, the stars aligned, and Stephenville captured its fifth state title. Striking on their first three possessions, the Jackets rested on a 21–0 lead with two minutes and fifteen seconds left in the opening quarter. However, El Campo rallied, putting the Ricebirds back in the game with a 35–21 halftime score. At third quarter's end, Stephenville led 49–35. Then the Jackets blew things open, posting twenty-one unanswered points after nose guard Kody Hook (Defensive MVP) and linebacker David Jackson stopped the Ricebirds short on a critical fourth and one with ten minutes and thirty-seven seconds left to play. On defense overall, Hook finished the contest with eight tackles. Linebackers Sam Macklin had seventeen and Jackson ten. Varnado added another nine (with one sack and a tackle-and-a-half for losses). The War Dog defense weathered an early-game injury that took the coach's son, sophomore linebacker Josh Gillespie, out of the contest. Others stepped up, including All-State defensive end Jonah Noah, lineman Jacoby Miller-Selem and linebackers Kobe Beavers and C.J. Cline. With five minutes and thirty-three seconds left and El Campo struggling to get back in the game, Jacket cornerback Tyler Pettit's fifty-five-yard pick-six iced the contest. It also tied Stephenville with Sulfur Springs (2008) and Aledo (2010) for the most points ever scored in an Eleven-Man Texas state final. Luis Garcia's subsequent point after made the final score 70–35, putting the Jackets into the record books once again. Moreover, Offensive MVP Tyler Jones became the first player in Eleven-Man finals to have a hand in nine scores (five passing and four as part of his 125 rushing yards). In all, Jones accounted for 547 of Stephenville's 621 yards of total offense, a poetically fitting end for the young man the Texas High School Press Box Services identified as the leader in total 2012 season offense—5,017 yards—regardless of conference.

Appropriately, Ric Renner of Fox Sports Southwest quipped, "I thought it was Jerry Jones that owned Cowboys Stadium—I didn't realize it was Tyler Jones!" In the final 2012 MaxPreps Medium Schools National Football Rankings, Jones and the Jackets finished fifth. Thus, after a thirteen-year absence, Stephenville returned to the finals with a vengeance and now looks to the future with five titles and counting.

ENNIS LIONS

Located one hundred miles east of Stephenville, the town of Ennis hosts the popular annual National Polka Festival and claims to be the "Bluebonnet Capital of North Texas." It even hosts an annual April bluebonnet festival to prove it. The town is also the home of the popular quarter-mile drag-racing facility known as the Texas Motorplex. In one respect, Ennis might well be considered a Dallas suburb. Its location thirty-five miles south-southeast of the Big D provides Ennis relatively easy access to the metropolis. But the city population of sixteen thousand, the 4A size of its student enrollment and rural character of the town itself make it a better fit with its Micro-Dynasty counterparts of Brownwood and Stephenville.

The rise of the Ennis football program began in the mid-1960s with the arrival of Coach Gerald Myers (1964–69), who took the Lions to the quarterfinals in 1966 and 1969. His successor, Don Berry (1970–71), took Ennis to the 1970 semifinals. Berry's assistant, Don Essary (1972–78), subsequently led the Lions.

Essary and his team secured the first Lion state title in 1975. It came against the two-time defending champion, number-one-ranked Cuero Gobblers, who were looking to extend a forty-four-game win streak and secure the three-peat under Coach Buster Gilbreth. The two teams met on A&M's Kyle Field in front of 8,652 spectators. The Lions' Gary Lillie returned the opening kickoff ninety yards for the score. Cuero posted ten straight third-quarter points before the Lions scored again. It ultimately took a ten-yard, fourth-quarter touchdown run by Ennis halfback Mark Grant to determine the outcome. The final score was 13–10, and the Lions, not the Gobblers, took home the 1975 title trophy. Ennis did not return to the playoffs until 1987.

The leap to dynasty status came with the arrival of Coach Sam Harrell (1994–2010), who compressed three state titles (2000–01 and 2004) into a five-year span. In an interesting echo out of Brownwood, "Sammy" Harrell had played his high school football under Gordon Wood. Harrell quarterbacked the 1974 Lions to an 11–1–1 record and a trip to that year's semifinal. A quarter-century later, Harrell parlayed his football savvy into elevating the Ennis program to unprecedented levels. Although barely perceptible at the time, the Lions' narrow semifinal loss to Stephenville in 1999 heralded a changing of the 4A guard. In 2000, the Yellow Jackets fell to Southlake Carroll in the second round. Meanwhile, early-season Ennis losses to Poteet and Marshall notwithstanding, Harrell's Lions breezed through their district schedule and then manhandled playoff opponents until meeting number-

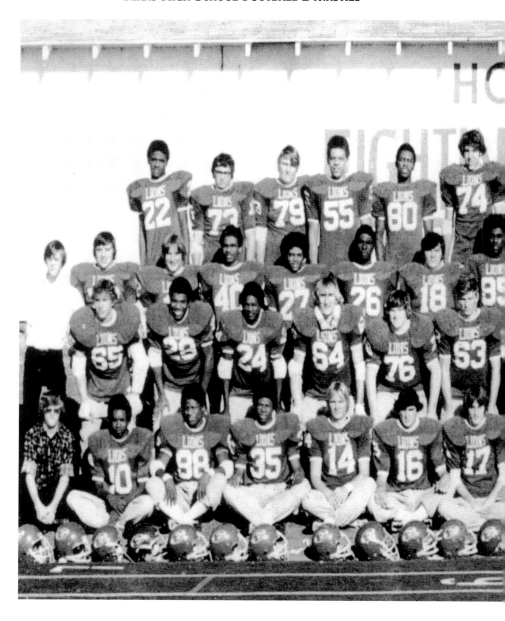

one-ranked Wichita Falls in the semifinal. What goes around comes around. As Stephenville snuck by Ennis with a three-point margin in 1999, the 2000 Lions took the semifinal crown by the same slender advantage. Lion quarterback Tate Wallis's last-minute touchdown pass to receiver Broderic Jones gave Ennis the win, 23–20. The following week, Harrell and the Lions breathed easier, taking a 31–0 halftime lead against number-one-ranked

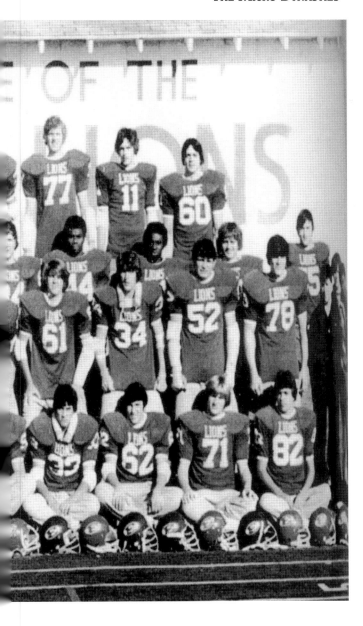

The 1975 Lions brought Ennis its first state title. To do so, they had to defeat the number-one-ranked, back-to-back defending state champions, the Cuero Gobblers. They were up to the task and took the contest 13-10.

West Orange-Stark. In the style of his Brownwood High School mentor's 1978 title win over Gainesville, Harrell and company ground out the clock in the second half, giving the Lions the 2000 4A D-2 title with a 34–28 win over the two-time state champion (1986–87) Mustangs.

As it had for ascendant Stephenville seven years earlier, the 2000 Lions momentum carried over into 2001. Ennis moved through the 2001 schedule, roundly defeating any and all comers. The Lions went to the quarterfinals undefeated but faced a strong Highland Park team steeped in football tradition and expecting to add a third state championship to the Scottie résumé. The Lions and Scots met in Texas Stadium in front of 25,515. Highland Park had come to play. With eight minutes and twelve seconds left in the contest, Ennis trailed 38–24. Coach Harrell's son and sophomore quarterback Graham Harrell turned the tide with two long scoring drives that tied the game with a little less than four minutes to play. Then, Highland Park turned the ball over on its own eleven-yard line. Graham Harrell got the game-winning score on a three-yard run. The 45–38 victory advanced Ennis to the semifinal, where the Lions convincingly defeated Southlake Carroll 49–17. The title game the following weekend was against Bay City at the Houston Astrodome. The Lion defense held the Black Cats to only 113 yards total offense. At the end of the day, Ennis came out ahead, 21–0, with back-to-back titles and three total championships. Similar to Converse Judson, Stephenville and Southlake Carroll, a father-and-son combination—Sam and Graham Harrell—helped move the Ennis program toward dynasty status.

Coming off two tremendously successful seasons and retaining the services of a state-winning quarterback, Ennis was the 4A team to beat in 2002. The Lions advanced to that year's semifinal but were beaten by a surging Denton Ryan in the midst of what would become four consecutive title appearances (2000–03). In 2003, the Lions played well but fell 38–28 to Highland Park in round three. That year marked the end of one of the most successful quarterback careers in Texas history. In his years as Lion signal caller, Graham Harrell rewrote state schoolboy records for single-season passing yards (4,825 in 2003), career passing yards (12,532), single-season touchdown passes (67 in 2003), career touchdown passes (167) and single-season pass completions (334 in 2003). He continued his illustrious career at Texas Tech, breaking gunslinger Kliff Kingsbury's standard with a new mark of 12,709 career yards. Harrell also set an NCAA career touchdown pass record (134) and won the 2008 Johnny Unitas Golden Arm Award. Following a brief experience with the Saskatchewan Roughriders of the Canadian Football League, Harrell signed a 2010 contract with that season's Super Bowl champion Green Bay Packers and in 2012 was 2011 NFL MVP Aaron Rodgers's backup.

In 2004, the year Graham Harrell left Ennis for college, the Lions returned to the 4A D-1 title contest. In that encounter, Ennis defeated two-time finalist and 1990 state champion Marshall 23–21. The Lions made playoff runs over their next four seasons, the best of which took them to the 2005

In 2001, it was the "Harrell and Harrell" show, as the head coach and starting sophomore quarterback, along with a host of Ennis Lions, shut out the defending 4A D-2 Bay City Black Cats 21–0. In the 2001 team photo above, coach's son Graham Harrell (#6) appears in the sixth row from bottom, seventh from left.

Graham and Sam Harrell immediately after the 2003 Ennis-Mesquite Horn contest. In that game, Graham set a new state record for touchdown passes. *Courtesy of Sam Harrell.*

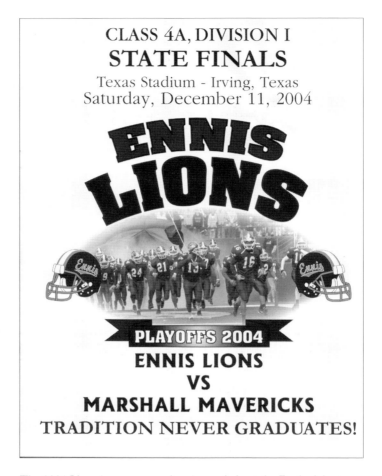

The 2004 Lions (see program above) rounded out the Ennis claim to dynastic status. Meeting East Texas powerhouse Marshall, the Lions bested the Mavericks 23–21, narrowly securing a fourth state title.

quarterfinals. In May 2010, Sam Harrell stepped down from coaching for health reasons and accepted a job as the Ennis ISD director of career and technology education. During his sixteen-year Ennis coaching tenure, Harrell posted a 146–46 record (76 percent). His teams made thirteen consecutive playoff appearances and won three state titles. Reflecting on his rewarding career, Harrell observed, "I'm stepping away from this great profession with no regrets, because I leave with so many wonderful memories of teams and players and with so many great relationships with coaches and athletes."[46] Indeed, during the Harrell era in Ennis, the locals were never lacking great excitement in the fall.

CHAPTER 5

MIGHTY MITES

With limited local cultural, entertainment and recreational options, micropolitan dynasties draw strong community support for their local high school football programs. How much more so in even smaller Texas towns? Six such cities dubbed (to borrow from the old nickname formerly affixed to the team from Fort Worth Masonic Home) the Mighty Mites have captured four or more conference 1A through 3A titles. These Lilliputian football giants might struggle if pitted against their larger 5A and 4A counterparts with enrollments of one thousand to four thousand. But the adage "size doesn't matter" applies well to this list of smaller conference super teams. Such schools have even produced the likes of 3A Sealy's Eric Dickerson, who holds the NFL single-season rushing record with 2,105 yards. Dickerson, Billy Sims from 2A Hooks and at least a few other small-school superstars have moved to the next level with ease, effectiveness and expertise.

Dynasties on the Mighty Mite honor roll are broadcast across the state: Goldthwaite and Mart in Central Texas, Sonora in West Texas, Daingerfield in East Texas, Sealy in Southeast Texas fifty miles west of Houston and Stamford in the North Central part of the state. The demographic profiles of these towns bear resemblance to the 4A dynasties of Chapter Four. With high hopes of adding yet another title, townsfolk from all six communities come together every August to rally behind their Boys of Fall.

Town	Median Household Income / Percentage Below Poverty Line	Population Breakdown
Goldthwaite	$26,731 / 18.7%	87.0% white, 0.4% black, 18.4% Hispanic
Mart	$26,603 / 20.8%	68.3% white, 27.5% black, 5.8% Hispanic
Sonora	$36,272 / 16.7%	71.0% white, 0.3% black, 53.4% Hispanic
Daingerfield	$28,333 / 23.5%	67.5% white, 26.1% black, 5.3% Hispanic
Sealy	$34,277 / 15.6%	75.1% white, 12.3% black, 30.4% Hispanic
Stamford	$24,079 / 22.0%	75.7% white, 8.4% black, 26.9% Hispanic

GOLDTHWAITE EAGLES

Located along Highway 183, Goldthwaite is an agricultural community of 1,800, well loved for the white-tailed deer that bring hunters to Mills County each November. Its median household income is just under $27,000, and its poverty rate is 18.7 percent.

Goldthwaite made its first trip to the final in 1985, taking the 1A title 24–7 over Runge. Coach Chan Priest, running the wishbone offense, set the Goldthwaite compass for the future, but at season's end, he accepted an offer from Ballinger to become head coach there. Priest's twenty-eight-year-old assistant, Gary Proffitt, had grown up in Ballinger and happily expected to follow his boss out west. That was not to be. Goldthwaite offered Proffitt the head coaching position, a job he held until September 2012. Over the ensuing twenty-six years, Proffitt brought the Eagles to the dynastic status that they enjoy today. In twenty of those seasons, the low-key, even-tempered coach took Goldthwaite to the playoffs, including two quarterfinals, a closely fought 7–0 semifinal loss against a Chad Morris team from Elysian Fields and five finals. The Eagles won three of their five championship rounds. In his own youth as a Ballinger Bearcat, Proffitt played on teams that only narrowly missed the 1974 and 1975 playoffs. He reflected in later years, "I still had that itch to help other kids get to the

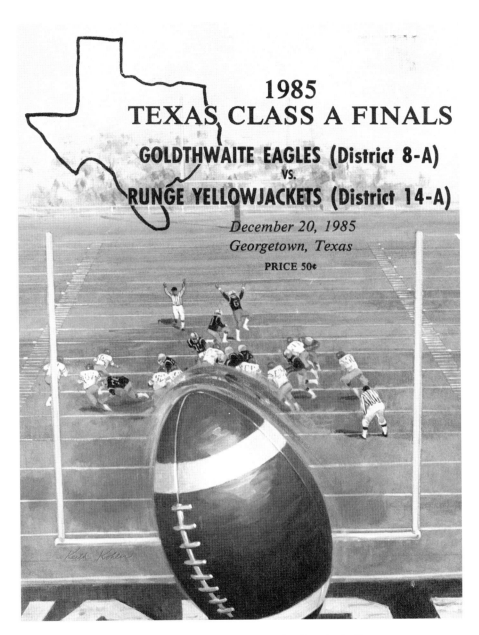

1985
TEXAS CLASS A FINALS
GOLDTHWAITE EAGLES (District 8-A)
VS.
RUNGE YELLOWJACKETS (District 14-A)

December 20, 1985
Georgetown, Texas
PRICE 50¢

A program from the 1985 1A title game that brought Goldthwaite its first state championship after defeating Runge 24–7. Shortly thereafter, Eagle coach Chan Priest left Goldthwaite for a coaching position in Ballinger. His twenty-eight-year-old assistant, Gary Proffitt, subsequently began a coaching tenure that would establish Goldthwaite as one of the most prominent small school football dynasties.

Coach Gary Proffitt (left) took Goldthwaite to three consecutive finals (1992–94), winning the last two over Omaha Paul Pewitt and Schulenburg. His Eagles returned to the final in 2009 and 2010. Proffitt appears with son and assistant coach, Greg Proffitt, who played for Goldthwaite's 1999 and 2000 playoff teams. The duo poses together after Goldthwaite's 34–0 win over Joaquin in the 2009 semifinal in Ennis. *Courtesy of Gary Proffitt.*

playoffs. I wanted to be a part of playoff teams."[47] Subsequently, Proffitt did so in spades.

Proffitt's 1992 team made the first of three consecutive final appearances. The Eagles lost 35–20 to Schulenburg in that outing but then earned back-to-back titles. The first came after a 21–8 win in 1993 over Omaha Paul Pewitt. The Eagles then avenged their 1992 defeat by Schulenburg, winning the 1994 title contest over the Shorthorns, 20–16. Even in the face of Texas high school football's evolving offensive theory, Proffitt retained the wishbone offense inherited from his predecessor. Throughout his tenure as Eagle head coach (1985–2011), when most successful teams were running the popular spread, Proffitt affirmed his belief in this old-fashioned run-centered offense. The Eagles instead retained a physical, smash-mouth style, running straight at opposing defenses and controlling the tempo of the game.

The now-archaic style has worked—at least in Goldthwaite, where in 2008, Proffitt notched his 200th win with a 57–0 shutout of nearby Valley Mills. Proffitt's program remains rich in tradition with strong community support. His coaching staff included Jeffrey Head, the quarterback on the Eagles 1985 state champion team, and the coach's own son, Greg Proffitt, who played for Goldthwaite's 1999 and 2000 playoff teams. A significant part of Proffitt's success is highly autobiographical. Having lost his father at a young age, he learned from personal experience what a powerful positive influence coaches can have in the lives of their players.

The Eagles made back-to-back title appearances in 2009–10. On the way to the championship round, the 2009 team pitched eight shutouts, including three of the first four playoffs games. In some respects, the final played in Lubbock's Jones AT&T Stadium was not the typical Goldthwaite win. The Eagles' wishbone offense scored three of its four touchdowns not on runs but on Tyler Horton passes. Goldthwaite took a 20–6 lead early in the third quarter, but its opponent, Canadian, abruptly revived. With eight minutes and fifteen seconds left in that same quarter, the Wildcats scored, making it a one-possession game. Shortly after the fourth quarter began, another Canadian touchdown made the score 27–25. Hoping to tie the game, the Wildcats went for the two-point conversion. Goldthwaite's Hunter Melton picked off the Canadian pass and took the ball all the way back to the end zone, giving the Eagles a 29–25 lead. Although the Wildcats battled back, they remained unable to score. Goldthwaite linebacker Kiefer Wilson intercepted a Canadian pass to seal the win with only one minute and twelve seconds left in the contest. In the end, the Eagles celebrated a perfect 15–0 season and Goldthwaite's fourth state title.

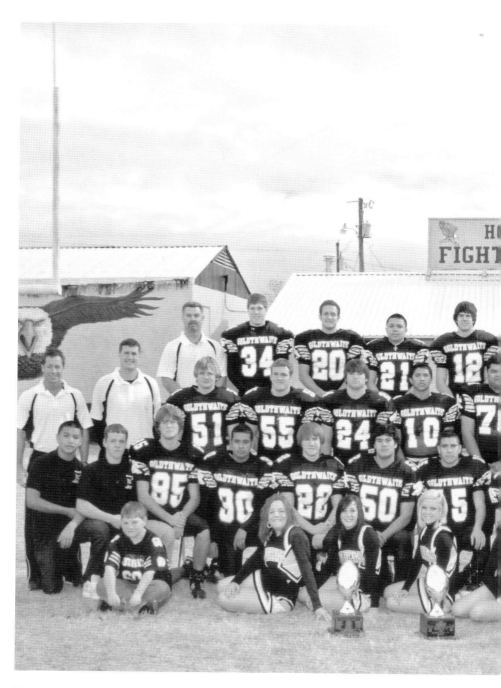

From 1992 through 2010, Coach Gary Proffitt took his Eagle teams to five finals, winning three of them. The 2009 Eagle team (above) won the championship over Canadian. Every time Goldthwaite pulled away, the Wildcats rallied back, but in the end, the Eagles prevailed 29–25.

Goldthwaite's return to the final the following season was less successful, as the route to the championship round was much more challenging than the previous year. The Eagles took an 11–2 record into the 2010 1A D-1 semifinal against the Garrison Bulldogs. Junior quarterback Tyler Horton ran for two touchdowns and passed for one, but more significant were five Bulldog turnovers and two blocked punts. After an explosive first half, Goldthwaite led 28–7. The Eagles protected the lead thereafter and emerged victorious, 35–7. They were not so fortunate the following week when they faced fellow-1A dynasty Mart in the final. The Panthers beat the Eagles 28–7, notching their fifth championship win.

MART PANTHERS

McClennan County's Mart, eighteen miles east of Waco, is home to close to 2,300. During the 1870s, the community was known as Willow Springs. In 1880, a resident expecting the settlement to grow into a bustling commercial center changed the town's name to Mart. And the community did indeed grow over the next five decades. Discontinuation of railroad service during the Great Depression reversed that trend in the 1930s. Gradually, the town's population declined from a 1929 high of 3,800 to 2,273 in 1950. In this small-town 1A high school setting, Mart laid the foundation for a formidable high school football dynasty.

Mart's Panthers first visited the finals in 1957. They had marched through the first three playoff rounds easily, dispensing with Joinerville Gaston, Garrison and Jourdanton. Mart entered the championship game undefeated. The only blemish on an otherwise perfect Panther season was a 7–7 tie with White Oak in the 1A 1957 championship game. Mart led for most of the contest, but the Roughnecks scored late to secure a title share. Jerry Hopkins, named by the *Waco Herald-Tribune* as part of the 1958 Cen-Tex Super Squad, was a member of that 1957 championship team. After his exceptional high school career (1956–58), Hopkins played linebacker for Texas A&M (1960–62) and later for the Denver Broncos (1963–66), Miami Dolphins (1967) and Oakland Raiders (1968).

The 1969 Panthers, under Coach Ed Burleson, returned to the final and won their first outright title. On the way to the championship game, Mart's defense left opposing offenses frustrated. The Panthers shut out five of its ten regular-season and district opponents. It opened the playoffs with a 37–0 win over Leander and subsequently allowed only seven points apiece to its next three playoff adversaries: Rogers, White Oak and Poth. The Panthers were even stingier in the final played in Austin. Capitalizing on four interceptions and three fumble recoveries, Mart's physical defense shut out defending 1A state champion Sonora 28–0.

With a few exceptions, Mart football was largely mediocre over the next seventeen seasons. Burleson's 1976 squad went 13–3 but fell to Barbers Hill in that year's semifinal. The 1980 team, coached by Leonard Tolbert, reached round two. Positive momentum began to build in 1982 when the Panthers, under Coach Len Williams, made it to round three. Williams took his 1984

Jerry Hopkins was a member of Mart's first state-title team in 1957. After high school, he enjoyed a successful football career at Texas A&M and later in the NFL, where he played for the Denver Broncos, the Miami Dolphins and the Oakland Raiders.

team to the quarterfinals. Finally, in 1986, he brought the Panthers back to the title game, this time played against Shiner. Although Mart had moved with relative ease through the 1986 playoffs, Shiner's Comanches pitched their ninth shutout of the season in the final. The quick Comanche defense denied all Panther attempts to score, and the game ended in an 18–0 Mart loss.

Williams remained in Mart for one more season, during which he took the Panthers three deep into the playoffs. The subsequent administration of Casey Rodgers (1988–93) yielded two bi-district and two quarterfinal appearances in six seasons. In 1995, Terry Cron came to Mart with a praiseworthy record, including the 1A state title of his 1992 Bartlett Bulldogs. Cron took Mart to six consecutive playoff trips, including a 1998 semifinal appearance. In the 1998 season opener against Groesbeck, Mart won 28–16. No one would come that close to them again until Mart's final regular-season contest. Mart's 53–0 victory over district opponent Blooming Grove was the Panthers' biggest win and representative of how little difficulty they otherwise experienced in 1998. The Brookshire Royal Falcons, however, brought the Panther run to an abrupt and premature end, defeating Mart 23–21 in the semifinal.

Cron's Panthers made amends in 1999, enjoying a 15–0 run through all opponents. In its first ten games, Mart scored between forty-one and sixty-seven points in every contest, simultaneously denying double-digit scores to seven of those ten opponents. Its path through the playoffs was scarcely less difficult. In the five games from bi-district through the final, the Mart defense allowed a mere forty points, while the Panther offense averaged nearly forty-five points per game. In the championship contest, Mart pounded the Boyd Yellow Jackets 40–7, securing a third Panthers title.

The following season, Mart returned to the championship round but faced the 2A D-2 juggernaut Celina. The formidable Bobcats were coached by the legendary G.A. Moore. While the Panthers boasted a thirty-game win streak going into the final, the Bobcats had won forty in a row. Moore had gathered six state titles in contrast to Cron's "mere" two. Moreover, in the previous week's semifinal match against Refugio, Mart had scrapped to recover from a 20–0 first-quarter deficit. In the final minute of play, Mart quarterback and future Longhorn great Quan Crosby made a two-point conversion to give the Panthers a slender 21–20 victory. In the final, the Panthers fell 21–17. After the 2000 season, Terry Cron moved to Commerce, where he coached his third state championship team in 2001, thus becoming the only Texas coach to win state titles at three different schools in three different conferences.

Over the next five seasons, the Panthers returned to the playoffs three times, making it three deep each time. Championship times returned in 2006 when the new Mart coach, Rusty Nail, took the helm. In his first season as head coach, Nail guided the Panthers to the final. The only Panther loss—a 35–33 Groesbeck victory—came early in the season. In the grand climax of a near-perfect season, Mart met Cisco for the championship. The Panthers earned a fourth state title, defeating the Loboes 23–13. Two years later, in a battle of big cats at Wichita Falls Memorial Stadium, the Panthers fell 38–7 in the 2008 final to Panhandle adversary Canadian, as the Wildcats outscored them 38–7. In spite of a 9–5 record the following season, Nail took his Panthers to the quarterfinals again in 2009.

The 2010 Panthers overcame two pre-district losses, moving through their district schedule undefeated. They then marched efficiently through their playoff bracket to the final, allowing a total of only thirty combined points to opponents. The championship at Mansfield's Newton Stadium

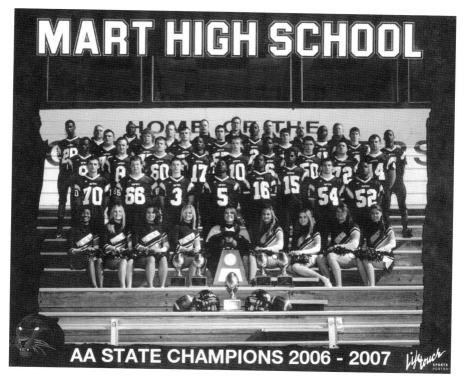

MART HIGH SCHOOL

AA STATE CHAMPIONS 2006 - 2007

Mart's fourth state title came in 2006 against the Cisco Loboes, whom they defeated 23–13. *Courtesy of Lifetouch Austin.*

promised top-quality drama, pitting Mart against Goldthwaite—two teams both aiming to secure a fifth state title. The contest was all the more exciting in that the Panthers and Eagles had collided early in the season, when Gary Proffitt's Goldthwaite dealt Mart a 29–23 defeat. That win came after a second-half Eagle comeback that rescinded a 23–7 first-half Panther lead. The rematch had the quality and character of the irresistible force meeting the immoveable object. Throughout the season, the Eagle defense had allowed a meager 10.2 points per game. Mart's explosive, high-octane offense averaged 43.1 points. In the Panthers' favor, the Mart defense also had eight shutouts to its credit and had allowed only 8.4 points per game. Moreover, Coach Nail knew that the Eagle wishbone offense predisposed Goldthwaite to the run. Both Panther defense and offense stepped up when it counted most. At the end of the day, Mart added a fifth championship trophy to the display case, overcoming Goldthwaite 28–7.

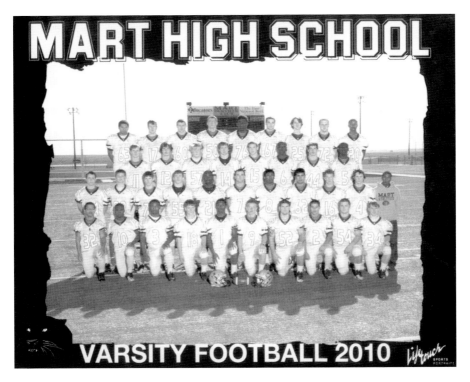

Mart earned its most recent state title in 2010 at a final played against the Goldthwaite Eagles. The Panthers won the contest 28–7. *Courtesy of Lifetouch Austin.*

The following season, Mart lost 47–28 in the semifinal to Stamford, which advanced to its fifth finals appearance. Mart got the opportunity for payback when the Panthers and Bulldogs converged in Arlington for the 1A D-1 2012 title round. In Cowboys Stadium, Rusty Nail's Panthers made Mart's ninth title appearance, armed with a youthful, talented team including freshman D'Marcus Cosby (Quan's cousin) and speedy sophomore quarterback D'Nerian Thomas. While the game went down to the wire and ended in a 35–28 Mart loss, the Panther future looks quite bright for the 2013 season.

SONORA BRONCOS

Mart had been fortunate in 1969 when it shut out the Sonora Broncos in the final. Mart's win that year was all the more impressive in that Sonora, some 250 miles to its west-southwest, had won the title twice in the past three seasons (1966 and 1968). In that decade, Sonora's "Red Hosses" rapidly laid the foundation of its 1A football dynasty. The architect of Sonora's success was Jerry Hopkins. As small schools go, perhaps Hopkins had a little more to work with than his 1A, 2A and 3A counterparts. With almost three thousand residents and a median family income of $36,272, Sutton County's Sonora is the wealthiest of today's six small-school dynasties.

Ahead of his time, the twenty-five-year-old Hopkins changed the local culture in Sonora in his first year (1960). Starting Primo Gonzales as Bronco quarterback because Gonzales was the best player for the job, Hopkins challenged contemporary attitudes toward race. In a day when few recognized the crucial importance of the practice, he also introduced rigorous, regular weight lifting as a standard feature of the Sonora training program. Hopkins also exploited the advantage of smallness. Sonora's 2A size enabled him to control the Bronco program from stem to stern via a highly effective feeder system that started in junior high school. Seventh graders learned the Hopkins system together, and by the time they concluded their high school careers, they had become a well-oiled football machine. From 1965 to 1971, Hopkins's Broncos never lost a district game. His career record was 229–92–8 (86.1 percent). From 1966 to 1970, Sonora made four finals.

In his seventh season at Sonora, Hopkins took the Broncos to their first final. For the 1A title, the 1966 Broncos faced the Schulenburg Shorthorns. Both teams were first-time finalists. At season's end, three Bronco players received first-team all-state recognition: quarterback Laney Cook, receiver Noe Chavez and sophomore halfback Ed Lee Renfro. In the 1966 final, however, it was Mike Gosney, powering Sonora with his four touchdowns, that helped the Broncos to best their bovine opponents 40–14. Both teams became regular finalists in years to come, but Sonora won more often and returned sooner.

The 1967 Broncos made the playoffs but lost to Seagraves in the second round. In spite of two losses in pre-district 1968 competition, the Broncos moved undefeated through the remainder of their regular season, posting three shutouts and allowing only Ozona to score in double digits. Following tight contests against Coahoma and Sudan, the Bronco defense held remaining opponents scoreless. Sonora's semifinal win over Clifton was a decisive 47–0. The next week, the Broncos met Poth in San Marcos for the title match. Senior Bronco halfback and future Texas Tech star Ed Lee Renfro rushed for 188 yards and scored the game's only touchdown. At the end of the day, Sonora secured its second state title, beating the Pirates 9–0.

The following season, the Broncos were again slow out of the gate, losing pre-district games to Reagan County and Ballinger. In the image of 1968,

Ed Lee Renfro (third row, far right, #22) was a star on the 1968 Sonora Bronco state-champion squad. The team's 9–0 win over Poth in San Marcos was the second Bronco championship.

they found their stride thereafter and shut out six of their remaining regular-season opponents. The Bronco defense continued performing well, blanking Van Horn and Seagraves in the first two playoff rounds. Clarendon and Honey Grove were hardly more successful, each posting only six points apiece in the quarter and semifinals. Seven Sonora turnovers in the final undermined Bronco hopes for a happy season ending. Mighty Mart, earning its first full championship, shut out the 1969 Broncos 28–0, thus denying Sonora back-to-back titles. But another chance for that was soon to come.

In 1970, Hopkins took the Broncos back to the final for the third consecutive season. The Sonora defense did its usual duty, shutting out half of the Broncos regular-season opponents and allowing only sixteen points throughout the district schedule. Sonora was almost as stingy during the playoffs, although the quarterfinal round proved perhaps the most challenging game of the season. That contest ended in a 19–19 tie with Honey Grove, but Sonora was the team that advanced. The Broncos exploited that good fortune, destroying Petersburg 49–8 in the semifinal. The following week at San Angelo Stadium, a Sonora offense led by Milton Noel overwhelmed the previously undefeated Pflugerville Panthers, 45–6. It was Sonora's third state title in five short years. But the Broncos were not yet done.

The 1971 Broncos won that year's co-championship along with Barbers Hill. They played to a 14–14 tie. It was Sonora's fourth title claim.

Coach Bill Scoggins took Sonora's helm in 1971. Having served as Emory Bellard's assistant coach for the 4A 1966 champion San Angelo Central Bobcats, Scoggins came to Sonora with excellent experience. The Broncos made the transition effectively, moving through ten regular-season contests undefeated. They continued efficiently through the first two playoff rounds. The quarterfinal against a determined Crowley presented a greater challenge, but Sonora came out on top, 19–12. The semifinal against White Deer was no easier. The Broncos won that contest 20–19, a victory advancing Sonora to its fourth finals appearance in as many years. In the final, the Broncos met Mont Belvieu's Barbers Hill. The previous week, the undefeated Eagles likewise barely advanced to the championship game. To get there, Barbers Hill battled Schulenburg to a 14–14 semifinal tie. Continuing that year's 1A playoff theme, Sonora and Barbers Hill finished the 1971 season in a deadlock, 3–3. If neither team found the outcome completely satisfying, both owned a piece of the title. For the Broncos, it was a fourth state championship trophy in a mere six years. But Sonora would not return to the championship for another twenty-nine, and when it did, it was again time to break out the can of red paint.

In the nineteenth century—an era in which Britain was the veritable "King of the World"—cartographers acknowledged each of England's

The most recent Bronco championship came in 2000, when Coach Jason Herring led his team to a 27–24 victory over the Blanco Panthers (see program above). Herring later led the Refugio Bobcats to the 2011 title.

imperial possessions by coloring recently acquired regions red on any and all world maps. The expression of speech "painting the map red" became the day's common shorthand for empire building. Although twenty-first-century Sonora, Texas is far, far away in both space and time from nineteenth-century imperial England, the two are at one when it comes to the red. In Sonora, there is "The Wall." Each new generation of Bronco football players leaves its record of achievements on the field house wall—an improvised monument of sorts—a tableau on which district titles are recorded in black. Only state championships are denoted in the school color red.

In 2000, Bronco coach Jason Herring had the pleasure of opening the red paint can once again. Sonora's most recent championship came courtesy of a perfect 15–0 season, which had concluded with a 27–24 victory over the Blanco Panthers. And it had come with an audible echo from the past. The roster of the Bronco team taking the field on December 16, 2000, bore familiar names: Renfro, Elliot, Thomas, Snodgrass and Bloodworth. Eight of these turn-of-the-new-century Bronco players were the sons, grandsons and nephews of the Broncos who had owned Conference 1A football some thirty years before. If Ed Lee Renfro helped to bring two trophies back to Sonora, his nephew Bill was no less a central factor in the 2000 resurrection of the city as a title town. The younger Renfro amassed 1,693 rushing yards and thirty-six touchdowns on the way to Sonora's fifth state title. He and his teammates entered the final at Waco ISD Stadium heavily favored against a Blanco team that was 10–4. But the Panthers had come to play. An early fourth-quarter touchdown gave Blanco a surprising 24–12 advantage. It took Bill Renfro's three-yard touchdown run with one minute and twenty-eight seconds left to play to give the Broncos the ultimate edge. Securing a 27–24 win, the happy Sonora football team returned home, ready, willing and entitled to break out the red paint for old time's sake.

DAINGERFIELD TIGERS

In northeast Texas, the 2,500 residents of the Morris County seat of Daingerfield have most recently reveled in the 2008–10 three-peat posted by their beloved Tigers. But the Tiger championship history long predates that championship run. The same season Sonora was angling for its second state trophy, some 450 miles northeast of the Bronco stomping grounds, Daingerfield began its equally impressive (if less compact) collection of state title trophies.

Daingerfield made the first of its nine trips to the finals in 1968. To get there, "Dangerous Daingerfield" built on two previously successful seasons during which the Tigers lost the 1966 semifinal to Granbury and the 1967 quarterfinal to powerful Plano (who, that year, won its second state title in the past three seasons). In 1968, Daingerfield entered the playoffs with only

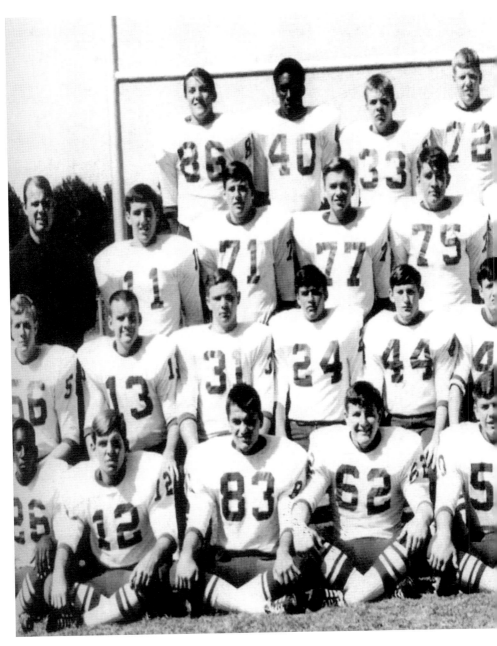

The 1968 Tigers were the first Daingerfield team to bring home a state championship.
They did it by defeating a tough 2A Lufkin Dunbar team. The Tigers won the contest when
Larry Duncan kicked a fourth-quarter point after, sealing a Daingerfield 7–6 win.

a single loss. The Tigers moved through their 2A bracket with ease until the final, where they met a Lufkin Dunbar team riding a thirty-nine-game win streak. It took a fourth-quarter Daingerfield touchdown on a muddy field to finally tie the contest. Daingerfield won 7–6 on Larry Duncan's twenty-fourth consecutive extra point. The Tigers would not return to the final for another fifteen years. When they did, their convincing victory in Waco was the capstone of a perfect 1983 season.

As UIL expanded the 1980s playoff system, more games were required to reach the championship. Coach Dennis Alexander's 1983 Tigers became the first Texas team to post a perfect 16–0 season record. Daingerfield

The "Terrible" 1983 Tigers took on the Sweeney Bulldogs for that season's 3A championship. Daingerfield's overwhelming 42–0 victory was a fitting conclusion to a season during which the Tiger defense allowed only eight points through the entire season. In an ever-expanding UIL playoff bracket system, the Tigers became the first-ever Texas team to win sixteen games in a single season.

scored 681 points, allowing only two teams to score in those sixteen contests. The "Terrible Tiger" defense surrendered a mere 8 points all year. After a blemish-free regular season, the Tigers hammered their way through the bracket, overwhelming the hapless Sweeney Bulldogs 42–0 in the 3A championship round. In addition to the sixteen wins, Daingerfield's 246 points scored in its six-game playoff run was an all-time Texas 3A record. The Tigers' thirteen straight shutouts to close the 1983 season also tied a seventy-year-old national mark set in 1913 by Maryland's Everett High School. In all, the Tigers shut out fourteen of their 1983 opponents, a mark that remains a national record today. The Tiger defense allowed only 1,037 yards total offense—64.8 yards per contest—all season long. Those same defenders recovered twenty-six fumbles and intercepted thirty-eight passes. If that were not enough, this defense also scored 72 points while allowing only a single touchdown to their larger 4A neighbor Carthage.

The successful 1983 season did much to hearten Daingerfield's otherwise discouraged East Texas population, which was languishing in financial crisis caused by the problems of the local steel mill. If vicarious fulfillment from football glory helped relieve depression in 1983, the next two seasons continued to provide Daingerfield residents much to look forward to on weekends. The 1984 Tigers were not the record-making machine that their predecessors were. But their solid, winning play earned them a return trip to the final, where they fell 21–13 to the Castroville Medina Valley Panthers.

A young 1985 Tigers team took Daingerfield to the championship round for the third straight season, having duplicated the perfect 16–0 season of the 1983 team. In Daingerfield's fourth-ever finals appearance, it met the 14–1 Cuero Gobblers, no stranger to the final themselves. In fact, the Gobblers had been to the championship round four previous seasons (1970, 1973–75)—and they would return the next two seasons (1986–87). The Gobblers left Waco's Baylor Stadium empty-handed in 1985, however, defeated 47–22 by a resurgent Tiger team that brought home Daingerfield's third title trophy. Although Daingerfield went three rounds deep once and advanced to the quarterfinals three times over the next four seasons, the Tigers did not make it back to the final for another thirteen years. When they did, the 1998 Tigers succumbed 21–0 to a fellow East Texas football power, the Newton Eagles.

A decade later, under head coach Barry Bowman, Daingerfield began a run producing the first Tiger three-peat. Bowman had been at Daingerfield as an assistant for the past three seasons. His 2008 Tigers enjoyed a near-perfect year, going 15–1 on their way to the 2A D-2 title. Daingerfield moved easily through the playoffs until the quarterfinal versus Newton. In the final against the Cisco Loboes, sophomore Tiger quarterback Tyler Boyd threw for two touchdowns to junior wide receiver Chris Jones. Boyd ran for another himself. Junior running back KoKo Smith scored a fourth-quarter touchdown, giving Daingerfield a comfortable 26–0 lead. The Loboes did not put any points on the board until the final two minutes of play. The contest ended at 26–8, with Daingerfield in possession of what became the first of three consecutive championships. The win also marked Daingerfield's fourth state title.

In 2009, the Tigers convincingly continued their run. With thirty returning members of the 2008 state champion team, success came as no surprise.

Thirteen of those players—seven on offense and six on defense—had previously started. Going into the season, the main unknown was the offensive line, of which five new starters had yet to be tested. They rose to the occasion. For the second year in a row, 2A Daingerfield entered the playoffs with only a single loss to Gilmer, the defending 3A D-1 champion. On the way to the title, the Tigers administered crushing defeats to all of their playoff opponents,

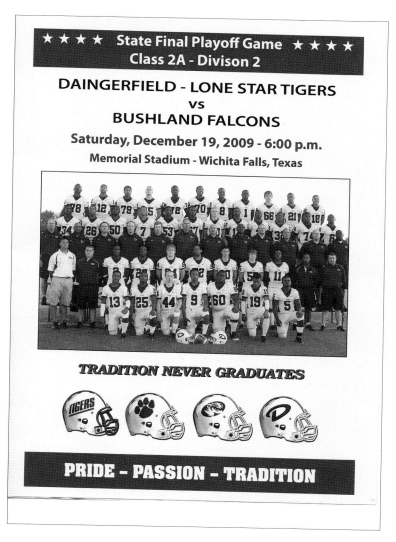

The 2009 Daingerfield Tigers overwhelmed the Bushland Falcons 62–14. As shown on the game program above, the contest took place at Memorial Stadium in Wichita Falls and was the second consecutive Tiger title win on the way to a three-peat completed in 2010.

scoring fifty-six points or more until reaching the quarterfinal. In the final at Wichita Falls Memorial Stadium before ten thousand spectators, Daingerfield met the undefeated Bushland Falcons. Both teams ran a spread offense, and both employed a three-man defensive front. Bushland had less experience, as the Falcons had appeared in only seven playoff games during the school's history (five of which had been in the current playoffs). The Tigers, however, had played in the postseason ninety-five times and had won sixty-seven of those contests. Exploiting superior speed, the Daingerfield offense posted 608 yards in the championship game. As he had the year before, junior Tyler Boyd contributed mightily to the win, throwing this time for 371 total yards. Chris Jones accounted for 67 of those receiving yards and, as he had the year before, hauled in two touchdown receptions. Teammate KoKo Smith also reprised his 2008 performance, this time taking the ball for 283 yards on just twenty carries. Meanwhile, the Daingerfield defense shut down a Falcon offense that had averaged over fifty points per game through the semifinal. At game's end, the Tigers led the Falcons 62–14.

The 2010 Tigers completed the eleventh Texas three-peat the following year with—who else—senior signal caller Tyler Boyd to lead the way, and what a way to end his high school career. Voted Offensive MVP, Boyd threw for 292 yards and four touchdowns and ran for an additional 140 yards. His first throw of the game was an 82-yard touchdown to Darrin Terry. At halftime, the Tigers enjoyed a comfortable 27–13 lead. Their opponents, the Cameron Yoe Yoemen, came alive in the fourth quarter. As the game approached conclusion, high drama prevailed. The Yoemen tied the contest at twenty-seven with just forty-seven seconds to play. Boyd responded with a touchdown strike to Keyarris Garrett with twenty-six seconds left on the clock. The Tiger defense held, and Daingerfield, beating Cameron 33–27, collected its sixth state title.

After three years at the helm and three championships, Bowman accepted a post as head football coach and athletic director at Paris High School. His career record at Daingerfield was an impressive 44–3 (91.5 percent). Meanwhile, the Tigers remained competitive, making their ninth finals appearance in 2012 under Coach Aric Sardinea. It was déjà vu all over again as the Tigers met their 2010 finals opponent, Cameron Yoe. The outcome, however, was different. A potent Yoemen offense and exceedingly stiff defense combined with several Tiger missteps in the first quarter put Daingerfield in a 28–0 halftime hole. The Tigers rallied in the second half, but not nearly enough, losing 38–20.

SEALY TIGERS

If three in a row is good, four is better. So would argue Sealy, with a population of over five thousand, making it the largest school among the Mighty Mites. And if the city's name has a familiar ring, it should. Cotton gin builder Daniel Haynes produced a cotton-filled mattress there in 1881, giving birth to today's nationally known Sealy Mattress Company. Not quite a century later, Sealy became known for something else as well: its formidable high school football program.

The undefeated 1978 Sealy Tigers converged at Waco's Baylor Stadium with the defending 2A state champion Wylie Pirates. There, the Tigers won their first of five state championships. The running game powered much of Sealy's undefeated season, as 773 Tiger carries set a new national record for single-season rushing attempts. Sealy's 42–40 finals win was powered by Eric Dickerson, who rushed for 296 yards and four touchdowns. The last was a memorable 32-yard pass reception during which he broke five tackles en route to the end zone. Those numbers brought his season totals to 2,642 rushing yards and thirty-seven touchdowns. Over Dickerson's three-year high school career, he rushed for 5,862 yards—clear evidence of greater things to come. From Sealy, Dickerson went to SMU, joining Houston Stratford's Craig James, whose team had won the 1978 4A state title. Together, from 1979 to 1982, the "Pony Express" set a still-best-ever NCAA standard of a combined 8,192 yards rushing and seventy touchdowns for a pair of college running backs. In 1984, as a Los Angeles Ram in only his second season in the pros, Dickerson set a still-standing NFL single-season rushing record of 2,105 yards. Six years earlier, on December 22, 1978, it mattered most that the road to "Titletown, Texas" was once and for all under construction.

Sealy's return to the final took sixteen years. When it came, it came in earnest. Coach T.J. Mills (1985–99) was the principal architect of a remarkable Sealy run. In 1985, he took over a program that had gone 223–304–2 in its fifty-seven-year existence. During the four seasons before Mills arrival, the Tigers had won only eight football games. In Mills's first year, Sealy went 3–7. His 1986 Tigers were 9–1. The 1989 team chalked up Sealy's first playoff win since the 1978 Tiger title. Five years later, the Tigers returned to the top of the heap.

The undefeated 1994 Tigers enjoyed a welcome guest on the sidelines of their round-three matchup against Groesbeck at College Station's Kyle Field. Tiger alumnus Eric Dickerson paid his special postgame respects to Tiger running back Fred Smith, who with 5,934 yards had surpassed

The 1978 Tigers won the first Sealy state title by defeating the 2A Wylie Pirates. While the entire Tiger team was good in its own right, the acknowledged star powering the Sealy offense was Eric Dickerson (back row, fourth from left, #19). After high school, Dickerson enjoyed record-setting college and professional careers.

Dickerson's career Tiger rushing record. That was not the only Dickerson record soon to fall. In Sealy's 3A final against Atlanta in the Astrodome, Smith ran wild for a title-game record 325 yards. As a team, the Tigers also rewrote a part of the title-game record book. With 534 yards of total offense, Sealy broke Converse Judson's standard set in the Rockets' 52–0 blowout of Euless Trinity in 1992. The 1994 Tiger championship win closed a perfect 16–0 season and set in motion Texas schoolboy football's first four-peat (not counting the one by Six-Man Fort Hancock in 1988–91).

The 1995 title game against Coach Steve Lineweaver's Commerce Tigers proved more difficult. Not only was the final score quite close, but the hitherto potent Sealy offense, led by field general Brad Burttschell and dynamic running backs Chris Tate and Jaron Dabney, found itself uncomfortably contained on the playing field in Waco. It was Sealy's impenetrable defense that decisively turned the tide, as senior linebackers Steve Newsome and Mario Tarver made big plays that proved decisive. On the first Commerce offensive play, Tarver knocked the ball loose, allowing teammate Newsome to make the recovery and race twenty-two yards into the end zone. When Commerce scored late in the game and went for the win and not the tie, Tarver made contact with the Commerce quarterback, whose pass fell incomplete. With fifty-three seconds left in the game, Sealy led 21–20. And

The 1994 Tigers became the first of Sealy's celebrated "Quad Squad." Their convincing 36–15 finals win over Atlanta was the front end of the first-ever four-peat in Texas Eleven-Man high school football.

that's how the 1995 "Battle of the Tigers" ended, increasing the Sealy win streak to thirty-two. Commerce and Sealy would meet again in the final, but not before the Tigers put another notch on their belt.

The 1996 Tigers would win that year's title, becoming the fifth Eleven-Man team ever to three-peat. Before they arrived, they sustained a disappointing homecoming loss that ended their win streak at thirty-five. LaGrange stunned Sealy 20–12 in a game in which the Leopards never trailed. The last time the Tigers had tasted defeat was the 1993 semifinal. Coach Mills made good on his postgame promise to get back up and start another streak. The Tigers did not lose again all season. The title game against Tatum was held in Houston's Astrodome, where 7,500 fans witnessed a turnover fest in which the Tigers lost the ball three times on their first five possessions. Fortunately for Sealy, the Eagles reciprocated with critical turnovers of their own. Tiger running back Jaron Dabney celebrated his eighteenth birthday by rushing for 173 yards and scoring three touchdowns. At the final gun, Sealy had completed its three-peat and collected a fourth state title. But the 36–27 final score belied the seesaw battle that made the Tigers work so hard to get the win.

In 1997, Sealy and Commerce—both undefeated—met again in the championship contest. In the Astrodome, supported by some eight thousand Sealy fans, senior quarterback Robbie Bozeman played in spite of a torn

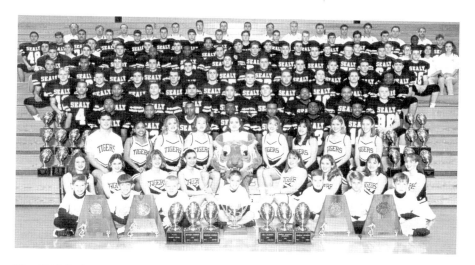

The 1997 Sealy Tigers display championship trophies aplenty. The team's 28–21 title win over Commerce made it four in a row. In 1999, Sealy returned to the final, where at long last, their Commerce adversary bested them by a score of 17–10.

This souvenir program dramatically highlights the significance of the Tiger's 28–21 victory over Commerce. For the first time in Texas schoolboy history, an Eleven-Man team had achieved the four-peat.

195

ACL sustained in the semifinal. Bozeman directed the sixty-eight-yard Sealy drive that concluded in senior running back Michael McDonald's game-winning touchdown. In a remarkable footnote to the larger story, McDonald played on all four Tiger title teams. Sealy's defense also contributed to the victory, including sophomore Wesley Martinez's third-quarter sixty-one-yard touchdown return of a Commerce fumble. Yet again, Sealy bested its Tiger opponent, with a final score of 28–21. The victory marked another perfect 16–0 season, a state record twenty-four consecutive playoff wins, Sealy's fifth state title and a Tiger four-peat (the first ever by an Eleven-Man Texas team).

Going back to the start of the 1994 season, Mills and his Tigers had mounted a remarkable 63–1 record. The 1997 win and four-peat inspired the moniker "Quad Squad" for the 1994–97 teams. Truly, these teams had etched their names into the schoolboy football annals. Postgame talk among Sealy supporters turned to five-peat. In spite of a 1998 roster laden with returning lettermen, including starters (six of whom were juniors-to-be), the 1998 Tigers fell in the bi-district playoff round to Vanderbilt Industrial. They were more successful in 1999 when they met Commerce in the title match for the third time in only five years. In a game at Texas Stadium pitting two undefeated sets of Tigers against each another for the 3A D-2 title, Sealy fell 17–10. The win for Commerce—its first title ever—was cathartic.

In the 1999 season's aftermath, Coach Mills accepted an offer from 5A Petro-Dynasty Odessa Permian, where he replaced the departing Panther coach, Randy Mayes. While Sealy remains competitive, it may be a long time before any future coach surpasses the 148–27 record (84.6 percent) that Coach Mills enjoyed over his fifteen years with the Tigers.

STAMFORD BULLDOGS

The city of Stamford, which sits along the border of Jones and Haskell Counties, took its name in 1900 from H. McHarg, president of the Texas Central Railroad, whose Connecticut hometown also bore that appellation. The turn-of-the-century town became a farming and ranching community, home for just under four thousand people. In 1935, the discovery of oil near Stamford strengthened and diversified the local economy. On the one hand, Stamford might be placed among the Petro-Dynasties of the 1950s, but on the other, its ascent into the Four or More Club is of recent vintage.

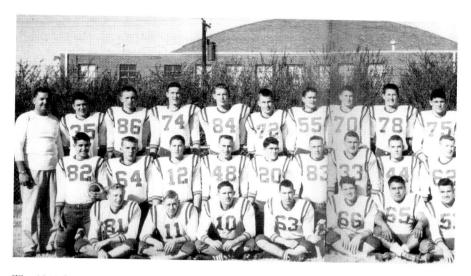

The 1955 Stamford team, coached by Gordon Wood (back row, far left), was the first Bulldog team to ascend to championship success. Their 1955 title was Wood's first as well. The Bulldogs went a perfect 15–0 and scored more than 4.5 points for every 1.0 posted by their opponents. *Courtesy of Stamford ISD and the Cowboy Country Museum.*

Although Stamford is the most recent addition to this elite fraternity, the Bulldogs would have arrived much sooner had a 1959 eligibility violation not stripped the Bulldogs of what would have been their fourth state title in only five seasons.

The first two titles came under the guidance of Gordon Wood, who coached the Bulldogs from 1951 through 1957, when the city's population numbered some 5,800. Wood came to Stamford from Winters, informing the Stamford board of trustees that he would coach for nothing less than the then-outrageous annual salary of $4,900 (about $39,200 in today's economy). School board president and prosperous community cotton farmer L.W. Stenholm declared that no coach in America was worth that sum. Nevertheless, under pressure from all the other board members, he relented. Had Stenholm seen just over the horizon, perhaps he would have been more supportive. On Gordon Wood's watch, Stenholm's son Charles became a three-sport letterman (all-district in both football and basketball), played both ways on the 1956 state champion Bulldogs and still later became a Blue Dog Democrat U.S. Congressman representing the 17th Congressional District of Texas from 1979 to 2004.

Wood's success at Stamford came quickly. During his first four seasons, Stamford lost only four games and reached the playoffs in both 1952

Mike McClellan was the mainstay of the 1955 and 1956 Bulldog offense. In addition to his membership on two state-title teams, the speedy McClellan found enormous success during the spring following football season, taking the individual 1A track titles in the 100-yard dash (1956–57), the 220-yard dash (1956) and the long jump (1957). McClellan's twenty-three-foot, eleven-and-a-quarter-inch leap remained a Texas state record for fifteen years. *Courtesy of Stamford ISD and the Cowboy Country Museum.*

and 1954. In 1955, the Bulldogs won it all. Before eleven thousand spectators in Abilene's Fair Park Stadium, Stamford rode to a comfortable 34–7 win over Hillsboro. Victory came largely courtesy of the fleet-footed, explosive running (and two touchdowns) of junior All-State halfback Mike McClellan, who later played at Baylor and Oklahoma University before joining the NFL's Philadelphia Eagles. Hillsboro's seven turnovers also helped the Stamford cause. Ironically, McClellan had begun the season as a Bulldog backup before starter Melvyn Stevenson went down with an early-season knee injury. The Bulldogs repeated in 1956, the first 2A team ever to do so. During the interim between titles, McClellan won both the 100- and 220- yard dashes at the 2A state track meet. He was again the star in 1956, scoring three times in Stamford's 26–13 title win over Brady. As the championship season ended, the Bulldogs rested on a thirty- two-game win streak that did not end until the fourth game of the following season.

Oklahoma University coach Bud Wilkinson was the featured

guest speaker at the March 1957 Stamford Quarterback Club and Chamber of Commerce football banquet honoring the champion Bulldogs. In 1957, Stamford endured a playoff interregnum. Those Bulldogs shut out all district opponents except for Seymour. The Panthers won that game and the sole playoff berth that came with the district title. Subsequently, Wood elected to try his luck in other places.

Wood's 1958 replacement, Larry Wartes, resurrected the old playoff momentum. Wood had hired the charismatic Wartes in 1955. Wartes's resume included membership on the 1947 semifinalist Amarillo Sandies basketball team, which also featured T. Boone Pickens—long before he became a legendary oilman, business magnate and financier. A decade later, Wartes guided his 1958 Bulldogs to a 13–1–1 season and their third state title in only four years. Stamford earned the championship by shutting out Angleton 23–0. In 1959, Stamford returned to the final, again meeting the Brady Bulldogs. Wartes's warriors prevailed, beating Brady 19–14 on the field. UIL withdrew the title, however, after it was proven that six-foot-four,

Stamford's third state title came in 1958, by which time Gordon Wood had moved on, leaving the Bulldogs in the capable hands of Larry Wartes (second from left) and assistant coaches Bill Anderson, O.M. Isbell and Keith Munnerlyn. In their five-game 1958 playoff run, the Bulldogs allowed only thirty-six points and shut out Angleton 23–0 in the championship. *Courtesy of Stamford ISD and the Cowboy Country Museum.*

250-pound All-State center/defensive lineman Wendell Robinson had been living at the local fire station after his parents had moved from Stamford about one hundred miles northwest to McAdoo.

It would be more than half a century before the Bulldogs returned to the state final. By that time, Stamford's population had fallen to a little more than 3,100, and the high school was competing in conference 1A. The mantle of Gordon Wood and Larry Wartes had fallen upon Wayne Hutchinson, whose talented

Stamford's "official" fourth title came in 2012. In this photo, the Bulldogs celebrate with their championship trophy in Cowboys Stadium after defeating perennial title contender Mart 35–28. The final score and win came largely courtesy of a Hagen Hutchinson touchdown run with only thirty-two seconds left to play in the contest. *Courtesy of Michael Marugg.*

son, junior Hagen Hutchinson, quarterbacked the modern-day Bulldogs. To even get to the 2011 championship round, Stamford had to defeat defending 1A D-1 state champion Mart in the semifinal. The Bulldogs did, but one week later, they met an ascendant group of Mason Punchers who authoritatively won their first state title 62–40. Undaunted, Stamford returned in 2012 for its third back-to-back finals appearance. Led by the 1A Player of the Year, Hagen Hutchinson, the Bulldogs finally secured that elusive fourth championship.

Stamford head coach Wayne Hutchinson is flanked by his two sons, Bulldog quarterback/safety Hagen (left) and backup quarterback/outside linebacker Wes (right). In the 2012 1A D-1 championship game against Mart, Hagen had a career night. His exploits on both sides of the ball made him the first Texas schoolboy to receive both Offensive and Defensive MVP honors in a title game. *Courtesy of Michael Marugg.*

The contest was a thrilling, closely fought affair with Mart. Hagen Hutchinson put on a remarkable display, going twenty-two of thirty for 248 yards and two touchdown passes, running for another 132 and two touchdowns and making sixteen tackles on defense (including one sack). Fittingly, Hutchinson received acknowledgment as both Offensive and Defensive Player of the Game. Supported by a talented cast of James Washington, Isaiah Llewellyn, Dalton Mathis, Bo Wimberly and a host of others, Stamford executed a come-from-behind win that included two fourth-quarter touchdowns. The game-winning Bulldog drive culminated in Hutchinson's nine-yard dash across the goal line with just thirty-two seconds left to play. Mart got the ball back and quickly moved it into Stamford territory, but it was too little, too late, as Hutchinson picked off a Panther pass on the final play of the game. At the gun, Wayne Hutchinson, in his seventh season as Stamford head coach, and Hagen met in a tearful embrace, rejoicing in the successful outcome that had eluded them only a year before. The Bulldogs won 35–28.

CHAPTER 6

SIX-MAN BALL

Six-Man football was the 1934 brainchild of Nebraskan Stephen Epler, who designed the game for schools with enrollments too small to field traditional Eleven-Man squads. The first Texas Six-Man football game—an exhibition contest put on for UIL—took place in the spring of 1938 between Prairie Lea and Martindale. One might argue that Six-Man and Eleven-Man football are two entirely different species. Not only are there fewer players on the field in the former, but the field itself has different dimensions: eighty yards long by forty yards wide (in contrast to the one-hundred- by fifty-yard Eleven-Man field). Quarters are ten minutes, not the usual twelve, and a first down requires advancing the ball fifteen yards rather than ten. While touchdowns still count for six points, field goals count for four. Points after are inverted. Kicks yield two, while advancing the ball on the ground or through the air produces only one. All six players on offense are eligible receivers, but the quarterback is not allowed to move the ball beyond the line of scrimmage after taking a direct snap. Since Six-Man ballgames are often wild and wooly shootouts, yet another provision—the "mercy rule"—stipulates that a game concludes if one of the two teams holds at least a forty-five-point lead by halftime or at any point thereafter. Nevertheless, under closer examination, Six-Man and Eleven-Man football are at least first cousins. And certainly, the followers and fans of the Six-Man variety are no less passionate than their Eleven-Man counterparts.

San Antonio Express-News staff writer David King observed, "The emphasis may be on offense, but it's still the Friday Night Lights experience,"

Jack Pardee, 1950s Six-Man football star from Christoval, wears the helmet and football gear typical of the time. Pardee is probably the best known Texas Six-Man football player because he later enjoyed successful college and professional careers. His alma mater, Christoval, is also widely known for its four appearances in the final (1985–86, 1990–91), none of which produced a title trophy.

particularly for small rural areas without a large population base. Reflecting on his personal Six-Man experience during the 1950s, Christoval's record-setting star Jack Pardee observed, "Football is a huge thing for a town, especially in six-man. The whole town got involved. It was like a big family, and they knew every time you did something. People knew about you and cared about you."[48] For anyone doubting the effectiveness of Six-Man football as a training ground for greater achievements, it should be known that the career of Jack Pardee sprang from Christoval Six-Man origins. Becoming one of Bear Bryant's famous "Junction Boys," Pardee continued his football career, becoming a Texas A&M All-American and an All-Pro linebacker for the NFL's Los Angeles Rams (1963) and Washington Redskins (1971). While Pardee is the only Texas Six-Man player to ever ascend to the NFL, Texas governor Rick Perry, who played quarterback on Paint Creek's Six-Man team in the 1960s, today affirms that his football experience taught him invaluable lessons about teamwork and leadership.

In 1972, UIL sponsored the first title matchups for both Eight-Man and Six-Man football teams. Eight-Man ball survived only four years (1972–75), while Six-Man ball continues to flourish four decades later. Six-Man's run-and-gun style and high-scoring contests delight spectators. Several Six-Man schools have separated themselves from the pack. In five and four title appearances respectively, both Borden County (1997, 2008–09) and Panther Creek (1992–93, 2000) have won three times. Marathon made a five-year title run (1973–77) that also produced three wins. Similarly, Marathon's 1970s rival, the Cherokee Indians, won three of their four title appearances (1973, 1975, 1978).

Coach Danny Medina (left) enjoys a Fort Hancock athletic banquet after one of his many successful seasons. Left to right are Jose "Lupe" Franco, who coached the Mustang defense during Fort Hancock's glory years, and Team Manager Aurelio "Red" Saldana. Medina led the Mustangs to their first state title in only their second year in Six-Man ball. *Courtesy of Danny Medina.*

Then there is Pardee's alma mater, the unfortunate Christoval. The Cougars made the Six-Man finals four different times, losing first to Jayton (1985) and the remaining three times to Fort Hancock (1986, 1990–91). Christoval's misfortune was largely the "blame" of Fort Hancock's extraordinary Danny Medina, who did double duty for Fort Hancock ISD, serving primarily as elementary school principal. *Fort Worth Star-Telegram* writer Whit Canning insightfully described Medina's impact as "a plague on the land and a glittering inspiration to a small West Texas town."[49]

FORT HANCOCK MUSTANGS

Only two Six-Man schools have captured four or more state titles—one is Fort Hancock in Hudspeth County; the other is Richland Springs. The former's 1,713 residents live some two miles north of the Texas-Mexico border, about an hour's drive down the Rio Grande River Valley southeast of El Paso. The unincorporated community sits in a stark semi-desert setting surrounded by picturesque, breathtaking mountains. Writing for the *Houston Post* on August 20, 1992, Kevin Newberry described Fort Hancock as "little more than a rest stop on Interstate 10," a place where "at 6 a.m., there are more stray dogs in the streets than cars."[50] Originally established as Camp Rice in 1882 by the Tenth U.S. Cavalry Buffalo Soldiers, the town was renamed in 1886 in honor of the Civil War hero of the Battle of Gettysburg, General Winfield Scott Hancock. Fort Hancock's population— over 90 percent Hispanic—earns a median household income just over $17,000. Some 47 percent of the city's residents live below the poverty line. The town's principal employment opportunities are found in the cotton fields nourished by the nearby waters of the Rio Grande, the railroad, the highway department or the border patrol. A few city residents work outside Fort Hancock and make the daily commute to El Paso.

This far-flung outpost's smallness in both population and wealth did not limit its football success. Over a seven-year span (1986–92), Coach Medina's Mustangs took five state titles, four of them consecutive (1988–91), as well as two national Six-Man championships (1986, 1991) and accumulated an incredible 92–4–1 record (94.8 percent). Fort Hancock's remarkable run included a seventy-game win streak that fell only two victories short of Hudson, Michigan's national record (1968–75). Predictably, this remote West Texas locale attracted deserved press coverage from newspapers not only in nearby El Paso but also in Dallas, Fort Worth, Houston and even *USA Today*, which, in a thinly veiled allusion to a similarly titled 1982 movie, authoritatively declared that Fort Hancock had "the best little *football team* [author's italics] in Texas."[51] There is a reason that the sign adjacent to the Fort Hancock football field reads "Welcome to the Stomping Grounds."

From the mid-1980s through the early 1990s, visiting opponents were trodden under foot as a matter of course. As success continued, the all-black Mustang uniforms elicited predictable comparisons with a dynastic Eleven-Man counterpart at Odessa Permian. Fort Hancock has commemorated its extraordinary football success with a Texas-shaped stone monument covered in plaques listing the names of every Mustang player on its five state-champion football teams. Considering the number of names that are included, it's a good thing that Texas is the largest state in the Lower Forty-Eight.

Fort Hancock earned the first of its five state titles in 1986. The ensuing "Mustang Mania" brought "The Fort" community together as one, abolishing distinctions of ethnicity and inspiring the vast majority of the city's population to vacate the town to follow their football boys to games that regularly took them two hundred miles or more away on any given fall Friday night. In 1992, manager of Fort Hancock's Mercantile Store Arturo Hernandez poignantly declared, "The community is united. Anglos, Hispanic...when push comes to shove, we're all together."[52] Football success imbued the community with an "immense pride—centered largely on an amazing dynasty of fleet young warriors playing a weird game that regularly boggles the minds of those accustomed to conventional football." Fort Hancock resident Jackie Hillin eloquently expressed the local view, observing, "Around here, the football team is the big deal."[53] Accumulating football success soon prompted improvements to the local playing field, physically abutted by cotton fields and occasionally known to provide a level thoroughfare for an indigenous rattlesnake or two.

Throughout the 1986 playoffs, few pundits expected the Mustangs to advance. Nevertheless, Fort Hancock enjoyed a convincing 51–22 semifinal win against West Texas powerhouse and recent two-time Six-Man state and national champion Jayton (1984–85). The outlines of a dynasty in the making were becoming clear. The following weekend in the final, the Mustangs beat Christoval 50–36. Reflecting on the 1986 team, Danny Medina identified both camaraderie and work ethic as central factors in Fort Hancock's leap to the highest level. And Mustang athletes knew how to work. Some of The Fort's best players earned summer income hoeing area cotton fields for a painfully paltry four dollars an hour. Mustang success was also the product of Coach Medina's innovative introduction of the spread offense in Six-Man football, a stark contrast to the tight Six-Man formations typical at that time. With creativity reminiscent of Waco's Paul Tyson during the 1920s, the Mustangs caught playoff opponents unprepared to stop such explosive firepower. Whit Canning explained the impact of Medina's spread offense as something "that makes the run-and-shoot look like a five o'clock traffic jam. The field took on the appearance of a black-and-white pinwheel—ends and backs in motion, center zigzagging, quarterback moving between a man under crouch and a shotgun stance, deep back drifting this way and that to run or throw, shovel passes zipping through the foe's belly."[54] Medina's "razzle-dazzle, big-play game based on darting speed" became the first of its Six-Man kind to win a title. Fort Hancock became so dominant that Medina declared in 1989, "Maybe the toughest team we've faced is our own JVs."[55]

The 1987 Mustangs advanced to the playoffs but foundered in bi-district, falling 40–29 to Jayton. Part of Fort Hancock's misfortune sprang from the loss of two key starters—Brett Bean and Kelly Legaratta—to injuries.

Fort Hancock enjoyed an extraordinary run of success from 1986 through 1992. During the course of this remarkable seven-year stretch, the Mustangs posted a seventy-game win streak. The 1986 team (above) initiated the run of six finals appearances. *Courtesy of Danny Medina.*

Nevertheless, in the contest, The Fort sported a 14–0 halftime lead and did not fall behind until the fourth quarter, when two critical fumbles undermined hopes of advancing. The 1988 Mustang team rebounded, initiating the first football four-peat in Texas schoolboy history. During the 1988 season, Mustang junior quarterback Jamie Aguilar threw for 3,567 yards and fifty-seven touchdowns, while his running back teammate Manny Galindo averaged nearly eleven yards per carry. The Mustang route through the playoffs to the final was impressive. Fort Hancock

moved efficiently past Grady, Trent, New Home and, finally, Christoval, averaging just under sixty-six points per contest. But the best was yet to come. In the title game against the Zephyr Bulldogs, Fort Hancock handily won 76–30. That Mustangs point count became the new high total in a Six-Man Texas championship contest (remaining so until 1995, when Amherst defeated Milford 78–42).

By 1989, the local popularity of the football program drew more than a quarter of the high school's eighty-seven students into its ranks. That year's team adopted the appropriate motto, "One More Time in '89!" Courtesy of the aforementioned mercy rule, through their first eight regular-season games, the Mustangs went no longer than five minutes into the third quarter. Two-time All-State quarterback and National Honor Society member

Jamie Aguilar did much to help The Fort earn back-to-back titles. In the championship match, the Mustangs won 48–24 over 1988 quarterfinalist Jayton-Girard. A Mustang three-peat came in 1990 with another finals victory over hapless Christoval. Behind the passing of Pancho Solis in a game played in Lobo Stadium at Monahans, Fort Hancock cruised to a 66–17 win.

The following year, the Mustangs pitched eight shutouts and posted 866 points while allowing only 149. Before season's end, eleven of the Mustang wins had come in games shortened by the mercy rule. In round two of the 1991 playoffs, Fort Hancock equaled Pflugerville's state record fifty-five-game win streak. The final occurred at Wink in front of 3,800 spectators. Yet again, the Mustangs met Christoval for the championship. Senior quarterback Arturo Nava scored the winning touchdown, invoking the mercy rule with two minutes and forty-two seconds remaining in the game. However, junior Mustang deep back Vincente "Cheetah" Ramirez stole the show. His jukes and ability to reverse his field effortlessly enabled him to rush for 229 yards on eighteen carries, including two touchdowns. For good measure, he also threw four touchdown passes. Meanwhile, the "No Name" Mustang defense stingily limited the Cougars to 180 yards of total offense. At the final gun, Fort Hancock had bested the Cougars 66–14, and the Mustang win streak stood at fifty-seven.

Fort Hancock returned for a fifth consecutive finals appearance in 1992 to much fanfare. Not only would a Mustang win put Fort Hancock a single victory away from tying the national consecutive win record, but it would also be the first-ever Texas football five-peat. In spite of the loss of nine seniors who had graduated the previous season, odds seemed good for another Mustang win. Going into the title game, many Mustang seniors were about to compete in their fourth finals contest. Fort Hancock was averaging sixty-five points per game (many of which ended early courtesy of the mercy rule). Senior running back Vince Ramirez had rushed for 2,890 yards (including thirty-eight touchdowns); passed for 1,018 yards (including thirty-six touchdowns) and made thirteen receptions for 314 yards (including six touchdowns). For good measure, Ramirez had also run back four kickoffs for scores. His counterpart in the backfield and lead blocker was six-foot-two, 220-pound Brent Henderson. The duo brought three years of championship experience, a seventy-game win streak and three state rings to the 1992 final. Moreover, they were coming off an 84–49 semifinal victory over the previously undefeated Lazbuddie Longhorns, who many Six-Man football pundits had predicted would knock the Mustangs off their title

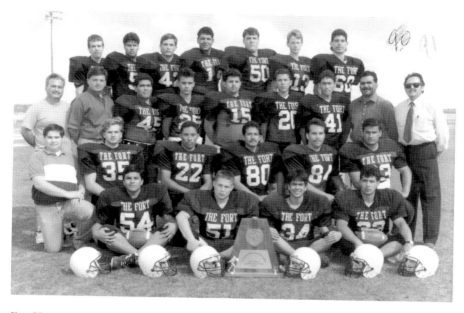

Fort Hancock's extraordinary period of dominance also produced the first-ever four-peat (1988–91) in Texas schoolboy football history. The 1991 title team (above) both completed the four-peat and earned a fifth Mustang championship. *Courtesy of Danny Medina.*

throne. Defeat did come, but not via the opponent they de-horned a week before the final.

Relative newcomer Panther Creek, located some seventy miles east of San Angelo, rose to the occasion. The Panthers, under Coach Alan Luker, made their first title bid only six years after Panther Creek had been created out of two adjacent rural school districts. To get to the final, the Panthers had to defeat District 11 rival Christoval for the first time ever. They did it twice in 1992—once during the regular season, 56–50, and again in the semifinal, 58–12. In the December 12, 1992 final played in Monahans, Panther Creek was not to be denied, winning the championship 54–26 in what became the first of three Panther titles (1992–93, 2000). The Panthers repeated as champions the following season, after which Coach Luker moved to Stephenville, where two of his sons won championship rings: Seth in 1994, giving him jewelry for both a Six-Man and an Eleven-Man 4A title, and Kelan, who had a 1998 record-setting senior season for the 4A D-2 state champion Yellow Jackets. Meanwhile, back in West Texas, after the 1994 biennial UIL realignment, The Fort found itself moved to Eleven-Man ball, and the Mustangs have not returned to the final since 1992.

RICHLAND SPRINGS COYOTES

A decade after the Mustangs relinquished their hold on the Six-Man throne, a new king assumed the crown. Some 450 miles east of Fort Hancock, Richland Springs sits near the center of Texas at the edge of San Saba County's picturesque Hill Country. This exquisite ranching and hunting country is not quite 40 miles south of an earlier Central Texas football dynasty, Brownwood. Richland Springs's population of 350 is one-fifth that of Fort Hancock's. Of its residents, 96.0 percent are white, while 14.3 percent are Hispanic. The median family income—$28,750—is larger than Fort Hancock's by 50 percent. Perhaps that financial advantage helps account for some of the Coyotes' recent football success. More likely, it is good coaching and enthusiastic community support. The Fightin' Coyotes have owned Six-Man football since 2004, taking six state titles (2004, 2006–07, 2010–12) and four national Six-Man championships (2004, 2006–07, 2011). To date, they are the twenty-first-century successor of the Fort Hancock Mustangs and the only Six-Man team surpassing The Fort in total state titles.

Richland Springs set the stage for its ascension as early as 1999, when it fell 73–38 to that year's eventual state champion, the Gordon Longhorns. That semifinal loss was the only 1999 Richland Springs defeat. Two years later, Coach Doyle Clawson's Coyotes made it one step further, reaching the final. To get there, they defeated Woodson in the 2001 semifinal, a game deemed by many Six-Man enthusiasts as an instant classic. With only twenty-five seconds elapsed in the contest, both teams had already scored. Thereafter evolved a seesaw battle in which the lead changed hands multiple times. Richland Springs won on the game's final play, a thirty-five-yard run by Jordan Hicks. His score gave the Coyotes a 55–54 victory. It was Hicks's sixth touchdown of the game. Not surprisingly, Hicks received recognition as the 2001 Six-Man Player of the Year. The 2001 final took place in Sweetwater's Mustang Bowl, in which Richland Springs met the Whitharral Panthers. Six-Man football is not ordinarily noted for defensive stands in championship matchups, but the Coyotes put on a remarkable display, holding the Panther offense scoreless on five consecutive possessions. Nevertheless, the Panthers won 27–20, denying the Coyotes their first title.

Although Richland Springs did not return to the final for another three seasons, the Coyotes continued to knock on the door. In 2002, Clawson's undefeated team advanced to the quarterfinals, where the only blemish on their otherwise perfect record was a loss to the Calvert Trojans, who won the title two weeks later. In 2003, new coach Jerry Burkhart took the helm. He

Richland Springs quarterback Tyler Ethridge (seen here in the midst of Coyote trophies won during his varsity career) was a four-year starter (2004–07) who took the Coyotes to three state championships. In the process, Ethridge passed for national records of 10,681 career yards and 230 career touchdowns. During his four years as signal caller, his team went 56–1. *Courtesy of Don Fowler.*

led his undefeated Coyotes to that season's semifinal, where Richland Springs fell 56–54 to the Strawn Greyhounds, who won the title the following week.

Burkhart and the Coyotes won it all in 2004. A central factor in the new Coyote success was freshman quarterback Tyler Ethridge. He and his teammates moved smoothly through the regular-season schedule, cruising toward a perfect record and their first state title. At Abilene's Shotwell Stadium, the Coyotes met Turkey Valley in the final. Ethridge dazzled his opponents, running for four touchdowns and passing for another four. At halftime, the Coyotes led 30–8, but the Patriots fought back valiantly. In the end, Ethridge's 245 yards running and precision passing (thirteen for nineteen for 159 yards) and a stiff Coyote fourth-quarter goal-line defense proved too much for Turkey Valley. At the final gun, Richland Springs led 58–38. The foundation for a dynasty had been laid.

The following season, the Coyotes "forty-fived" the opposition eleven times. Throckmorton, however, imposed a one-year interregnum, knocking the otherwise undefeated Coyotes out in the 2005 semifinal, 72–58. That loss would be the only one that Ethridge would suffer his entire high school career. Richland Springs returned with a vengeance in 2006, setting in motion a back-to-back title run. During the course of that season in a game against Eden, Ethridge completed his 149th touchdown toss (to his center, Jestin Fox, no less). The pass was believed to be a new all-time national record. Verification of the mark remains debatable since Six-Man recordkeeping across the country has often been sporadic. Coach Burkhart retrieved the record-setting football and later gave it to Ethridge, who in turn passed it on to Coyote offensive coordinator and his father, Harley Ethridge Jr. Richland Springs won that contest against Eden 96–0, a game stopped at halftime via the mercy rule. Those ninety-six points were a season high for the Coyotes. Even more impressive is the fact that their low score of the season was still a whopping fifty-two. Richland Springs played in that year's state final against Rule, the home of Art Briles and the site of Gordon Wood's second fulltime coaching assignment (1940–41). The Coyotes won the high-scoring shootout 78–58, securing their second state title and setting the stage for a 2007 Coyote-Bobcat rematch.

In a battle of the undefeateds, the 2007 Coyotes won an even more decisive victory, posting ninety-eight points to the Bobcats' fifty-four. At the end of the season, there were several significant story lines. Some football pundits anointed Richland Springs as that year's mythical Six-Man football national champion. Coach Burkhart also joined an elite father-and-son fraternity including the likes of D.W. Rutledge, Art Briles, Todd Dodge, Sam Harrell and G.A. Moore. Burkhart's son Haustin was among the players on the 2007 state-champion Coyote team. Indeed, Haustin caught a touchdown pass on the opening play of that year's title contest. Then there was Tyler Ethridge, the quarterback who threw Haustin the football. Ethridge was Offensive MVP in the title games of 2004, 2006 and 2007. During his senior year, he passed Chris Leak's national high school touchdown record of 185. (Leak later went on to star in the quarterback role for the Florida Gators.) During Ethridge's four years as Coyote signal caller (2004–07), he won fifty-six of fifty-seven games, passed for 10,681 yards and a national record 230 touchdowns, rushed for another 4,536 yards and took his team to three state titles. During his last two seasons, twenty-four of the twenty-eight Coyote wins were games shortened by the forty-five-point mercy rule.

The 2008 season ended in disappointment for the Coyotes. In a bi-district scoring fest played in Hico, Richland Springs fell 83–72 to subsequent finalist Strawn. The Greyhounds decisively knocked Richland Springs out

Richland Springs's Six-Man program has recently risen to take the place formerly held by Fort Hancock's Mustangs. The 2006–07 and 2010 teams earned state titles, beating Rule twice and Sterling City once. The 2011 Coyotes (above) celebrate after winning their fifth title. *Courtesy of Don Fowler.*

of the playoffs again in the following season's quarterfinal, 70–22. Richland Springs rebounded in 2010, putting together a perfect 15–0 season that included seven shutouts. The last two came in the semifinal and final. First, the Coyotes convincingly dispatched with Milford, 50–0. The following weekend, the final lasted a mere nineteen seconds into the fourth quarter, at which time an eighteen-yard touchdown run by Ben Vancleave brought the mercy rule into effect. Richland Springs secured its fourth state trophy with its 2010 shutout win—46–0—over Sterling City. It was the first-ever shutout in a Six-Man football final.

In 2011, Richland Springs made it back-to-back finals appearances, meeting the Six-Man D-2 2007 champion Motley County Matadors. The state title put an exclamation point at the end of a season during which Richland Springs forty-fived fourteen of their fifteen opponents. The Coyotes won 76–28. At Abilene's Shotwell Stadium, the unquestioned star of the show was Coyote quarterback Denim Reeves, who rushed for 295 yards on only a dozen carries and scored eight touchdowns. Reeves also

Offensive MVP Denim Reeves receives his award in the aftermath of the 2011 title game. His 295 rushing yards on a mere twelve carries resulted in eight touchdowns. *Courtesy of Don Fowler.*

Opposite, bottom: The 2012 Richland Springs team made Six-Man football history when it notched its forty-fifth straight win to three-peat and capture the sixth Coyote title in only nine seasons. *Courtesy of Don Fowler.*

threw a touchdown pass to teammate Danny Tillery. In all, the Coyote offense needed only twenty plays to close out their second consecutive perfect season. Reeves's twenty-five-yard touchdown dash on the third play of the third quarter ended the contest. The victory marked far more than a new state title. It was the fifth Richland Springs championship in seven years. During that stretch, the Coyotes put together back-to-back titles twice (2006–07, 2010–11). The 2011 title victory was the thirtieth consecutive Coyote win—and a victory that gave Coach Jerry Burkhart an impressive 120–5 career record (96 percent) at Richland Springs. That percentage improved as Burkhart's Coyotes rolled through the 2012 season, making it forty-five consecutive wins and a three-peat in championships.

On its way to a third straight title, Richland Springs outscored opponents 997–278, a run that included five shutouts. The drama of the 2012 championship game, watched by 4,748 at Shotwell Stadium, was even

Jerry Burkhart collects the 2011 title trophy—his fifth since becoming head football coach at Richland Springs in 2004. The sixth championship, which came the following year, placed Burkhart behind only Brownwood's Gordon Wood and Celina's G.A. Moore in terms of state titles won. *Courtesy of Don Fowler.*

greater than usual. Richland Springs's opponent was Follett, under first-year head coach Harley Ethridge, the father of Tyler Ethridge and Coyote offensive coordinator from 2004 through 2007. Nevertheless, neither the advantage of knowing his opponent nor his wide open offense could enable Coach Ethridge's Panthers to forestall a determined pack of Coyotes, intent on writing new Six-Man football history. Richland Springs's senior spreadback Chance Bush, who would be named Offensive Player of the Game, completed ten of eleven passes for 224 yards and three scores and rushed for another 61 yards and three more touchdowns. Defensive Player of the Game junior Coyote Ty Mann had six tackles (three of which were sacks), one interception and a forced fumble. In the image of the two recent state-title games, Richland Springs forty-fived its opponent for the third consecutive year. The final Coyote score came with five minutes and twenty-three seconds left in the third. The 60–14 Coyote victory broke the tie between Richland Springs and Fort Hancock for most Texas Six-Man championships earned. It also gave Coach Jerry Burkhart a sixth state title, placing him on the all-time winning coaches list behind only Gordon Wood (nine) and G.A. Moore (eight). It is to Coach Moore's exquisite handiwork we next will turn.

CHAPTER 7

CURRENT CO-REGENTS

In 509 BC, the ancient Romans drove out their foreign Etruscan king. They were thereafter so mistrustful of centralized executive power and monarchy that they created the co-consulship—two simultaneously sitting administrative magistrates disallowed from serving consecutive one-year terms. In its grandiose Coliseum, the ancient Roman polity, not unlike our own today, provided entertainment for the masses. In so doing, those Romans foreshadowed our magnificent twentieth- and twenty-first-century stadiums. If the metaphor of politics and football dissolves when pressed too far, in two important respects, there is an accord between old Roman history and Texas high school football. First, under normal circumstances, two administrative chiefs occupied the Roman consulship at once. Second, no one remained atop the chief political seat for long. Today's Texas high school football is similar. If Waco is the alpha, then one might argue that the omega, at least for now, could be the Celina Bobcats and Austin's Lake Travis Cavaliers.

To be sure, their tenure on the exalted football throne will not last forever. With good cause, Harold Ratliff entitled the thirty-third chapter of *Autumn's Mightiest Legions* "The Winningest Team—*For Now* [author's italics]." But at least for now, Lake Travis and Celina seem to sit simultaneously as current co-regents. Celina is the "winningest," and the Cavaliers have the longest, most recent consecutive string of title wins. With eight titles in ten finals appearances, the Bobcats are tied with Southlake Carroll for the most championships, but Celina reached eight first. Celina holds a narrow edge over Brownwood, Plano, Abilene and Katy, all with seven championship wins. The principal architect of Celina's success was G.A. Moore, who on November 8, 2002, displaced Gordon Wood as the winningest coach in Texas schoolboy football. After Pilot Point's 27–13 win against Van Alstyne, out came T-shirts that proudly proclaimed, "Texas High School Football's All-Time Winningest Coach—397 Wins." The Pilot Point superintendent, Cloyce Purcell, appropriately presented Moore with a commemorative plaque. With his signature humility, Moore declared, "I'm taking it home on behalf of two towns [Pilot Point and Celina] and a lot of great athletes."[56] Between 1974 and 2001, Moore took Celina to the title game six times and won them all (including four in a row from 1998 to 2001). His story is remarkable.

CELINA BOBCATS

G.A. Moore poses in front of some of his championship memorabilia and many trophies. As the winningest high school football coach in the Lone Star State, he compiled a career record of 423–97–9, including eight state championships. Six of his titles came while coaching at Celina, while the other two came during his stint at his alma mater, Pilot Point. *Courtesy of G.A. Moore.*

At Pilot Point High School, G.A. Moore was a four-sport letterman in football, basketball, track and baseball. After graduating in 1957, Moore attended North Texas State University (now the University of North Texas) on a football scholarship. Upon his 1962 graduation, he took a coaching position at Bryson High School. The following season, Moore returned to his high school alma mater, where he coached from 1963 to 1970 without a losing season.

Moore took the head football coaching position at Celina in 1972. He put together a string of winning seasons over the next six years that included a trip to the 1974 Class B finals. Moore's first state title was a 0–0 tie that conferred the co-championship on both the Bobcats and Big Sandy Wildcats. That particular championship game is rich in football history. It was the second of three consecutive Wildcat titles (1973–75). In the previous 1973 title game—the second Class B title game ever—the Wildcats defeated Rule, quarterbacked by future coaching great Art Briles. Big Sandy won 25–0, powered by Wildcat Bobby Mitchell, who scored all three touchdowns. Mitchell finished the 1973 season with a whopping 3,070 rushing yards. A year after the 1974 Bobcat-Wildcat title match, Big Sandy's 1975 team set a then–single-season national scoring record of 824 points. The Wildcat defense allowed a meager fifteen points and imposed eleven shutouts, including one in the 1975 title game against Groom. Two Wildcats on that team had extraordinary NFL careers: Miami Dolphin David Overstreet and 2006 Super Bowl LXI Chicago Bears coach Lovie Smith, who coincidentally received induction with G.A. Moore into the Class of 2011 Texas Sports Hall of Fame.

As for the 1974 Celina-Big Sandy title game, G.A. Moore led the Bobcats to their first of a current Texas record eight state titles. The 1974 Celina co-championship was also the start of extraordinary things for Moore. In 1977—three years after bringing Celina a championship—Moore returned to Pilot Point, where he revived an anemic program that had gone 1–9 during the 1976 season. He ultimately delivered Bearcat fans back-to-back state titles (1980–81). The first, like his previous championship at Celina, was shared, as the Tidehaven Tigers battled the Bearcats to a 0–0 co-title. In 1981, Pilot Point won the championship free and clear with a 32–0 shutout of the Garrison Bulldogs. The victory capped a perfect 15–0 Pilot Point season. Over Moore's second tenure as coach for the Bearcats (1977–85), he went 106–9–3 (89.8 percent). In his last season during this Pilot Point tour of duty, he took the Bearcats to a 1985 quarterfinals appearance against Electra. The next two seasons, Moore turned around a 4A program at Sherman that had gone winless in 1985. He took Sherman (also the Bearcats) to a 6–4 season that included a win over the number-four-ranked Gainesville Leopards. For his trouble, Moore received distinction as the 1986 Dallas Area Coach of the Year.

In 1988, Moore returned to Celina, which for a decade had been without a district title. There, he delivered not only district titles but also five more state championships. The first came in 1995 with a 32–28 win over Alto. A crowd of ten thousand watched the game in Texas Stadium. The win capped an undefeated 15–0 Bobcat season. Junior tailback Jarrod Martin rushed for 120 yards and two touchdowns, including a 90-yard kickoff return. For good measure, Martin intercepted two Yellow Jacket passes, scored a

Coach G.A. Moore prepares his Celina team for its 1974 title match against Big Sandy. In the subsequent battle between the Bobcats and Wildcats, the two teams fought to a scoreless tie. The game gave Coach Moore claim to his first state championship. Seven more would follow, including a 1998–2001 four-peat. *Courtesy of G.A. Moore.*

two-point conversion and caught the go-ahead fourth-quarter touchdown pass. That toss was thrown by all-state senior quarterback Gary Don Moore, the coach's son. Thus, G.A. Moore joined an elite head coach-quarterback/father-and-son-state-champion fraternity that then included D.W. Rutledge (and would later admit Art Briles, Todd Dodge, Sam Harrell and Wayne Hutchinson into its ranks). Gary Don completed his high school career with forty-one wins as Bobcat signal caller. He eventually became part of his father's 2001 Celina coaching staff.

Celina performed well after its 1995 state title, advancing over the next two seasons to round three and the quarterfinals, respectively. Moore's 1998 Bobcats initiated a four-peat (the second ever in Eleven-Man ball), as Celina blanked Chad Morris's Elysian Fields Yellow Jackets 21–0. A second Bobcat-Yellow Jacket matchup came in 1999. Celina convincingly won 38–7, but Morris would be heard from again as the schoolboy coach taking both Bay City (2000–01) and Austin Lake Travis (2008–09) to the finals. Morris won three of those four encounters. Meanwhile, the Bobcats continued to roll in 2000, securing the eighth three-peat in Texas schoolboy history in their 21–17 victory over perennial powerhouse Mart. This contest had more than the usual amount of drama in that it was a battle between defending champions. The previous season, Mart had taken the 2A D-1 title, while Celina had earned the D-2 title. Celina got the four-peat in 2001, becoming the second (behind Sealy) Eleven-Man team to reach that milestone. The 40–7 Bobcat win over Valley

From left to right: Sam Warren, G.A. Moore, Pat Hunn and Gary Don Moore enjoy the successful aftermath of Celina's fourth consecutive state championship. The 2001 Bobcats defeated Garrison's Bulldogs 41–35. Gary Don, the son of Coach Moore, was the All-State Bobcat quarterback on Celina's 1995 state champion team. *Courtesy of G.A. Moore.*

View during the 2001 regular season put Moore past Chuck Moser's forty-four-year-old, forty-nine-game state-record win streak (excepting, of course, a 1958–62 fifty-five-game run by Pflugerville that included a dozen wins in Eight-Man football). In the 2001 final, the Bobcats beat Garrison's Bulldogs 41–35. That championship—Moore's eighth in all, with six at Celina and two at Pilot Point—was his final title win.

In 2002, Moore left Celina in the midst of a fifty-seven-game win streak. He returned to coach at nearby Pilot Point, his alma mater and Celina's archrival. Taking the post as athletic director and head football coach, he hoped to rebuild a program that failed in 2001 to reach the playoffs. Back at Celina, whoever stepped in to replace Moore would be confronted with the challenge of continuing the streak. And winning would be more difficult because in 2002, Celina jumped from 2A to the larger 3A conference. Under the capable direction of Moore's assistant coach of twenty-five years, Butch Ford, Celina's excellent program happily endured.

Ford extended the Bobcat win streak to sixty-eight. In Celina's first 2002 game against a 3A opponent, Pottsboro, the Bobcats overcame a 21–8 halftime deficit and won the contest 29–21. In a subsequent high-profile district game in which the student met the teacher, Ford's Bobcats shut out Moore's Bearcats 10–0. In round two of the 2002 playoffs before seven thousand fans in Garland, the Bobcats met 3A D-2 powerhouse Daingerfield. There, the Tigers brought an end to the Bobcat state record

Before his 2002 departure from Celina for Pilot Point, Coach Moore (left) stands beside Rex Glendenning. To their right are Celina coaches Butch Ford and Bill Elliott. Ford took the Bobcat helm in 2002, later leading Celina to four straight finals appearances (2005–08) and two state titles (2005, 2007). *Courtesy of G.A. Moore.*

win streak running from 1998 to 2002. Daingerfield led 14–0 at halftime. In spite of a valiant fourth-quarter Bobcat effort that produced thirteen points, a missed Celina point after gave Daingerfield the one-point victory. Included in the scrutinizing media coverage during Ford's first season as head coach, his 2002 Bobcat team was featured in the documentary *Power, Passion and Glory: The Real Story of Texas Football Madness* (2004).

Celina's 2002 defeat at Daingerfield hands notwithstanding, Coach Ford enjoyed uninterrupted playoff appearances after taking the helm. Celina made it to bi-district in 2003 and round two in 2004. The Bobcats returned to the final in 2005, this time besting Omaha Paul Pewitt 28–12. The Celina win was the first of four consecutive trips to the final, although the most recent run was a split decision rather than a second four-peat. In the 2006 title contest, Liberty Hill outscored the Bobcats 22–19. In the 2007 final, Celina beat three-time finalist China Spring 21–14, thus making the Bobcats the first Texas team to record an eighth title win.

On September 12, 2008, Daingerfield cut short another Bobcat streak, this time defeating Celina to end a ten-year, forty-five-game run of home-game victories. However, the home loss did not prevent Celina's return to the 2008 final. With high hopes and lofty expectations, Celina made its tenth title appearance. In this high-scoring contest, Carthage (in what became the front end of the twelfth-ever three-peat) won 49–37. In 2009, Ford recorded his 100th win, and he continued to produce playoff Bobcat teams until his retirement in May 2012.

There remains an important postscript on G.A. Moore. He is a man of staunch faith who at one time even considered entering the Christian ministry. In all aspects of his coaching, Moore consistently emphasized strong family ties, as well as Christian principles and religious values. In 1999, Moore even boldly challenged the U.S. Fifth Circuit Court of Appeals ruling against public prayer at football games and other school events. During that year's football season, Moore personally offered the prayer preceding a regular-season Celina home contest against Denton Liberty Christian, leaving instructions with his fellow coaches to carry on should he be arrested. Once the U.S. Supreme Court upheld the lower court's ruling, Celina agreed to live within the law of the land. The 1999 anecdote richly documents how Moore's inimitable style left an enduring impact on the Celina program. Although Moore moved on, Coach Ford, the Celina program and the Celina community maintained a Christian persona, aiming to teach life lessons through the vehicle of sport. In the midst of the late 1990s controversy over prayer in public school, one popular T-shirt seen on campus and at football games revealingly read, "Celina Football: They Pray Before They Play."

Meanwhile, when Moore departed Celina for the final time, his career win record put him within reach of Gordon Wood's state record of 396. Not surprisingly, Moore and Gordon Wood were friends. A November 6, 2001 Josh Gajewski article in the *Houston Chronicle* quoted the latter predicting that Moore would end his career with 425 wins. Wood wryly concluded that if Moore did not, "I'll see about getting him fired." Wood's prediction came close to the mark. In Moore's 2003 season at Pilot Point, he crossed the 400-win threshold with a 24–14 victory over Lake Dallas. It made him 400–77–9. At the time, Moore became only the third American high school coach in history to win 400 or more games. Moore retired at Pilot Point in 2004 but returned to coaching in 2009, this time at 2A Aubrey High School. Not surprisingly, he took the Chaparrals to a school record 11 wins and round three of the 2009 2A playoffs. At Moore's

In this priceless photograph, Coach G.A. Moore is flanked by the celebrated Brownwood coaching duo of Morris Southall (left) and Gordon Wood. Coach Moore's November 8, 2002 win over Van Alstyne marked his 397th career victory, moving him ahead of Coach Wood as the winningest coach in Texas high school football history. *Courtesy of G.A. Moore.*

departure from Aubrey after the end of the 2011 season, his composite record stood at 423–97–9 (80 percent), making Gordon Wood's forecast only two short.

LAKE TRAVIS CAVALIERS

Around the 2011 season's midpoint, Fox Sports Southwest's host of *High-School Scoreboard*, Ric Renner, declared, "In Austin, it's Lake Travis… and everybody else." The "LT" championship ascent is not only a recent development; it is a story compressed into a compact five years. At the turn of the twentieth century, Lake Travis was a tiny farming and ranching region about twenty minutes west of downtown Austin. The 1941 completion of the twenty-seven-story-high, seven-thousand-foot-long Mansfield Dam created today's magnificent 1,900-acre lake and has drawn some 12,840 residents to form the scenic Lake Travis residential community. This recreational mecca provides opportunity to water-ski, scuba dive, sail, fish and swim. At a comfortable $74,293, the median household income is almost double the national average. In 2007, *Newsweek* ranked Lake Travis High School 503rd among all American high schools. The strong Lake Travis academic program is the bedrock on which the school's achievements securely rest, but in a manner that would deeply gratify one-time UIL director and "Father of Texas High School Sports" Roy Bedichek, Lake Travis provides rich opportunities to develop both body and mind. In a special fashion, today's LT football program contributes to the 2007 *Newsweek* ranking.

The first Cavalier title came the same year as Lake Travis High School's laudatory praise from *Newsweek*. The championship was the happy culmination of a successful LT run beginning at the start of the twenty-first century. From 2000, the Cavaliers began collecting either district titles or playoff wins (oftentimes both). These successes notwithstanding, before 2007, the twenty-three-year-old Lake Travis football program had yet to advance in the playoffs beyond round two. In spite of a 2007 regular-season 18–10 loss to perennial neighborhood football power Austin Westlake (the alma mater of Super Bowl XLIV champion quarterback Drew Brees), LT took the District 25-4A title and moved with relative ease through the playoffs into the championship round. Coach Jeff Dicus (2003–07) took his team to Waco's Floyd Casey Stadium, where the Cavs met the undefeated Highland Park Scots, a program that had won its third state title as recently as 2005. Cavalier junior quarterback Garrett Gilbert entered the contest having already thrown that season for 4,466 yards and forty-nine touchdowns. By the end of the title game, he increased those totals to 4,827 and fifty-two. The former broke the existing state yards-in-a-single-season record set in 2003 by Ennis gunslinger Graham Harrell. The All-State Gilbert also rewrote the single-season standards for pass attempts (556) and completions (360). In the final, he and his fellow Cavaliers turned back the Scotties 36–34.

Coach Dicus departed after the championship season, taking head coaching duties at Duncanville. If the coach was gone in 2008, the quarterback Gilbert returned with impressive company. In 2007, running back Chris Aydam had carried the ball for 1,491 yards and twenty touchdowns. Wide receiver Cohl Walla had receiving yardage of 1,072 and thirteen scores. Perhaps even more important was the arrival of Chad Morris from Stephenville, where from 2003 to 2008, he had compiled a 49–10 record (83.1 percent), including a narrow 41–38 semifinal loss to Highland Park in 2005. His résumé also included four previous finals trips, two with Elysian Fields and another two with Bay City. Morris, Gilbert and company did not disappoint.

The 2008 Cavaliers returned to the final under new direction—Coach Chad Morris—but with Garrett Gilbert still calling signals. The second of their back-to-back wins came with greater ease than the first Cavs title, as they handily defeated the Longview Lobos 48–23. During the contest, Gilbert broke Graham Harrell's career total yardage record. *Courtesy of John C. Jacob, TSS Photography.*

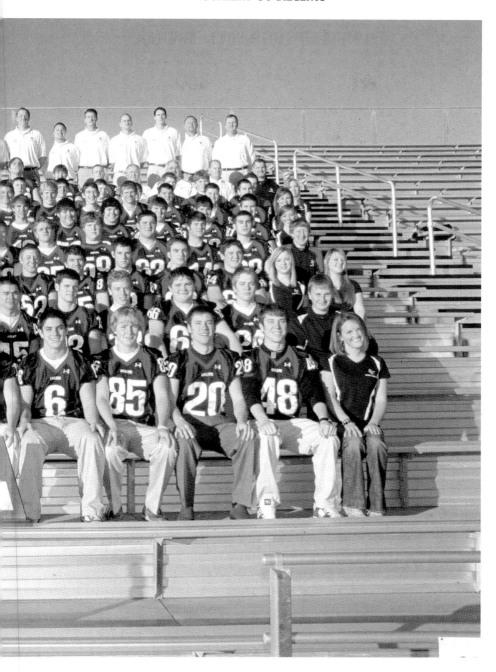

Good things happened early on the way to a perfect season. In a high-profile interstate contest with Shreveport, Louisiana football factory Evangel High School, the Cavs convincingly bested the opposition 46–31. They then breezed through their District 25-4A schedule, scoring fifty or more points in every contest save one (a game in which they posted forty-two). In the playoffs, Lake Travis hammered its first three opponents, setting the stage for a blowout 71–9 quarterfinal victory over Killeen's Kangaroos. At Kyle Field in College Station, the Cavaliers next dispensed with semifinal opponent Friendswood. The Longview Lobos were next in line. The final again took place at Floyd Casey Stadium. On the last Cavalier drive, Gilbert broke his own single-season passing record, moving the mark to 4,854 yards. By a scant few yards, he also passed Graham Harrell's career record with a total of 12,537. In the championship game itself, Gilbert had a banner day, passing for four touchdowns to Cade McCrary, Chris Aydam and Conner Floyd and running for another two. The final score—48–23—obscured the lopsided nature of the win, as two of the Lobo scores had come in the fourth quarter. With considerable satisfaction, the Cavs looked back on back-to-back state titles, as well as their first-ever 16–0 undefeated season. Over the course of those games, they outscored opponents 784–256. And as Garrett Gilbert closed out his high school career, he looked back on national rankings in six separate statistical categories in which he was positioned from fifth through eleventh: passing yards in a season and career, career passing attempts and completions, single-season completions and career touchdown passes.

The successes of 2007–08 only whetted Cavalier appetites. As they had the previous season, the Cavs moved decisively through the regular season, winning their sixth consecutive district title. On the pathway through the playoffs, Lake Travis destroyed their adversaries, including semifinal contender Pearland Dawson. On College Station's Kyle Field, the Cavaliers made short work of the Eagles, emerging victorious, 57–12. A stiff Cavalier defense forced five Pearland turnovers. Gilbert's replacement, Michael Brewer, was involved in seven touchdowns (five rushing and two passing), setting up a finals rematch again at Floyd Casey against the Longview Lobos. It was the sixth trip to the finals in eleven years for Coach Chad Morris. The 2009 Lobos proved a more formidable challenger than their 2008 counterpart, but in the end, the Cavaliers reprised their previous performance. A third-quarter Lake Travis fumble recovery helped set up an Andy Erickson touchdown (one of two that he scored), giving the Cavaliers a 24–10 lead. Longview cut the margin to a single score with just over two and a half minutes left in the contest, but the Lobos could not recover their

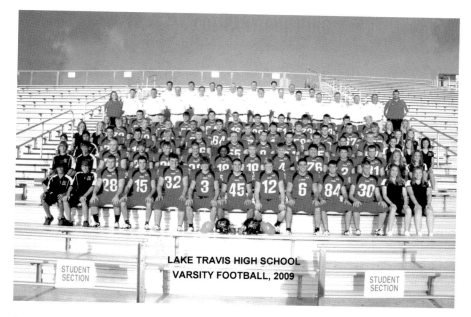

In 2009, Lake Travis returned to the finals for the third straight season, as Chad Morris and his Cavs faced Longview once again. Although the contest was closer than the one fought the previous year, the Cavs nevertheless prevailed, coming home victorious with a 24–10 win over the Lobos. *Courtesy of John C. Jacob, TSS Photography.*

subsequent onside kick. The game ended 24–17. Victory in the final marked LT's forty-sixth consecutive win. At season's end, the Cavs had posted another perfect 16–0 season. In the process, they scored 761 points to the opposition's 227.

In 2010, Morris departed. During his eighteen years at five different high schools, he compiled a 169–38 cumulative record (82 percent). At his final schoolboy assignment at Lake Travis, he was a perfect 32–0. Even bigger things were in store. Morris moved to the University of Tulsa for a one-year tour as Hurricane offensive coordinator and associate head coach. He experienced instant success, contributing to a 28–27 regular-season 2010 win over storied Notre Dame, as well as a 62–35 victory over the Hawaii Warriors at the Hawaii Bowl. His good work in Oklahoma inspired Clemson's head coach Dabo Swinney to offer Morris offensive coordinator duties for the 2011 Tigers. The Clemson season ended with an Atlantic Coast Conference championship, a BCS Orange Bowl appearance and a number-twenty-two national ranking in the final BCS, AP and *USA Today* polls. Things only got better in 2012. The Tigers had their first eleven-win season since 1981 and received a bid to the Chick-fil-A Bowl. Going into the bowl game, number-

Before leaving high school coaching for the college ranks, Chad Morris took his teams to six state finals and three state titles. Here, he appears more recently as Clemson's innovative offensive coordinator after the Tigers' thrilling 25–24 bowl win over LSU at the Georgia Dome. Tiger quarterback Tajh Boyd (to the right of Morris) poses with his coach and the 2012 Chick-fil-A Bowl Most Outstanding Offensive Player award. *Courtesy of Chad Morris.*

fourteen-ranked Clemson met number-eight-ranked LSU. In a thrilling finish, a Clemson field goal on the final play of the contest gave the Tigers a 25–24 win and a boost to eleventh and ninth in the final 2012 AP and Coaches Top 25 respective rankings. Fittingly, Ed Cunningham, ESPN commentator for the bowl game, concluded, "Chad Morris, the offensive coordinator, is one of the most inventive minds in the game."

Three years earlier, Hank Carter, who played football and basketball for Morris during the latter's first coaching job at tiny Eustace High School, had replaced Morris at Lake Travis. Carter had previously served as Morris's defensive coordinator at Bay City, Stephenville and LT. In his two years as Cavalier DC, he turned the LT defense into a formidable force. During his first season, the Cavs allowed an average of only 16.0 points per game. In 2009, it was even stingier, giving up a paltry 14.8. The 2010 Cavaliers entered the season with the motto, "One More Makes Four." That goal seemed well within reach as Lake Travis rolled over its first opponent, 5A Austin Westlake, 32–21 in the Air Force Great American Rivalry Series Game. The victory, however, was Pyrrhic. In the contest, top Cavalier senior receiver Conner Floyd suffered what appeared to be a season-ending broken leg. The following week, in a 34–24 win over Pflugerville Hendrickson, 2009 all-state honorable mention quarterback Michael Brewer sustained a shoulder injury that took him out of the next three games, including a big week-three contest pitting the 2008 4A D-1 and D-2 champions, Lake Travis and Aledo, against one another. Winning 14–10, the Bearcats ended the Cavalier win streak at forty-eight. Thereafter, Lake Travis scored convincing wins against all opponents until the final game of district play. In that contest, the Cavs lost both the game (35–21) and the District 25-4A championship, which would have been LT's eighth in a row. LT fell to the undefeated Cedar Park Timberwolves. Against seemingly strong odds, Lake Travis then cobbled together five consecutive playoff wins. In round three against Victoria East at the Alamodome, Conner Floyd's return greatly boosted spirits. The following weekend, decisively settling old scores with District 25-4A champion and number-two-ranked Cedar Park, the Cavs secured a quarterfinal win in Austin's Darrell K. Royal-Texas Memorial Stadium. The contest was closely fought, but Lake Travis emerged a 21–20 victor. The Cavalier semifinal margin of victory over Friendswood—24–3—proved far more comfortable.

Some 20,487 fans gathered on December 18, 2010, in Arlington's Cowboys Stadium to watch Lake Travis in the final against the undefeated Denton Ryan Raiders. Pregame press coverage celebrated both the vaunted Raider offense and defense, providing valuable bulletin board material that fired up the Cavaliers. Much had been made by the media about a Raider defense allowing only 12.1 points per game. In a postgame interview with *Austin American-Statesman* sportswriter Rick Cantu, first-year LT head coach Hank Carter explained that his players had a "chip on their shoulders. No one was talking about Lake Travis." The game's Offensive MVP Michael Brewer rushed for a team high 88 yards and two touchdowns. He also threw the ball for another 211 yards, 88 of which were to leading Cavs receiver junior Griffin Gilbert (Garrett's younger brother and an all-state honorable-mention). On the other side of the ball, Cavalier defensive play was stellar. First-team, all-state inside linebacker and finals Defensive MVP Austin Williams led the way. The heretofore-potent Raider offense gained only 22 yards in the first half and did not make a first down until the game's third quarter. In the end, Brewer's two scores were an ample margin of victory. The 27–7 Cavalier 4A D-1 win marked the third Eleven-Man four-peat ever and the only one in any conference above 3A. The Cavaliers ended the 2010 season with twenty-four consecutive playoff wins, second only to Celina's state record twenty-five.

Again, the best was yet to come. The 2011 Cavalier motto was the "Drive for Five." LT moved through its pre-playoff schedule with little difficulty, seriously challenged only by district rival Cedar Park in the final game of the

The 2011 Cavaliers, celebrating above in the aftermath of their newly acquired state title, made history. Their 22–7 victory over the Hewitt Midway Panthers gave the Cavs the first-ever five-peat in Texas schoolboy football. In addition, the state title win set a new Lone Star State record of thirty consecutive playoff victories. *Courtesy of Diane Wrinkle.*

regular season. The Cavs beat the Timberwolves 24–21, winning back the district title that Cedar Park had taken from them the year before. A 2011 bi-district 58–7 blowout of Austin McCallum placed Lake Travis in a tie with Celina for most consecutive playoff wins. The following week, a 42–21 win over Smithson Valley in San Antonio's Alamodome gave the Cavaliers their state-record-setting twenty-sixth consecutive playoff victory. In round three, they added another, topping Corpus Christi Flour Bluff 58–15. In the highly anticipated quarterfinal, Lake Travis again faced the bothersome bunch out of District 25-4A, Cedar Park's Timberwolves. After a closely fought contest ending in a 14–9 Cavalier victory, Lake Travis advanced to the semifinal, where in an echo of 2009, they handily dispensed with Pearland Dawson 45–14. The grand finale came on December 16, 2011, when the Cavaliers had their rendezvous with Texas high school football history. At Cowboys Stadium before 32,314 spectators, Lake Travis met Midway High School, from the Waco area, in its first-ever finals appearance.

Instrumental in the Lake Travis five-peat was three-year starter Griffin Gilbert (#7). In the 2011 state final against Midway, Gilbert's leaping second-quarter catch in the back of the end zone gave the Cavs a lead that they held throughout the contest. *Courtesy of Diane Wrinkle.*

Opposite, bottom: Coach Hank Carter and his defensive coordinator, Randall Edwards, displaying their championship rings. Carter holds five (one from Bay City and four from Lake Travis), while Edwards has earned eight (four from Stephenville and another four from Lake Travis). *Courtesy of Hank Carter.*

Like Griffin Gilbert, Colin Lagasse (#4) was a three-year starter for the Cavs. In the 2011 final against Midway, Lagasse rushed for 210 yards and two touchdowns, a performance that earned him Offensive MVP honors in his final high school football game. *Courtesy of Diane Wrinkle.*

There was little scoring by either team during the first half. With seven minutes and forty-one seconds left in the second quarter, Baker Mayfield threw a 17-yard touchdown strike in the back of the end zone to a leaping Griffin Gilbert. Still later in the quarter, Cavalier kicker Kevin Marcotte hit a 26-yard field goal, giving Lake Travis a 10–0 halftime lead. But Midway opened the second half with a 90-yard kickoff return for a touchdown. The Cavaliers rallied, however, as the LT defense stepped up and never allowed the Panthers to score again. Defensive MVP Jacob Standard came up with both an interception and a fumble recovery. Offensive MVP Colin Lagasse contributed 210 rushing yards, as well as a 2-yard touchdown run that secured the victory with four minutes and forty seconds left in the contest. At game's end, Mayfield had a hefty 293 yards through the air. The Cavaliers won 22–7. At the end of the season, the 2011 Fab 50 conferred a number-nine national ranking on Lake Travis. The "Drive for Five" successfully completed, Cavalier coaches, players and fans looked back on an extraordinary 77–3 run from 2007 to 2011.

The Cavs began their "Search for Six" with a record-setting five consecutive titles and thirty consecutive playoff wins, now elevated for the 2012 season to Conference 5A. Entering the playoffs hindered by critical injuries, the Lake Travis bid for a sixth straight title ended in round one of the playoffs against Pflugerville. As time expired, Baker Mayfield hit Grant Foster on a fifty-five-yard strike in the back of the end zone—a score that would have won the game—but the front of Foster's foot was just out of the end zone. Nevertheless, regardless of conference, the Cavaliers promise to field contending football teams long into the foreseeable future.

CONCLUSION

W hat will the future bring? Kingdoms rise, and kingdoms fall. Which teams of the future will crowd their way to the top? Southlake Carroll and Celina will no doubt make it a race to see which program is the first to grab a ninth state title. And if four state titles is today's definition of a dynasty, a host of teams—twenty-two in number, including recent powerhouses like Euless Trinity, Highland Park, Carthage, Refugio, Newton, Munday, Throckmorton and Borden County—are all on the cusp. If reigning monarchs necessarily give place to eager usurpers, one thing will remain the same. In Texas, high school football is king. It will remain so from one end of the Lone Star State to the other as long as loyal football fans flock to watch their hometown heroes.

APPENDIX

Top Consecutive Appearances in State Final

Conferences assigned according to relative placement by 2012 alignment standards

High School	Conference	Consecutive Years	Wins	Losses
Waco	5A	6 (1922–27)	4	2
La Marque	4A	6 (1993–98)	3	3
Marathon	Six-Man	5 (1973–77)	3	2
Fort Hancock	Six-Man	5 (1988–92)	4	1
Southlake Carroll	5A	5 (2002–06)	4	1
Lake Travis	4A	5 (2007–11)	5	0
Wichita Falls	5A	4 (1958–61)	2	2
Sonora	2A	4 (1968–71)	3 (1 co-title)	1
Sealy	3A	4 (1994–97)	4	0
Celina (1 of 2)	2A	4 (1998–01)	4	0
Denton Ryan	4A	4 (2000–03)	2	2
Celina (2 of 2)	2A and 3A	4 (2005–08)	2	2
Amarillo	5A	3 (1934–36)	3	0
Port Neches-Groves	4A	3 (1953–55)	2	1
Abilene	5A	3 (1954–56)	3	0

High School	Conference	Consecutive Years	Wins	Losses
Big Sandy	1A	3 (1973–75)	3 (1 co-title)	0
Cuero (1 of 2)	4A	3 (1973–75)	2	1
Cherokee	Six-Man	3 (1973–75)	2	1
Wheeler	1A	3 (1977–79)	2	1
Daingerfield (1 of 2)	3A	3 (1983–85)	2	1
Cuero (2 of 2)	3A	3 (1985–87)	1	2
Groveton	2A	3 (1983–85)	1	2
West Orange-Stark	4A	3 (1986–88)	2	1
Goldthwaite	2A	3 (1992–94)	2	1
Denison	4A	3 (1995–97)	0	3
Midland Lee	5A	3 (1998–2000)	3	0
Tatum	3A and 2A	3 (2005–07)	2	1
Canadian	2A and 1A	3 (2007–09)	2	1
Katy	5A	3 (2007–09)	2	1
Carthage	3A	3 (2008–10)	3	0
Daingerfield (2 of 2)	2A	3 (2008–10)	3	0
Aledo	4A	3 (2009–11)	3	0
Throckmorton	Six-Man	3 (2010–12)	2	1
Richland Springs	Six-Man	3 (2010–12)	3	0

NOTES

1. Reinert, *Rites of Fall*, 173–74.
2. Bissinger, *Friday Night Lights*, back cover.
3. Reid, *Vain Glory*, 4, 12, 17, 31.
4. Wilson, *Home Field*, 76.
5. Ratliff, *Autumn's Mightiest Legions*, iv.
6. Bissinger, *Friday Night Lights*, 236.
7. Wilson, *Home Field*, foreword, 83–84.
8. Bedichek, *Educational Competition*, 342.
9. Ratliff, *Autumn's Mightiest Legions*, 9.
10. Bedichek, *Educational Competition*, vii, xi, 5, 8–9, 358.
11. Ratliff, *Autumn's Mightiest Legions*, foreword.
12. Bedichek, *Educational Competition*, 367.
13. Information adapted from Bedichek's *Educational Competition* and Ratliff's *Autumn's Mightiest Legions*.
14. Bedichek, *Educational Competition*, 343–44.
15. Breazeale, *Tops in Texas*.
16. *The Best of Dave Campbell's Texas Football 1960–1989*, 156.
17. Ratliff, *Autumn's Mightiest Legions*, 55.
18. Ibid., 50–55.
19. Reinert, *Rites of Fall*, 28.
20. Bissinger, *Friday Night Lights*, 238.
21. Reid, *Vain Glory*, xv, 4, 32.
22. Grant, *Warbirds*, 2.
23. Ibid., 81.
24. Bynum, *King Football*, 133.
25. Pickett and Mitchell, *Brother's Keeper*, 130.
26. Harris, *Passion for Victory*, 46.
27. Reid, *Vain Glory*, 7, 13–14, 34.

28. Reinert, *Rites of Fall*, 28.

29. McMurray, *Texas High School Football*, 388.

30. *Houston Chronicle*, September 27, 1992.

31. Reid, *Vain Glory*, 16.

32. Ibid., xv.

33. Bissinger, *Friday Night Lights*, xiv, 36, 237.

34. McCally, *Secret of Mojo*, 13, 223.

35. Bynum, *King Football*, 547.

36. Todd Hveem, "Johnston Reflects on Career," *Houston Chronicle*, July 12, 2007.

37. Katy Tigers Football, http://katyathleticboosterclub.org/tigertradition.htm.

38. Melanie Saxton, "The Man Behind the Katy Tigers," *Katy Magazine*, Fall 2008.

39. Benne, *The Best High School Football in the Country*, 175.

40. Bedichek, *Educational Competition*, 373.

41. Babb Giles, "Unofficial and Insufficient History of Judson Rocket Football."

42. Records adapted from "Lone Star Gridiron" (http://lonestargridiron.com/history-records/coaching-wins-all-time-leaders/), Dave Campbell's Texas Football (http://www.texasfootball.com/highschool-news/view/5265), "Six-Man Winningest Coaches" (http://www.texassixmancoachesassociation.com/6-ManWinningestCoaches.html), various newspaper articles and individual input from several coaches.

43. Carver, *Coach of the Century*, 174.

44. Ibid., 169.

45. Ibid., 360–61.

46. Brandon George, *Dallas Morning News*, December 3, 2010.

47. Mike Lee, "Goldthwaite Football Coach Reaches 200-Wins Plateau," *San Angelo Standard-Times*, October 31, 2008.

48. David King, "The Six-Man World," *San Antonio Express-News*, October 14, 2006.

49. Whit Canning, "A Football Dynasty Born of Despair," *Fort Worth Star-Telegram*, October 19, 1989.

50. Kevin Newberry, "6-Man Domination Puts Town on Map," *Houston Post*, August 20, 1992.

51. Jim Myers, "Mustangs Cause 6-Man Stampede," *USA Today*, November 9, 1989.

52. Kevin Newberry, "6-Man Domination Puts Town on Map," *Houston Post*, August 20, 1992.

53. Whit Canning, "A Football Dynasty Born of Despair," *Fort Worth Star-Telegram*, October 19, 1989.

54. Ibid.

55. Jim Myers, "Mustangs Cause 6-Man Stampede," *USA Today*, November 9, 1989.

56. Bynum, *King Football*, 356.

BIBLIOGRAPHY

Books

Bedichek, Roy. *Educational Competition: The Story of the University Interscholastic League*. Austin: University of Texas, 1956.

Benne, Bart. *The Best High School Football in the Country: A History of Plano, Texas High School Football from 1900 to the Present*. Dallas, TX: Taylor Publishing Company, 1989.

Bissinger, H.G. *Friday Night Lights: A Town, a Team, and a Dream*. New York: Addison-Wesley, 1990.

Breazeale, George. *Tops in Texas: Records and Notes on UIL State Football Champions, 1920–1992*. Austin, TX: Martin Communications, 1993.

Bynum, Mike. *King Football: Greatest Moments in Texas High School Football History*. Epic Sports Classics, 2003.

Carver, John. *Coach of the Century: An Autobiography by Gordon Wood as Told to John Carver*. Plano, TX: Hard Times Cattle Company Publishing, 2001.

Cashion, Ty. *Pigskin Pulpit: A Social History of Texas High School Football Coaches*. Austin: Texas State Historical Association, 1998.

Dent, Jim. *The Junction Boys: How Twelve Days in Hell with Bear Bryant Forged a Championship Team*. New York: St. Martin's Griffin, 2000.

_____. *Twelve Mighty Orphans: The Inspiring True Story of the Mighty Mites Who Ruled Texas Football*. New York: St. Martin's Press, 2007.

Gholson, Nick. *Hail to Our Colors: A Complete History of Coyote Football*. Wichita Falls, TX: Times Record News, 1999.

Grant, Michael. *Warbirds: How They Played the Game*. N.p.: Lone Star Sundries, 2004.

Harris, Jack "Sleepy." *A Passion for Victory: The Coaching Life of Texas Legend Joe Kerbel*. Dallas, TX: Taylor Publishing Company, 1990.

McCally, Regina Walker. *The Secret of Mojo*. Self-published, 1986.

McMurray, Bill. *Texas High School Football*. South Bend, IN: Icarus Press, 1985.

Pickett, Al. *Team of the Century: The Greatest High School Football Team in Texas*. Buffalo Gap, TX: State House Press, 2004.

Pickett, Al, and Chad Mitchell. *Brother's Keeper: The Story of the 2009 Abilene High State Championship*. Abilene, TX: Picket Publications, 2010.

Ratliff, Harold. *Autumn's Mightiest Legions: A History of Texas Schoolboy Football*. Waco, TX: Texian Press, 1963.

_____. *Texas Schoolboy Football: Champions in Action*. Austin, TX: University Interscholastic League, 1972.

Reid, Jan. *Vain Glory*. Fredericksburg, TX: Shearer Publishing, 1986.

Reinert, Al. *Rites of Fall: High School Football in Texas*. Austin: University of Texas, 1979.

Sherrod, Ricky L. *Stephenville Yellow Jacket Football*. Charleston, SC: Arcadia Publishing, 2011.

Stowers, Carlton. *Friday Night Heroes: A Look at Texas High School Football*. Austin, TX: Eakin Press, 1983.

Wilson, Gene. *Cotton & Co.: The Story of a Texas High School Coaching Legend*. Self-published, 2002.

Wilson, Jeff. *Home Field: Texas High School Football Stadiums from Alice to Zephyr*. Austin: University of Texas Press, 2010.

Newspapers and Magazines

Abilene Reporter-News
Amarillo Globe-News
Austin American-Statesman
Brownwood Bulletin
Charleston Post and Courier
Cleburne Times-Review
Conroe News
The [Galveston] *Daily News*
Dallas Morning News
Dave Campbell's *Texas Football*
Denton Record-Chronicle
El Paso Times
Fort Worth Star-Telegram
Galveston News
Groesbeck Journal

BIBLIOGRAPHY

Herald Democrat
Houston Chronicle
Houston Post
Katy Magazine
Killeen Daily Herald
Lake Travis View
Longview News-Journal
Lubbock Avalanche-Journal
New American
The Old Coach
Round Rock/Pflugerville Community Impact Newspaper
San Angelo Standard-Times
San Antonio Express-News
Sports Illustrated
Stephenville Empire-Tribune
Upshur Advocate
USA Today
Victoria Advocate

ONLINE RESOURCES

Babb, Giles. "Unofficial and Insufficient History of Judson Rocket Football." http://www.judsonrocketball.com/.

CelinaBobcats.org. "Celina Bobcat Football Season Records." www.celinabobcats.org/records.

Davis, Lucas. "Top 10 High School Football Programs of All-Time." Bleacher Report. www.bleacherreport.com/articles/49223-top-10-high-school-football-programs-of-all-time.

FootballScoop.com. "Philip Montgomery—2011 Quarterbacks Coach of the Year." http://www.footballscoop.com/coaching-awards/2011-coaches-of-the-year/2011-quarterbacks-coach.

GarlandOwls.com. "All-Time Coaching Records." http://www.garlandowls.com/football/team/coaches/all-time_coaches.

High School Football Database. "Historical High School National Football Champions." www.hsfdatabase.com/nationalchampions.htm.

Lone Star Football Network. http://lonestarfootball.net.

Lone Star Gridiron. "Texas High School Football All-Time Coaching Wins." http://lonestargridiron.com/history-records/coaching-wins-all-time-leaders.

PlanoFootball.com. "Unbeaten Teams." http://www.planofootball.com/history/teams.

SealySports.com. "Tigers at the Next Level." http://www.sealysports.com/ Sealy_STSN/Tigers_At_The_Next_Level.html.

SixManFootball.com. "History." http://sixmanfootball.com/history.php.

Smoaky.com. "Most H.S. Football State Championships." http://www. smoaky.com/news/View.php?ArticleID=2336.

Stephenville Yellow Jackets. http://stephenvilleyellowjackets.com/index.php.

TexasHSFootball.com. "Ennis Lions Football: Over a Century of Football." www.texashsfootball.com/board/index.php?showtopic=25072.

Texas Six-Man Coaches Association. "Hall of Fame Coaches." http://www. texassixmancoachesassociation.com/6-ManHallofFameCoaches.html.

———. "Winningest Texas 6-Man Coaches." http://www. texassixmancoachesassociation.com/6-ManWinningestCoaches.html.

TXPrepsFootball.com. "State Records." http://txprepsfootball.com/ archives/state-records.

UILTexas.org. "Prairie View Interscholastic League Football Records." http://www2.uiltexas.org/athletics/archives/football/pvil_records.html.

Wichita Falls High School Coyote Football. http://www.wfhscoyotes.com.

INDEX

A

Abilene
  Abilene Cooper 60, 79, 146, 147, 148
  Abilene High 33, 39, 53, 54, 60,
    85, 146
Albany 45, 64
Aledo 16, 21, 87, 88, 91, 127, 128,
    129, 130, 132, 133, 138, 158,
    160, 233, 242
Amarillo 15, 20, 21, 42, 48, 49, 50, 51,
    52, 53, 64, 69, 102, 158, 199, 241
Arlington
  Cowboys Stadium 18, 113, 130, 131,
    158, 160, 178, 233, 236
Arnold, Frank 115
Austin
  Anderson High 72, 73
  Austin High 25
  Cedar Park 233, 236
  Clark Field 18, 25
  Darrell K. Royal Texas Memorial
    Stadium 129, 233
  McCallum High 236
  Nelson Field 101
  Reagan High 20, 60, 68, 78, 123
  Westlake High 113, 227, 232

B

Bartlett 139, 175
Bartosh, Gil 79
Bay City 147, 158, 164, 222, 227, 232
Bedichek, Roy 9, 22, 25, 227
Bellard, Emory 53, 65, 66, 67, 68, 78,
    79, 139, 140, 181
Bible, Dana X. 51
Big Sandy 20, 21, 37, 107, 108, 154,
    220, 221, 242
Bissinger, H.G. 18, 19, 52, 77, 78, 84
Borden County 204, 239
Bowman, Barry 188, 190
Boyd 188
Brady 36, 140, 198, 199
Breazeale, George 10, 22
Breckenridge 10, 14, 20, 40, 45, 48,
    50, 53, 57, 58, 61, 62, 63, 64,
    65, 67, 68, 70, 71, 89, 138, 139,
    140, 142, 152
Brence, Gerald 106
Brenham 125, 129
Bridge City 142
Briles, Art 118, 124, 136, 138, 150, 152,
    153, 156, 157, 214, 221, 222
Brown, Gordon 94

Brown, Joe 152
Brownwood 10, 14, 20, 40, 53, 63,
        91, 94, 102, 123, 135, 136, 139,
        140, 141, 143, 146, 147, 148,
        149, 150, 152, 154, 156, 158,
        161, 212, 219
Buchanan, Tim 87, 128, 132, 133, 138
Burkhart, Jerry 137, 212, 213, 214,
        216, 218
Burleson, Edd 174, 175

C

Canadian 164, 171, 176, 242
Carter, Hank 10, 232, 233
Carthage 21, 188, 225, 239, 242
Cedar Hill 99, 114
Celina 10, 14, 20, 21, 99, 114, 137,
        176, 219, 220, 221, 222, 223,
        224, 225, 233, 236, 239, 241
Cherokee 204, 242
Cherry, Blair 48, 49, 50, 51, 89
Chicago Fenger 40
China Spring 127, 224
Christoval 204, 205, 207, 209, 210, 211
Cisco 45, 53, 54, 152, 176, 188
Clark, John 18, 25, 102, 103
Cleburne 18, 26, 37, 53, 67, 91, 154
Clyde 45
College Station
  Kyle Field 143, 161, 191, 230
Comanche 23, 24, 73, 175
Commerce 107, 138, 139, 176, 193,
        194, 196, 199
Converse Judson 10, 14, 20, 73, 86, 88,
        106, 114, 115, 121, 122, 124,
        137, 164, 192
Copeland, Mike 9, 154, 156, 157, 158
Copperas Cove 19, 128
Corpus Christi 22, 24, 26, 37, 40, 49,
        57, 59, 71, 89, 150, 236
Corsicana 33, 36, 39, 131
Cotton Palace. *See* Waco
Cron, Terry 138, 139, 175, 176
Crosslin, Donnell 76, 77
Cuero 20, 108, 147, 161, 188, 242

Curtis, Chuck 49, 89, 91, 128, 138
Curtis, Eck 40, 62

D

Daingerfield 10, 21, 167, 168, 183,
        186, 188, 189, 190, 223, 224,
        225, 242
Dallas
  Bryan Street High 26
  Carter High 85, 115, 117
  Cotton Bowl 40
  Dallas High 23, 24
  Fair Park 37, 49
  Forest Avenue (Madison) High 36, 37
  Highland Park 40, 60, 62, 69, 70, 71,
        104, 117, 164, 227, 239
  Highland Park High 40, 41, 47, 57
  Jesuit High 40
  Lake Dallas High 225
  Oak Cliff (Adamson) High 33, 36, 37
  Skyline High 114
  Washington High 72
  Wilmer-Hutchins High 153
  Woodrow Wilson High 146
Denison 20, 124, 154, 242
Denton
  Ryan High 125, 164, 233, 241
Dickinson 147
Dicus, Jeff 227
Dodge, Todd 98, 108, 110, 112, 113,
        118, 138, 214, 222
Duncanville 105, 120, 227

E

Eastland 45
Elysian Fields 158, 168, 222, 227
Ennis 10, 15, 135, 136, 156, 161, 163,
        164, 227
Erney, Fred 18, 37
Erwin, Bryan 125, 126
Essary, Don 161
Ethridge, Harley, Jr. 214
Euless Trinity 87, 107, 117, 122, 138,
        192, 239

Evangel High (Louisiana) 230
Everett High School (Maryland) 187

F

Florida Gators 113, 214
Ford, Butch 223, 224, 225
Fort Bend
  Dulles High 117
  Hightower 113
  Willowridge 19, 148
Fort Hancock 10, 15, 21, 137, 192, 205,
    206, 207, 210, 212, 218, 241
Fort Worth
  Amon Carter Stadium 58, 102
  Dunbar High 73, 131, 186
  Fort Worth High 24
  Masonic Home 49, 52, 167
  North Side 25, 48
  Panther Park 35
Frenship 156
Friendswood 230, 233

G

Gaines, Gary 84, 85, 86
Gainesville 107, 108, 147, 163, 221
Galena Park 74, 91
Garland 10, 15, 88, 89, 91, 97, 127,
    138, 223
Garrison 174, 221, 223
Gilbreth, Buster 147, 161
Gillespie, Joseph 9, 158
Gilmer 189
Golding, Joe 53, 69, 70, 74, 75, 76, 77,
    84, 137
Goldthwaite 10, 16, 167, 168, 171,
    174, 177, 242
Gordon 212
Granger 79
Grapeland 127
Greenville 50, 102
Gregory-Portland 102
Groesbeck 175, 176, 191
Grover Cleveland High (St. Louis,
    Missouri) 40

H

Hardin-Simmons 53
Harrell, Sam 10, 118, 136, 161, 162,
    163, 164, 166, 214, 222, 227, 230
Henderson, Roy 25
Highland Park. See Dallas
Hillsboro 126, 139, 198
Hollingshead, Tam 86
Hopkins, Jerry 179, 180
Houston
  Aldine High 85, 123
  Astrodome 91, 96, 97, 120, 153, 156,
    164, 192, 194
  Central (Sam Houston) High 23, 24,
    73, 74
  Christian High 98
  Davis High 37
  Heights High 26, 67
  Kashmere High 73, 74
  Lamar High 42, 47
  Rice Stadium 91
  Stephen F. Austin High 58
  Stratford High 104, 105, 191
  Worthing High 73
  Yates High 72, 83, 84
Hudson, MI 206
Hutchinson, Wayne 10, 118, 200, 222

I

Irving
  Texas Stadium 77, 115, 147, 155

J

Jacksboro 49, 89, 91, 117, 138
Jayton 205, 207, 210
Jeffries, Ted 69
Johnston, Mike 95, 96, 98
Joseph, Gary 10, 98, 99

K

Katy 10, 20, 21, 61, 88, 92, 94, 96, 97,
    98, 99, 106, 110, 112, 118, 122,
    219, 242

Kerbel, Joe 63, 64, 65, 79
Kilgore 125, 158
Kimbrough, Tommy 103, 104, 105, 106
Kuempel, Charles 60
Kuempel, Herbert "Hub" 60

L

Lake Travis 9, 10, 15, 21, 130, 158,
    219, 222, 226, 227, 230, 231,
    232, 233, 236, 238, 241
Lamar Junior College 69
La Marque 10, 15, 20, 21, 43, 88, 105,
    122, 123, 124, 125, 126, 130,
    153, 155, 241
Latin School (Chardron, Ohio) 39
Ledbetter, Bob 107, 108
Lewisville 119
Liberty Hill 224
Lineweaver, Steve 87, 107, 138, 193
Little Southwest Conference 57, 140
Longview 62, 69, 96, 105, 138, 230
Lubbock
    Estacado High 22, 146
    Jones AT&T Stadium 104, 171
    Lubbock High 40, 57
Lufkin 40, 63, 186
Luker, Alan 211
Lynch, Howard 51, 52

M

Mansfield
    Newton Stadium 176
    Summit High 131
Manvel 131
Manziel, Johnny 50
Marathon 204, 241
Marlin 33, 37, 53
Marshall, Jimmy 152
Mart 10, 139, 167, 168, 174, 175, 176,
    178, 180, 201, 202, 222
Massey, Hugh 123
Mayes, Randy 86, 196
Mayfield, Gene 78, 79
Mayhew, Dewey 39, 53, 54, 55, 57

McAllen 55
McKinney 110
Medina, Danny 10, 137, 205, 206, 207
Mesquite Poteet 130, 161
Meyers, Watty 89
Midland
    Midland High 57, 121, 122
    Midland Lee High 20, 21, 84, 85, 97,
        115, 242
Midway High 236, 238
Mills, T.J. 137, 191, 194, 196
Mobley, Jim 152
Monahans 146, 210, 211
Mont Belvieu Barbers Hill 175, 181
Moore, G.A. 7, 10, 118, 136, 137, 176,
    214, 218, 220, 221, 222, 223, 225
Morris, Chad 10, 158, 168, 222, 227,
    230, 231, 232
Moser, Chuck 53, 55, 57, 58, 60, 61,
    70, 75, 89, 110, 140, 150, 223
Motley County 19, 215
Murphy, Mike 152
Myers, Gerald 161

N

Nail, Rusty 176, 177, 178
National Championship 39, 85, 123, 152
No Pass, No Play (House Bill No. 72) 57
North Texas State University (University
    of North Texas) 78, 220
Notre Dame 33, 231
Nowotny, Larry 123

O

Odessa
    Mojo 19, 78, 81, 82, 83, 85, 100
    Odessa High 78
    Permian High 14, 18, 19, 20, 48, 68,
        77, 78, 79, 80, 81, 82, 83, 84,
        85, 86, 100, 104, 105, 108, 114,
        119, 196, 206
    Ratliff Stadium 18, 78
Omaha Paul Pewitt 171, 224
Orange Bowl 51, 55, 231

P

Pampa 57, 70
Panther Creek 204, 211
Pardee, Jack 204, 205
Paris 190
Patterson, Andrew "Pat" 72
Pearland Dawson 230, 236
Pflugerville 60, 61, 98, 180, 210, 223, 232, 238
Phillips, Oail Andrew "Bum" 52, 102, 139
Pilot Point 137, 220, 221, 223, 225
Plano 9, 14, 20, 84, 88, 96, 99, 100, 101, 102, 103, 104, 105, 106, 114, 117, 123, 127, 146, 147, 183, 219
Port Arthur 39, 41, 54, 61, 80, 83, 108, 110
Port Lavaca 141
Port Neches 64, 80, 89, 104, 156, 241
Poth 19, 175, 179
Prairie View Interscholastic League (PVIL) 72, 73, 74, 83
Price, Carl 41
Priest, Chan 168
Proffitt, Gary 10, 168, 171, 177

R

Rackley, Jim 121, 122
Ranger 45, 48, 54
Rapp, Tom 108
Ratliff, Harold 22, 35, 39, 45, 219
Raven, Travis 78
Refugio 22, 176, 239
Reid, Jan 17, 19, 52, 53, 69, 77
Reinert, Al 47, 72, 74
Richland Springs 10, 15, 21, 137, 212, 213, 214, 215, 216, 242
Robbins, Cooper 62, 63
Rockne, Knute 32, 33
Rockwall 110, 148
Rodgers, Casey 175
Rose Bowl 37, 98

Russell, Rusty 40, 49
Rutledge, D.W. 73, 115, 117, 118, 120, 121, 124, 137, 214, 222

S

San Angelo 40, 50, 53, 57, 68, 78, 85, 140, 148, 180, 181, 211
San Antonio
  Alamodome 18, 61, 98, 121, 125, 233, 236
  Alamo Heights 114, 125
  Brackenridge 22, 72, 114
  Jefferson 114
  Jefferson High 78
  Lee 114
  Lee High 76, 77, 78
  Marshall High 86
  Randolph High 102
Sanders, Jerry 115
Schulenburg 171, 179, 181
Scoggins, Bill 181
Scott, Verne 150
Sealy 10, 15, 20, 21, 104, 137, 167, 168, 191, 192, 193, 194, 196, 222, 241
Sherman 137, 153, 221
Shipley, Bob 150
Shotwell, Prince Elmer "Pete" 33, 35, 48, 53, 55, 57, 61, 62, 69, 138
Sixty-Mile Banquet 64
Smithson Valley 110, 236
Sonora 10, 167, 168, 175, 178, 179, 180, 181, 182, 183, 241
Southall, Morris 146
South Bend, IN 32
Southlake Carroll 10, 14, 21, 88, 98, 99, 106, 107, 108, 110, 111, 112, 113, 114, 127, 138, 155, 161, 164, 219, 239, 241
Stamford 10, 16, 47, 53, 65, 117, 136, 139, 167, 168, 178, 196, 197, 199, 200, 202
Steele High School (Dayton, Ohio) 39, 114
Stephen F. Austin (State University) 69

Stephenville 9, 10, 15, 20, 52, 124, 125, 130, 135, 136, 138, 150, 152, 153, 154, 155, 156, 157, 158, 160, 161, 163, 211, 227, 232
Stiteler, Harry 40, 41
Strawn 213, 214
Sundown 94
Sweetwater 47, 49, 54, 57, 152, 212

T

Tatum 194, 242
Temple 25, 35, 40, 52, 63, 69, 73, 127, 141, 152
Terrell High 152
Texarkana 78, 89
Texas Sports Hall of Fame 10, 32, 221
Throckmorton 19, 213, 239, 242
Trinity. *See* Euless Trinity
Tusa, Joe 73
Tyler 49, 58
Tyson, Paul 31, 32, 33, 35, 36, 37, 39, 40, 43, 44, 53, 54, 61, 89, 125, 137, 139, 207

U

University Interscholastic League (UIL) 18, 20, 22, 24, 25, 26, 27, 33, 45, 67, 73, 113, 116, 117, 186, 199, 203, 204, 211, 227

V

Victoria 123, 140, 146, 233

W

Waco
Floyd Casey Stadium 117, 120, 153, 227, 230
Moore High 72
Waco High 24, 31, 32, 33, 40, 43
Walker, Larry 124, 125
Warner, Glenn Scobey "Pop" 32, 33
Warren, Steve 54, 61
Wartes, Larry 199, 200
Wasson, Hal 113
Waxahachie 153
Weatherford 148
Weddell, Alan 123, 124
West Columbia 146
Whitaker, Bobby 25
Wichita Falls 15, 17, 19, 40, 47, 48, 50, 52, 57, 62, 63, 66, 69, 70, 71, 74, 76, 77, 137, 162, 176, 190, 241
Wilkins, John 79, 80, 83, 84
Wilson, Jeff 18
Wood, Gordon 161, 197, 200, 214, 218

ABOUT THE AUTHOR

Rick Sherrod teaches dual-credit and advanced-placement history classes at Stephenville High School. He is the author of two Arcadia Images of America volumes: *Stephenville* and *Stephenville Yellow Jacket Football*. He has also published extensively in state historical journals on nineteenth-century southern kinship studies. A lifelong football fan, Sherrod grew up in Arlington, Texas, whose Colts won the 1951 state title when he was only one year old. Sherrod learned early that the entire town became near vacant on football Friday nights for away games. While his allegiance today lies with the Stephenville team and program, his love for high school football, and especially the good it produces within players and communities, spans the boundaries of the Lone Star State.